Mastering Object-Oriented Programming in C++: From Foundations to Advanced Techniques

Amir Keivan Shafiei

DEDICATION

This book is dedicated to all the aspiring programmers and curious minds who embark on the journey of mastering object-oriented programming in C++. Your dedication to learning, your persistence in problem-solving, and your passion for creating elegant and efficient software solutions have inspired us to compile this comprehensive guide. May your dedication lead you to new heights of knowledge and empower you to shape the future of technology with your skills and creativity.

To those who have nurtured the spirit of programming and embraced the challenges it brings, this book is a tribute to your unwavering commitment. Your thirst for knowledge and your desire to unravel the mysteries of code have set you on a path of continuous growth. As you delve into the world of C++ and object-oriented programming, may this book serve as a faithful companion, providing you with the guidance and insights you need to excel.

To the educators and mentors who tirelessly share their wisdom and expertise, shaping the next generation of programmers, we extend our deepest gratitude. Your passion for teaching and your dedication to fostering a love for programming are the driving forces behind the success stories of countless learners. This book is a testament to the impact you make and a token of appreciation for your invaluable contributions to the world of education.

May this book stand as a beacon of knowledge, illuminating the intricate concepts of object-oriented programming and guiding you through the exciting challenges that lie ahead. As you flip through its pages, may you find inspiration, clarity, and the confidence to embrace the art of coding and shape a future where innovation knows no bounds.

With heartfelt dedication,

Amir Keivan Shafiei

CONTENTS

ACKNOWLEDGMENTS

Bringing a comprehensive book to life is a collaborative effort that involves the dedication and support of numerous individuals. As we present this work on object-oriented programming in C++, we wish to express our heartfelt gratitude to those who have contributed to its creation.

First and foremost, we extend our deepest appreciation to the programmers, both seasoned and aspiring, whose curiosity and enthusiasm continue to fuel the world of software development. Your questions, insights, and passion have shaped the content of this book, and it is our sincere hope that it provides you with the guidance and knowledge you seek.

To our esteemed colleagues and mentors, thank you for sharing your expertise and wisdom. Your insights have enriched the content, and your guidance has been invaluable in ensuring its accuracy and relevance. Your commitment to nurturing a culture of learning and growth is a true inspiration.

We would also like to acknowledge the dedicated educators who have selflessly imparted knowledge and ignited the spark of curiosity in countless learners. Your influence extends far beyond the classroom, shaping the future of programming one student at a time.

Last but not least, we express our heartfelt thanks to our families and loved ones for their unwavering support and understanding throughout this journey. Your encouragement, patience, and belief in us have been the driving force behind our endeavors.

As we present this book to the world, we recognize that it is the culmination of the collective efforts of a diverse and dedicated community. To each and every individual who has played a role, no matter how big or small, in the creation of this book, we extend our sincere appreciation. May the knowledge shared within these pages inspire innovation and foster a lifelong love for programming.

1 AN OVERVIEW OF THE BASICS OF PROGRAMMING

1.1 INTRODUCTION

In the modern world, where technology plays a pivotal role in our daily lives, programming has emerged as a vital skill. Whether it's developing software applications, creating websites, or automating processes, programming enables us to harness the power of computers and accomplish complex tasks efficiently.

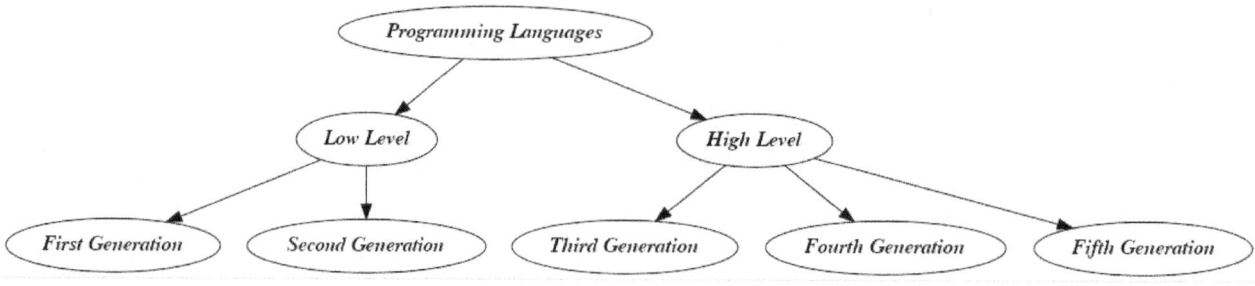

Figure 1Evolution of Programming Languages

Programming, at its core, is the process of writing instructions that tell a computer how to perform specific tasks. These instructions, known as code, are written in programming languages that are understood by both humans and machines. Over the years, programming languages have evolved, becoming more powerful and versatile, enabling programmers to create intricate and sophisticated software systems.

EXAMPLE:

Let's consider a simple example to illustrate the essence of programming. Imagine you want to create a program that calculates the area of a rectangle. To achieve this, you would write a series of instructions that specify how to perform the necessary calculations. Here's an example of code written in a programming language like C++:

```cpp
#include <iostream>
using namespace std;

int main() {
    float length, width, area;
```

```
cout << "Enter the length of the rectangle: ";
cin >> length;

cout << "Enter the width of the rectangle: ";
cin >> width;

area = length * width;

cout << "The area of the rectangle is: " << area << endl;

    return 0;
}
```

In this example, the program prompts the user to enter the length and width of a rectangle. It then calculates the area by multiplying the length and width values, and finally displays the result to the user. This simple program showcases the fundamental elements of programming: input, processing, and output.

Understanding programming requires grasping the fundamental concepts that form the foundation of the discipline. These concepts provide the necessary tools to solve problems and create functional programs. In the following sections, we will explore these concepts in more detail, including syntax, control flow, variables, functions, and the software development life cycle.

Throughout this book, we will focus on the C++ programming language to illustrate these concepts. However, the principles discussed can be applied to other programming languages as well. By understanding the basics of programming, you will acquire a solid foundation that will serve as a springboard for advanced programming techniques and methodologies.

Table 1: Programming Paradigms Comparison

Paradigm	Characteristics	Use Cases
Imperative	Sequential instructions, mutable state	Procedural programming, system software
Functional	Pure functions, immutable data	Mathematical computations, data analysis
Object-Oriented	Objects, encapsulation, inheritance	Large-scale software development

As we progress through this book, you will gain a deeper understanding of programming concepts and paradigms, allowing you to approach programming challenges with a structured and logical mindset. Let's embark on this journey to explore the intricacies of programming and unlock your full potential as a programmer.

1.2 FOUNDATIONS OF PROGRAMMING

Programming is built upon a solid foundation of fundamental concepts and principles that provide the framework for creating efficient and reliable software systems. In this section, we will explore the essence of programming, the different programming paradigms, and the importance of choosing the right paradigm based on the requirements of a given project.

1.2.1 THE ESSENCE OF PROGRAMMING

At its core, programming involves the creation of step-by-step instructions, known as algorithms, that guide a computer in performing specific tasks. These algorithms serve as a blueprint for solving problems and achieving desired outcomes through a series of logical and precise instructions.

The essence of programming can be distilled into three key components: input, processing, and output. Input refers to the data or information provided to a program, which could be entered by a user, retrieved from a file, or obtained from other sources. Processing involves manipulating and transforming the input data using predefined operations, calculations, and logical operations. Finally, output refers to the result produced by the program, which could be displayed on a screen, saved to a file, or used as input for subsequent operations.

Two essential elements of the C++ programming language that play significant roles in the process of creating algorithms are the semicolon (;) and the scope resolution operator (::).

The semicolon (;) is used in C++ to indicate the end of a statement. It serves as a delimiter, separating individual instructions within a program. Each line of code in C++ typically ends with a semicolon to mark the completion of that particular statement.

The scope resolution operator (::) is used in C++ to access members of a class, including variables, functions, and nested classes. It allows you to specify the scope or context from which a particular member is being accessed. By using the scope resolution operator, you can differentiate between members with the same name that exist in different scopes.

EXAMPLE:

Consider a program that calculates the average of a set of numbers. The input for this program would be a series of numbers provided by the user. The program would then process these numbers by summing them and dividing the sum by the total count. Finally, the output would be the calculated average displayed to the user.

Here's an example of code written in C++ to illustrate this:

```cpp
#include <iostream>
#include <vector>
int main() {
    std::vector<double> numbers;
    double total = 0.0;
    int n;
    std::cout << "Enter the number of elements: ";
    std::cin >> n;
    for (int i = 0; i < n; ++i) {
        double num;
        std::cout << "Enter a number: ";
        std::cin >> num;
        numbers.push_back(num);
        total += num;
    }
    double average = total / n;
    std::cout << "The average is: " << average << std::endl;
    return 0;
}
```

Let's go through the code line by line:

1. `#include <iostream>`: This line includes the necessary library for input and output operations in C++.
2. `#include <vector>`: This line includes the vector container class from the Standard Template Library (STL) in C++. We use it to store the numbers entered by the user.
3. `int main() {`: This line is the entry point of the program. It declares the main function, which is required in every C++ program.
4. `std::vector<double> numbers;`: This line declares a vector named "numbers" that stores double precision floating-point numbers.
5. `double total = 0.0;`: This line initializes the variable "total" to 0.0. It will be used to calculate the sum of the numbers entered by the user.
6. `int n;`: This line declares the variable "n" to store the number of elements to be entered by the user.
7. `std::cout << "Enter the number of elements: ";`: This line displays the prompt asking the user to enter the number of elements.
8. `std::cin >> n;`: This line reads the user's input for the number of elements and stores it in the variable "n".
9. `for (int i = 0; i < n; ++i) {`: This line starts a for loop that iterates "n" times, where "i" is the loop variable.
10. `double num;`: This line declares the variable "num" to store each number entered by the user.
11. `std::cout << "Enter a number: ";`: This line displays the prompt asking the user to enter a number.
12. `std::cin >> num;`: This line reads the user's input for a number and stores it in the variable "num".
13. `numbers.push_back(num);`: This line adds the entered number to the vector "numbers" using the `push_back` function.
14. `total += num;`: This line adds the entered number to the running total.
15. `double average = total / n;`: This line calculates the average by dividing the total by the number of elements.
16. `std::cout << "The average is: " << average << std::endl;`: This line displays the calculated average.
17. `return 0;`: This line indicates the end of the main function and returns 0, indicating successful program execution.

The code takes user input for the number of elements and the corresponding numbers, stores them in a vector, calculates the average, and then outputs the result.

In the code snippet, the meaning of << and >> in std::cout << "Enter a number: " and std::cin >> num; respectively, can be explained as follows:

The << operator in std::cout << "Enter a number: " is the stream insertion operator. It is used to insert data into the output stream std::cout. In this case, the string "Enter a number: " is inserted into the output stream, allowing it to be displayed on the screen or console.

The >> operator in std::cin >> num; is the stream extraction operator. It is used to extract data from the input stream std::cin and store it in the variable num. In this case, it reads the user's input for a number and assigns the entered value to the variable num.

By using these stream operators, you can interact with the user by displaying prompts and reading input from the console, enabling input and output operations within your program.

1.2.2 PROGRAMMING PARADIGMS

Programming paradigms represent different approaches to structuring and organizing code. Each paradigm embodies a set of principles and practices that dictate how programs are designed, written, and executed. Understanding the various paradigms is essential for selecting the most suitable approach based on the requirements and constraints of a specific project.

The three main programming paradigms are:

1. Imperative Programming: This paradigm focuses on describing a sequence of steps or commands that the computer should execute. It emphasizes mutable state and direct manipulation of data. Procedural programming, where programs are structured as a collection of procedures or functions, is a prominent example of imperative programming.

2. Functional Programming: Functional programming treats computation as the evaluation of mathematical functions. It emphasizes immutability and the absence of side effects. Programs are composed of pure functions that take inputs and produce outputs without modifying any external state. Functional programming languages often provide powerful tools for working with collections and performing high-level abstractions.

3. Object-Oriented Programming (OOP): Object-oriented programming revolves around the concept of objects, which encapsulate data and the operations or behaviors that can be performed on that data. OOP promotes modularity, reusability, and code organization by grouping related data and functions into classes. Inheritance and polymorphism are key features of OOP, enabling code reuse and flexibility.

Choosing the appropriate programming paradigm depends on factors such as the nature of the problem, the scalability requirements, the team's expertise, and the available resources. A thorough understanding of each paradigm enables programmers to make informed decisions and design software systems that align with the desired goals.

By grasping the foundations of programming and familiarizing yourself with different paradigms, you lay the groundwork for becoming a proficient programmer. In the next section, we will delve into the syntactical aspects of programming and explore the control flow mechanisms that govern how instructions are executed in a program.

1.3 SYNTAX AND CONTROL FLOW

Syntax and control flow are fundamental aspects of programming that dictate how instructions are written and executed in a program. In this section, we will explore the syntax rules of the C++ programming language and examine various control flow structures that enable programmers to create dynamic and efficient programs.

1.3.1 SYNTAX: THE LANGUAGE OF PROGRAMS

Programming languages, including C++, have a specific syntax that defines the rules and conventions for writing valid code. The syntax governs how statements and expressions are structured, how variables and functions are declared, and how control flow structures are defined. Adhering to the correct syntax is crucial for writing error-free programs.

In C++, statements are typically terminated with a semicolon (;), and blocks of code are enclosed within curly braces ({ }). Proper indentation and formatting enhance code readability and maintainability. C++ is case-sensitive, so uppercase and lowercase letters are distinct.

EXAMPLE:

Let's examine a simple C++ program that calculates the sum of two numbers:

```cpp
#include <iostream>
int main() {
    int num1, num2, sum;
    std::cout << "Enter the first number: ";
    std::cin >> num1;
    std::cout << "Enter the second number: ";
```

```
    std::cin >> num2;
    sum = num1 + num2;
    std::cout << "The sum is: " << sum << std::endl;
    return 0;
}
```

In this example, the program declares three variables (num1, num2, and sum) to store the input and the sum of the two numbers. It uses the std::cout and std::cin objects from the iostream library to perform input and output operations. The << and >> operators are used to display messages and read input from the user.

1.3.2 CONTROL FLOW

Control flow structures determine the order in which statements are executed within a program. C++ provides various control flow structures, including conditional statements and looping structures, to enable decision-making and repetition in code execution.

Conditional Statements: Conditional statements allow the program to make decisions based on certain conditions. The most common conditional statement is the if-else statement, which executes a block of code if a given condition is true and another block of code if the condition is false.

EXAMPLE:

Consider a program that determines whether a number entered by the user is positive or negative:

```
#include <iostream>

int main() {
    int number;
    std::cout << "Enter a number: ";
    std::cin >> number;
    if (number > 0) {
        std::cout << "The number is positive." << std::endl;
    }
    else if (number < 0) {
        std::cout << "The number is negative." << std::endl;
    }
    else {
        std::cout << "The number is zero." << std::endl;
    }
    return 0;
}
```

In this example, the program prompts the user to enter a number. It then uses the if-else statements to check whether the number is positive, negative, or zero. Based on the condition evaluation, the corresponding message is displayed to the user.

Looping Structures: Looping structures allow the repetition of a block of code until a certain condition is met. C++ offers several looping structures, such as the while loop, do-while loop, and for loop.

EXAMPLE:

Let's consider a program that calculates the factorial of a given number using a for loop:

```cpp
#include <iostream>

int main() {
    int number, factorial = 1;

    std::cout << "Enter a number: ";
    std::cin >> number;

    for (int i = 1; i <= number; ++i) {
        factorial *= i;
    }

    std::cout << "The factorial of " << number << " is: " << factorial << std::endl;

    return 0;
}
```

In this example, the program prompts the user to enter a number. It then uses a for loop to calculate the factorial of the number by multiplying each integer from 1 to the entered number. The result is displayed to the user.

Understanding and utilizing control flow structures is essential for creating programs that can handle different scenarios and iterate over data efficiently.

By mastering the syntax and control flow of the C++ programming language, you gain the necessary building blocks to create robust and functional programs. In the next section, we will explore the concepts of variables and data types, which enable programs to store and manipulate different types of data.

1.4 FUNDAMENTAL PROGRAMMING CONCEPTS

1.4.1 VARIABLES AND DATA STORAGE

Variables play a vital role in programming as they provide a means to store and manipulate data. In this section, we will explore the concept of variables, the different data types available in C++, and the process of memory allocation and variable initialization.

1.4.1.1 UNDERSTANDING VARIABLES

A variable is a named storage location that holds a value. It serves as a container for data that can be accessed and modified during the execution of a program. Variables allow programmers to store information such as numbers, characters, or boolean values and use them in calculations, comparisons, and other operations.

In C++, variables must be declared before they can be used. The declaration specifies the variable's name and its data type, which determines the kind of values the variable can hold. Variables can be assigned values using the assignment operator (=).

1.4.1.2 DATA TYPES

C++ provides various data types to cater to different kinds of data. Here are some common data types:
   • Numeric Data Types: Numeric data types include integers, floating-point numbers, and

characters. Integers represent whole numbers, while floating-point numbers are used to store decimal values. Characters represent individual characters and are enclosed in single quotes (' ').

Table 2: Numeric Data Types

Data Type	Description	Range
int	Integer values	-2,147,483,648 to 2,147,483,647
float	Single-precision floating point	Approximately ±3.4E±38 with 6 decimal places of precision
double	Double-precision floating point	Approximately ±1.7E±308 with 15 decimal places of precision
char	Individual characters	-128 to 127

- Boolean Data Type: The boolean data type represents logical values and can have two possible values: true or false. It is often used in conditions and logical operations.
- Derived Data Types: C++ also provides derived data types, such as arrays, strings, and structures, which allow for more complex data storage and manipulation.

1.4.1.3 MEMORY ALLOCATION AND VARIABLE INITIALIZATION

When a variable is declared, memory is allocated to store its value. The size of memory allocated depends on the data type of the variable. C++ automatically manages memory allocation and deallocation for variables.

Variable initialization refers to assigning an initial value to a variable at the time of declaration. Initializing variables is good practice to prevent accessing uninitialized values, which can lead to undefined behavior.

EXAMPLE:

```
int age;        // Variable declaration
age = 25;       // Variable assignment (without initialization)

float pi = 3.14;  // Variable declaration and initialization

char grade = 'A'; // Variable declaration and initialization
```

In this example, the variable `age` is declared and assigned a value later, while the variables `pi` and `grade` are both declared and initialized in a single step.

1.4.2 FUNCTIONS AND MODULARIZATION

Functions provide a way to organize code into reusable blocks, enhancing code readability, reusability, and maintainability. In this section, we will delve into the concept of functions, including declaration, definition, and invocation, as well as the benefits of modularization.

1.4.2.1 CONCEPT OF FUNCTIONS

A function is a self-contained block of code that performs a specific task. It encapsulates a series of statements, often with input parameters and a return value. Functions can be invoked (called) multiple times from different parts of the program, promoting code reuse and modularity.

1.4.2.2 FUNCTION DECLARATION, DEFINITION, AND INVOCATION

To use a function, it must be declared before it is called. Function declaration provides information about the function's name, return type, and parameter types (if any). The function definition, on the other hand, contains the actual implementation of the function.

Function invocation is the process of calling a function to execute its code. Arguments can be passed to a function through its parameters, and the function can return a value back to the calling code.

EXAMPLE:

```cpp
#include <iostream>
using namespace std;
// Function declaration
int addNumbers(int a, int b);

// Function definition
int addNumbers(int a, int b) {
    return a + b;
}

int main() {
    // Function invocation
    int sum = addNumbers(5, 3); // sum will be 8
    cout << "Sum: " << sum << endl;
    return 0;
}
```

In this example, the function **addNumbers** is declared with two integer parameters. Its definition specifies that it returns the sum of the two parameters. The function is then invoked with arguments 5 and 3, and the returned value is assigned to the variable **sum**.

1.4.2.3 MODULARIZATION AND CODE ORGANIZATION

Modularization involves breaking down a program into smaller, manageable modules or functions. Each module focuses on a specific task, making the overall program structure clearer and easier to understand. Modular code promotes code reusability, simplifies maintenance, and enhances collaboration among programmers.

By utilizing functions and modularizing code effectively, programmers can create well-structured and maintainable programs.

1.4.3 INPUT AND OUTPUT OPERATIONS

Input and output (I/O) operations allow programs to interact with users by receiving input and displaying output. In this section, we will explore the mechanisms of handling user input and performing output operations using the standard input/output streams.

1.4.3.1 HANDLING USER INPUT

User input can be obtained through the standard input stream, **std::cin**, in C++. The **std::cin** object is used in conjunction with the extraction operator (**>>**) to read input from the user and store it in variables.

EXAMPLE:

```cpp
#include <iostream>
using namespace std;

int main() {
    int age;
    cout << "Enter your age: ";
    cin >> age;
    return 0;
}
```

In this example, the program prompts the user to enter their age. The `std::cin` statement reads the input entered by the user and assigns it to the `age` variable.

1.4.3.2 DISPLAYING OUTPUT

Output can be displayed to the user using the standard output stream, `std::cout`, in C++. The `std::cout` object is used in conjunction with the insertion operator (`<<`) to output values or messages to the console.

EXAMPLE:

```cpp
#include <iostream>
using namespace std;

int main() {
    int age = 25;
    cout << "Your age is: " << age << endl;
    return 0;
}
```

In this example, the program displays the message "Your age is: " followed by the value of the age variable using the std::cout statement.

Understanding input and output operations is essential for creating interactive programs and providing meaningful feedback to users.

By mastering variables, data types, functions, and input/output operations, programmers gain a solid foundation in fundamental programming concepts. These concepts form the building blocks for developing sophisticated and efficient software systems.

1.5 THE SOFTWARE DEVELOPMENT LIFE CYCLE

1.5.1 REQUIREMENTS GATHERING AND ANALYSIS

Requirements gathering and analysis are crucial stages in the software development life cycle (SDLC). In this section, we will explore the process of understanding user requirements and specifications, as well as analyzing the problem domain and defining the scope of the software project.

1.5.1.1 UNDERSTANDING USER REQUIREMENTS AND SPECIFICATIONS

The first step in developing any software system is to gather and understand the requirements of the users or stakeholders. This involves actively communicating with the end-users or clients to identify their needs, expectations, and desired functionalities of the software. The requirements can be collected through interviews, surveys, and discussions.

Once the requirements are gathered, they need to be documented in a clear and concise manner. This documentation, often referred to as a requirements specification or software requirements document (SRD), serves as a reference for the development team and helps ensure that the software meets the users' needs.

1.5.1.2 ANALYZING THE PROBLEM DOMAIN AND DEFINING THE SCOPE

Analyzing the problem domain involves gaining a thorough understanding of the environment in which the software will be used. It includes studying the existing systems, processes, and constraints related to the problem that the software aims to solve. This analysis helps in identifying potential challenges, opportunities, and constraints that may impact the development process.

Defining the scope of the software project is crucial to ensure that the project remains focused and achievable within the available resources and time. The scope defines the boundaries of the project and outlines what functionalities and features will be included in the software. It helps in setting realistic goals and expectations for the development team and stakeholders.

1.5.2 DESIGN AND PLANNING

The design and planning phase of the SDLC involves creating a blueprint for the software system based on the gathered requirements. This phase focuses on high-level and low-level design approaches, considering modularity, reusability, and efficiency.

1.5.2.1 HIGH-LEVEL AND LOW-LEVEL DESIGN APPROACHES

High-level design involves creating a conceptual overview of the software system. It identifies the main components, modules, and their interactions. This design phase helps in defining the architecture of the software and how different components will work together to achieve the desired functionalities.

Low-level design, also known as detailed design, involves specifying the internal structure of each component or module identified in the high-level design. It includes defining data structures, algorithms, interfaces, and implementation details. Low-level design focuses on how each component will be implemented and how they will communicate with each other.

1.5.2.2 DESIGN CONSIDERATIONS: MODULARITY, REUSABILITY, AND EFFICIENCY

During the design phase, it is important to consider design principles such as modularity, reusability, and efficiency. Modularity ensures that the software is divided into independent and cohesive modules, making it easier to develop, test, and maintain. Reusability promotes the use of existing code or modules to minimize duplication and improve development efficiency. Efficiency focuses on optimizing the performance and resource usage of the software system.

1.5.2.3 PLANNING THE IMPLEMENTATION PROCESS

In the planning stage, the development team determines the overall timeline, milestones, and resource allocation for the project. It involves creating a project plan that outlines the tasks, dependencies, and responsibilities of team members. The plan helps in managing the development process, tracking progress, and ensuring that the project stays on schedule.

1.5.3 IMPLEMENTATION AND CODING

The implementation and coding phase involves translating the design into executable code. It is the stage where programmers write the actual code using the selected programming language, in this case, C++. This phase focuses on applying programming concepts and paradigms to create a functional and efficient software system.

During the implementation phase, it is important to follow coding standards and best practices. This includes writing clean and readable code, using meaningful variable names, adding comments for documentation, and applying coding conventions specific to the chosen programming language.

1.5.4 TESTING AND DEBUGGING

Testing and debugging are essential steps to ensure the quality and reliability of the software system.

1.5.4.1 IMPORTANCE OF TESTING FOR IDENTIFYING AND FIXING ISSUES

Testing helps in identifying defects or issues in the software before it is released to the users. It involves executing the software with various inputs and comparing the actual outputs against expected results. Testing helps in uncovering bugs, logic errors, and performance issues, ensuring that the software functions correctly and meets the specified requirements.

1.5.4.2 TYPES OF TESTING: UNIT TESTING, INTEGRATION TESTING, AND SYSTEM TESTING

Different types of testing are performed at various stages of the development process. Unit testing focuses on testing individual units or components of the software in isolation to ensure their correctness. Integration testing verifies the interaction and compatibility of different modules or components when combined. System testing evaluates the complete system against the requirements to ensure that it functions as expected.

1.5.4.3 DEBUGGING TECHNIQUES AND TOOLS FOR LOCATING AND RESOLVING ERRORS

Debugging is the process of locating and fixing errors or bugs in the code. It involves identifying the root cause of the issue and making necessary modifications to eliminate the problem. Various debugging techniques and tools, such as breakpoints, stepping through the code, and logging, aid in identifying and resolving errors efficiently.

By following a systematic approach to the software development life cycle, from requirements gathering and analysis to testing and debugging, programmers can ensure the successful development of reliable and high-quality software systems.

1.6 THE FUTURE OF PROGRAMMING

The field of programming is constantly evolving, driven by emerging trends and advancements in technology. In this section, we will explore some of the key areas that are shaping the future of programming.

1.6.1 EMERGING TRENDS AND TECHNOLOGIES IN PROGRAMMING

1.6.1.1 MOBILE AND WEB DEVELOPMENT

With the increasing popularity of smartphones and the internet, mobile and web development have become prominent areas in programming. Developers are focusing on creating responsive and user-friendly applications for mobile devices and web browsers. Technologies such as JavaScript frameworks (e.g., React, Angular), Progressive Web Apps (PWAs), and mobile app development platforms (e.g., Flutter, React Native) are gaining traction in the development community.

1.6.1.2 CLOUD COMPUTING AND SERVERLESS ARCHITECTURE

Cloud computing has revolutionized the way software applications are deployed and managed. It offers scalability, flexibility, and cost-effectiveness for hosting applications and services. Serverless architecture, a subset of cloud computing, enables developers to build applications without the need to manage infrastructure. Platforms like Amazon Web Services (AWS) Lambda and Microsoft Azure Functions are examples of serverless computing platforms that are simplifying application development and deployment.

1.6.1.3 INTERNET OF THINGS (IOT)

The Internet of Things (IoT) refers to the interconnection of everyday objects or devices with the internet. This technology trend is opening up new possibilities for programming, as devices become smarter and more connected. IoT applications often involve collecting and analyzing large amounts of data from sensors and devices. Programmers are working on developing efficient algorithms and data processing techniques to handle the massive influx of IoT data.

1.6.1.4 DATA SCIENCE AND BIG DATA

Data science and big data analytics have gained significant attention in recent years. With the increasing availability of data, organizations are seeking professionals who can analyze and extract valuable insights from large datasets. Programming languages like Python and R, along with frameworks such as Apache Hadoop and Spark, are widely used in data science and big data analytics. Programmers with expertise in these areas are in high demand.

1.6.2 THE IMPACT OF ARTIFICIAL INTELLIGENCE AND MACHINE LEARNING

Artificial Intelligence (AI) and Machine Learning (ML) are transforming various industries and have a profound impact on programming. AI algorithms and ML models are being developed to automate tasks, make predictions, and improve decision-making processes. Programmers are involved in creating intelligent systems that can learn from data and make intelligent decisions. Popular frameworks like TensorFlow and PyTorch are used for building and training machine learning models.

1.6.3 THE EVOLVING ROLE OF PROGRAMMERS IN A DIGITAL AGE

In a digital age where automation and AI are gaining momentum, the role of programmers is evolving. Programmers are not only responsible for writing code but also for understanding the broader context and implications of their work. They need to collaborate with other professionals, such as data scientists, UX designers, and domain experts, to develop comprehensive solutions.

Additionally, programmers are expected to embrace continuous learning and keep up with the latest technologies and trends. They need to adapt to new programming paradigms and tools, as well as develop skills in areas like cybersecurity, cloud computing, and data analysis.

EXAMPLE:

One example of the impact of emerging technologies in programming is the development of a smart home automation system. Programmers can utilize IoT technologies to connect various devices in a home, such as lights, thermostats, and security systems, to a central hub. By developing custom software applications, users can control and monitor these devices remotely through their smartphones or other connected devices.

In conclusion, the future of programming is characterized by emerging trends and technologies such as mobile and web development, cloud computing, IoT, and data science. The integration of artificial intelligence and machine learning is revolutionizing the way programmers approach problem-solving and decision-making. As technology continues to advance, programmers must adapt and acquire new skills to thrive in the digital age.

1.7 CONCLUSION

In this chapter, we have explored the fundamentals of programming and gained a solid understanding of the key concepts that serve as the foundation for advanced programming. Let's recap the main points covered in this chapter and conclude with an encouragement to continue the journey into advanced programming.

1.7.1 RECAP OF KEY CONCEPTS

Throughout this chapter, we have covered a range of essential topics that form the building blocks of programming:

1. An overview of the basics of programming, including the purpose and importance of programming in problem-solving and software development.

2. The top-down design approach, which provides a structured methodology for problem-solving and program development.

3. The basic concepts of object orientation, such as real-based modeling and encapsulation, which enable us to manage complexity in medium and large-sized programs.

4. The fundamental structures of object-oriented programming, including objects and constructors, which allow for the creation and manipulation of data and behavior.

5. Inheritance and polymorphism, powerful concepts that facilitate code reuse, modularity, and flexibility in object-oriented programming.

6. An introduction to memory management and dynamic data structures, which play a vital role in efficient memory allocation and utilization.

7. The concept of generic programming, which enables the creation of reusable algorithms and data structures that can work with different data types.

8. Handling errors and exceptions, essential techniques for robust error handling and graceful recovery from unexpected situations in program execution.

9. Input and output operations, including handling user input and displaying output, utilizing the standard input/output streams.

1.7.2 ENCOURAGEMENT TO CONTINUE THE JOURNEY

As you have now gained a solid foundation in the basics of programming, it's important to recognize that this is just the beginning of your journey into advanced programming. The concepts covered in this chapter provide a strong groundwork upon which you can build more complex and sophisticated programs.

Programming is a vast and ever-evolving field, and there is always more to learn and explore. As you continue your journey, you will encounter new programming paradigms, languages, tools, and technologies that will expand your horizons and open up exciting opportunities.

Remember to practice your programming skills regularly. Write code, experiment with different techniques, and solve real-world problems. Embrace challenges and seek opportunities to deepen your understanding and refine your programming abilities.

Throughout this book, we will delve into advanced programming concepts, techniques, and best practices. By mastering these advanced topics, you will gain the skills and knowledge necessary to tackle complex programming tasks and develop high-quality software solutions.

So, I encourage you to stay committed, be curious, and continue your exploration into the world of advanced programming. With dedication and perseverance, you will become a proficient and successful programmer.

Example:

Imagine you are developing a banking application in C++. You would utilize the concepts covered in this chapter to design and implement the application. You would use object-oriented programming to model customer accounts, transactions, and various banking operations. Memory management techniques would ensure efficient utilization of resources, while error handling would provide a robust and reliable system. Input and output operations would enable users to interact with the application, making deposits, withdrawals, and balance inquiries.

In conclusion, this chapter has provided a comprehensive overview of the basics of programming. By understanding these foundational concepts, you are equipped to embark on a journey into advanced programming. Embrace the challenges, stay curious, and continue exploring the vast world of programming possibilities that lie ahead.

2 INTRODUCTION TO C++ PROGRAMMING

2.1 OVERVIEW

Welcome to Chapter 2 of our book, Introduction to C++ Programming. In this chapter, we will explore the fundamental concepts of C++ programming, providing you with a solid foundation for writing efficient and robust code. We will cover the syntax of the language, data types, variables, operators, control flow, and functions. Understanding these core concepts is essential for becoming a proficient C++ programmer.

2.2 C++ SYNTAX

In C++, understanding the syntax is essential for writing valid and understandable code. The syntax of a programming language defines the rules for constructing statements and expressions. It determines how the code should be written, organized, and structured. In this section, we will explore some important aspects of C++ syntax.

2.2.1 STATEMENTS AND BLOCKS

A **statement** in C++ is a complete instruction that performs a specific action. It can include variable declarations, assignments, function calls, loops, conditionals, and more. Each statement ends with a semicolon ; to indicate its completion. Here is an example of a simple C++ statement:

```cpp
int x = 5;
```

In the above example, the statement declares a variable named x of type int and assigns it the value 5.
Statements can be grouped together using blocks. A **block** is a set of statements enclosed within curly braces {}. Blocks allow multiple statements to be treated as a single unit, often used in loops, conditionals, and function bodies. Here is an example of a block of code:

```cpp
{
    int x = 5;
    int y = 3;
    int sum = x + y;
    cout << "The sum is: " << sum << endl;
}
```

In the above example, the block of code declares two variables x and y, calculates their sum, and then outputs the result to the console.

2.2.2 COMMENTS

Comments in C++ are used to add explanatory notes or annotations within the code. They are ignored by the compiler and have no effect on the program's execution. Comments are helpful for providing descriptions, clarifying code logic, and making the code more readable for other developers.

C++ supports two types of comments: **single-line comments** and **multi-line comments**.

Single-line comments begin with **//** and continue until the end of the line. Anything written after **//** on the same line is treated as a comment. Here is an example of a single-line comment:

```
// This is a single-line comment
```

Multi-line comments start with **/*** and end with ***/**. They can span multiple lines and are often used for longer explanations or to temporarily disable a block of code. Here is an example of a multi-line comment:

```
/*
    This is a multi-line comment.
    It can span multiple lines.
    Comments are ignored by the compiler.
*/
```

Comments are useful for documenting your code, providing context, and making it easier for others (including your future self) to understand the code.

Understanding and following the syntax rules in C++ is crucial for writing correct and well-structured programs. By adhering to the syntax guidelines, you ensure that your code is readable, maintainable, and can be successfully compiled. In the next sections, we will explore more aspects of C++ programming, including data types, variables, operators, control flow, and functions.

2.3 DATA TYPES, VARIABLES, AND LIBRARIES

In C++, **data types** define the nature and characteristics of data that can be stored in **variables**. Each data type specifies the **size** and **format** of the data, as well as the **operations** that can be performed on it. In this section, we will explore **different data types** available in C++, learn how to **declare variables** of these types, and introduce the concept of **libraries** and the #include directive.

C++ provides several **built-in data types**, including **numeric types**, **character types**, **Boolean types**, and more. Let's take a look at some **commonly used data types**:

1. **Numeric Data Types:**
   - int: Represents **integers** (whole numbers) without decimals. For example:

```
int age = 25;
```

   - **float**: Represents floating-point numbers with decimals. For example:

```
float pi = 3.14159;
```

   - **double**: Represents double-precision floating-point numbers. It can store larger and more precise decimal values compared to **float**. For example:

```
double distance = 1234.56789;
```

1. **Character Data Types:**
   - char: Represents a **single character**. It can store letters, digits, or special symbols enclosed in single quotes. For example:

```
char grade = 'A';
```

1. **Boolean Data Type:**
   - bool: Represents a **Boolean value**, which can be either **true** or **false**. For example:

```
bool isStudent = true;
```

It is important to note that when declaring a variable, you need to **specify its data type** before the variable name. This allows the compiler to allocate the appropriate amount of memory for the variable and **enforce type safety**.

Now, let's introduce the concept of libraries and the #include **directive. Libraries** in C++ are collections of **pre-compiled code** that provide **additional functionality** to your programs. They contain **ready-to-use functions, classes,** and other components that can be utilized to simplify and enhance your code.

To use a library in your program, you need to **include its header file** using the #include directive. The header file contains the **declarations and definitions** of the functions and types provided by the library. By including the header file, you make the library's functionality accessible to your program.

Here is an example that demonstrates the usage of libraries and the #include directive:

```cpp
#include <iostream> // Library for input/output operations
#include <cmath>    // Library for mathematical functions

using namespace std;

int main() {
    int radius = 5;
    double area = M_PI * pow(radius, 2); // Using the math library function

    cout << "The area of the circle is: " << area << endl;

    return 0;
}
```

In the above example, we include two libraries: <iostream> for input/output operations and <cmath> for mathematical functions. We then use the *cout* object from the <iostream> library to display the calculated area of a circle. The M_PI constant from the <cmath> library is used to represent the mathematical constant π.

Note: In C++, namespaces are used to organize code and prevent naming conflicts. The "std" namespace is the standard namespace used in C++ to include many standard library functions, objects, and features. When you write "using namespace std;" at the beginning of your program, you are telling the compiler that you want to use all the elements (functions, objects, etc.) from the "std" namespace directly in your code, without having to specify the "std::" prefix each time.

2.4 OPERATORS

In C++, operators are symbols that represent specific actions to be performed on operands (variables, constants, or expressions) to produce a result. They allow you to perform various operations, such as arithmetic calculations, logical comparisons, and assignment of values. In this section, we will explore different types of operators in C++ and their usage.

1. Arithmetic Operators:
    - **+** (Addition): Adds two operands together. Example:

```
int sum = 5 + 3;
```

    - **-** (Subtraction): Subtracts the second operand from the first. Example:

```
int difference = 8 - 4;
```

    - ***** (Multiplication): Multiplies two operands. Example:

```
int product = 6 * 2;
```

    - **/** (Division): Divides the first operand by the second. Example:

```
float result = 10.0 / 3.0;
```

    - **%** (Modulus): Returns the remainder of the division. Example:

```
int remainder = 10 % 3;
```

2. Relational Operators:
    - **==** (Equal to): Checks if two operands are equal. Example:

```
bool isEqual = (5 == 5);
```

    - **!=** (Not equal to): Checks if two operands are not equal. Example:

```
bool isNotEqual = (5 != 3);
```

    - **>** (Greater than): Checks if the first operand is greater than the second. Example:

```
bool isGreater = (10 > 5);
```

    - **<** (Less than): Checks if the first operand is less than the second. Example:

```
bool isLess = (3 < 8);
```

    - **>=** (Greater than or equal to): Checks if the first operand is greater than or equal to the second. Example:

```
bool isGreaterOrEqual = (7 >= 7);
```

    - **<=** (Less than or equal to): Checks if the first operand is less than or equal to the second. Example:

```
bool isLessOrEqual = (4 <= 6);
```

3. Logical Operators:
    - **&&** (Logical AND): Returns true if both operands are true. Example:

```
bool result = (true && false);
```

- || (Logical OR): Returns true if either operand is true. Example:

```
bool result = (true || false);
```

- ! (Logical NOT): Reverses the logical state of the operand. Example:

```
bool result = !true;
```

4. Assignment Operators:
    - = (Assignment): Assigns the value on the right-hand side to the variable on the left-hand side. Example:

```
int x = 5;
```

    - += (Addition assignment): Adds the value on the right-hand side to the variable on the left-hand side and stores the result in the variable. Example:

```
x += 3; // equivalent to x = x + 3;
```

    - -= (Subtraction assignment): Subtracts the value on the right-hand side from the variable on the left-hand side and stores the result in the variable. Example:

```
x -= 2; // equivalent to x = x - 2;
```

    - *= (Multiplication assignment): Multiplies the variable on the left-hand side by the value on the right-hand side and stores the result in the variable. Example:

```
x *= 4; // equivalent to x = x * 4;
```

    - /= (Division assignment): Divides the variable on the left-hand side by the value on the right-hand side and stores the result in the variable. Example:

```
x /= 2; // equivalent to x = x / 2;
```

It is important to note that operators have precedence, which determines the order in which operations are performed. You can use parentheses to enforce a specific order of evaluation when needed.

By understanding and utilizing the different types of operators available in C++, you can perform a wide range of computations, comparisons, and assignments in your programs. In the next section, we will explore control structures, such as conditional statements and loops, which allow you to control the flow of execution based on certain conditions.

2.5 ARRAYS AND POINTERS

In C++, arrays and pointers are fundamental concepts that allow you to work with collections of data and manipulate memory addresses. Arrays provide a way to store multiple values of the same data type, while pointers enable you to manipulate and access memory locations directly. In this section, we will explore arrays and pointers in C++ and understand their usage.

1. **Arrays**: An array is a collection of elements of the same data type, arranged in contiguous memory locations. Each element in the array can be accessed using its index, which represents its position within the array. Arrays in C++ are zero-indexed, meaning the first element has an index of 0. Here's an example of declaring and accessing elements in an array:

```
#include <iostream>

using namespace std;
```

```cpp
int main() {
  // Declaration of an integer array with 5 elements
  int numbers[5];

  // Assigning a value to the first element
  numbers[0] = 10;

  // Assigning a value to the second element
  numbers[1] = 20;

  // Assigning a value to the third element
  numbers[2] = 30;

  // Assigning a value to the fourth element
  numbers[3] = 40;

  // Assigning a value to the fifth element
  numbers[4] = 50;

  // Accessing and printing the values of the array elements
  cout << "Element at index 0: " << numbers[0] << endl;
  cout << "Element at index 1: " << numbers[1] << endl;
  cout << "Element at index 2: " << numbers[2] << endl;
  cout << "Element at index 3: " << numbers[3] << endl;
  cout << "Element at index 4: " << numbers[4] << endl;

  return 0;
}
```

Output:

```
Element at index 0: 10
Element at index 1: 20
Element at index 2: 30
Element at index 3: 40
Element at index 4: 50
```

In the above example, we declare an integer array numbers with 5 elements. We then assign values to each element using the index notation (numbers[index] = value). Finally, we access and print the values of the array elements using the same index notation.

```
              0   1   2   3   4  ◄──────── Array Indices
            ┌───┬───┬───┬───┬───┐
            │10 │20 │30 │40 │50 │
            └───┴───┴───┴───┴───┘
  numbers   [0] [1] [2] [3] [4] ◄──────── Array Members
```

- **Pointers**: A pointer is a variable that stores the memory address of another variable. It allows you to indirectly access and manipulate the value of the variable it points to. Pointers are useful for dynamic memory allocation, passing arguments by reference, and working with arrays. Here's an example of declaring and using pointers:

```cpp
#include <iostream>

using namespace std;

int main() {
    // Declaration of an integer variable
    int number = 10;

    // Declaration of a pointer variable
    int* pointer;

    // Assigning the address of 'number' to 'pointer'
    pointer = &number;

    // Printing the values of 'number', 'pointer', and the value at the address pointed by 'pointer'
    cout << "Value of 'number': " << number << endl;
    cout << "Address of 'number': " << &number << endl;
    cout << "Value of 'pointer': " << pointer << endl;
    cout << "Value at the address pointed by 'pointer': " << *pointer << endl;

    return 0;
}
```

Output:
```
Value of 'number': 10
Address of 'number': 0x7ffeedb14d64 (memory address may vary)
Value of 'pointer': 0x7ffeedb14d64 (memory address may vary)
Value at the address pointed by 'pointer': 10
```

The symbol * in C++ is typically pronounced as "star" or "pointer to." The symbol & is usually pronounced as "ampersand" or "address of."

In the provided example, we have demonstrated how to declare and use pointers in C++. Let's go through the code step by step:

1. We start by including the necessary header file iostream to perform input and output operations.

2. We declare an integer variable named number and assign it the value 10.

3. Next, we declare a pointer variable named pointer. This variable will store the memory address of the integer variable number.

4. To assign the address of number to pointer, we use the address-of operator &. It allows us to retrieve the memory address of a variable.

5. We then use the cout object from the iostream library to print the following information:

   • The value of number: Prints the value of the variable number (which is 10 in this case).

- The address of number: Prints the memory address of the variable number, represented as a hexadecimal value (e.g., 0x7ffeedb14d64).
- The value of pointer: Prints the memory address stored in the pointer variable (the address of number).
- The value at the address pointed by pointer: Prints the value stored at the memory address pointed by pointer. In this case, it prints the value 10, which is the value of number.

By understanding arrays and pointers, you can efficiently work with collections of data and manipulate memory addresses in your C++ programs. In the next section, we will delve into control structures, such as loops and conditional statements, which allow you to control the flow of execution based on certain conditions.

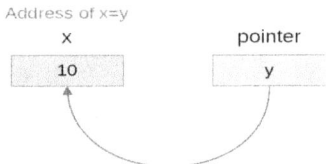

2.6 CONTROL FLOW

Control flow in programming refers to the order in which statements are executed. It allows you to control the flow of execution based on certain conditions or loops. In C++, there are several control flow statements that help you make decisions and repeat actions. In this section, we will explore these control flow statements and understand their usage through examples.

1. Conditional Statements:

Conditional statements allow you to execute a block of code based on a certain condition. The most commonly used conditional statements in C++ are:

- The **if statement**: The if statement evaluates a condition and executes a block of code if the condition is true. It has the following syntax:

```
if (condition) {
    // code to execute if the condition is true
}
```

Example:

```
#include <iostream>

using namespace std;

int main() {
    // Declaration of an integer variable
    int x = 10;

    // Conditional statement
    if (x > 5) {
        // Print a message if x is greater than 5
        cout << "x is greater than 5." << endl;
    }
```

```
    return 0;
}
```

- The **if-else statement**: The if-else statement allows you to execute different blocks of code based on the outcome of a condition. It has the following syntax:

```
if (condition) {
    // code to execute if the condition is true
} else {
    // code to execute if the condition is false
}
```

Example:

```
#include <iostream>

using namespace std;

int main() {
  // Declaration of an integer variable
  int x = 3;

  // Conditional statement
  if (x > 5) {
    // Print a message if x is greater than 5
    cout << "x is greater than 5." << endl;
  } else {
    // Print a message if x is less than or equal to 5
    cout << "x is less than or equal to 5." << endl;
  }

  return 0;
}
```

- The **if-else if-else statement**: The if-else if-else statement allows you to evaluate multiple conditions and execute different blocks of code based on the outcome of these conditions. It has the following syntax:

```
if (condition1) {
    // code to execute if condition1 is true
} else if (condition2) {
    // code to execute if condition1 is false and condition2 is true
} else {
    // code to execute if both condition1 and condition2 are false
}
```

Example:

```
int x = 10;

if (x < 5) {
    cout << "x is less than 5." << endl;
} else if (x < 10) {
    cout << "x is less than 10." << endl;
} else {
    cout << "x is greater than or equal to 10." << endl;
}
```

- **Looping Statements:**

Looping statements allow you to repeat a block of code multiple times. The two main looping statements in C++ are:

- The **while loop:** The while loop executes a block of code repeatedly as long as a condition remains true. It has the following syntax:

```
while (condition) {
    // code to execute
}
```

Example:

```
int count = 0;

while (count < 5) {
    cout << "Count: " << count << endl;
    count++;
}
```

- **Basic for Loop::** The for loop allows you to execute a block of code for a specific number of times. It has the following syntax:

```
for (initialization; condition; update) {
    // code to execute
}
```

Example:

```
for (int i = 0; i < 5; i++) {
    cout<< "i: " << i << endl; }
```

- **Range-based for Loop:** The range-based for loop is used to iterate over elements in a container, such as an array, vector, or other sequence-like data structure. It automatically iterates through each element without needing an index variable.

```
for (data_type variable : container) {
    // Code to be executed for each element
```

```
}
```

Example:

```
std::vector<int> numbers = {1, 2, 3, 4, 5};
for (int num : numbers) {
    std::cout << num << " ";
}
```

3. Control Flow Keywords:

C++ provides additional keywords that allow you to control the flow of execution within control flow statements:

- The **break** keyword: The break keyword is used to exit a loop or switch statement prematurely. When encountered, it terminates the current loop iteration or exits the switch statement.

Example:

```
for (int i = 0; i < 10; i++) {
    if (i == 5) {
        break; // exit the loop when i is equal to 5
    }
    cout << "i: " << i << endl;
}
```

- The **continue** keyword: The continue keyword is used to skip the rest of the current iteration of a loop and move to the next iteration. It allows you to bypass certain code within the loop.

Example:

```
for (int i = 0; i < 10; i++) {
    if (i == 5) {
        continue; // skip the rest of the iteration when i is equal to 5
    }
    cout << "i: " << i << endl;
}
```

- The **return** keyword: The return keyword is used to exit a function and return a value (if applicable) to the calling code. It can also be used to terminate the execution of a program if placed in the main function.

Example:

```
int addNumbers(int x, int y) {
    return x + y; // return the sum of x and y
}
```

The return keyword is used to pass the result of the addition back to the calling code.

By utilizing conditional statements and looping statements, you can create dynamic and flexible programs that adapt to different scenarios. Control flow statements and keywords allow you to make decisions, repeat actions, and control the flow of execution in your C++ programs. In the next chapter, we will explore functions, which provide a way to encapsulate reusable code and enhance the modular structure of your programs.

Switch Statement:

The switch statement allows you to perform different actions based on the value of a variable or expression. It provides an alternative to using multiple if-else if-else statements when dealing with multiple possible values. The syntax of the switch statement is as follows:

```cpp
switch (expression) {
    case value1:
        // code to execute if expression equals value1
        break;
    case value2:
        // code to execute if expression equals value2
        break;
    ...
    default:
        // code to execute if expression does not match any case
}
```

Example:

```cpp
int day = 3;
string dayName;

switch (day) {
    case 1:
        dayName = "Monday";
        break;
    case 2:
        dayName = "Tuesday";
        break;
    case 3:
        dayName = "Wednesday";
        break;
    case 4:
        dayName = "Thursday";
        break;
    case 5:
        dayName = "Friday";
        break;
    default:
        dayName = "Invalid day";
}

cout << "Day: " << dayName << endl;
```

In this example, the switch statement evaluates the value of the **day** variable and assigns the corresponding day name to the **dayName** variable.

- Control Flow with Keywords:

C++ provides additional keywords that can be used in control flow statements to modify their behavior:

- The **break** keyword: As mentioned earlier, the **break** keyword is used to exit a loop or switch statement prematurely.
- The **continue** keyword: The **continue** keyword, as mentioned earlier, is used to skip the rest of the current iteration and move to the next iteration of a loop.
- The **goto** keyword: The **goto** keyword allows you to transfer the control flow to a specified label within the same function. However, the use of **goto** is generally discouraged due to its potential to create complex and hard-to-understand code.

Example:

```cpp
int x = 0;

while (x < 10) {
    if (x == 5) {
        goto end;
    }
    cout << "x: " << x << endl;
    x++;
}


end:
cout << "End of program" << endl;
```

In this example, when **x** is equal to 5, the **goto** statement transfers the control flow to the **end** label, skipping the remaining iterations of the loop.

Understanding control flow is essential in creating programs that can make decisions, iterate over data, and perform different actions based on conditions. By utilizing conditional statements, loops, and switch statements, you can effectively control the flow of execution in your C++ programs. In the next section, we will dive into functions, which play a crucial role in modularizing code and promoting code reusability.

6. Control Flow Best Practices:

When working with control flow statements, it is important to follow certain best practices to ensure code readability and maintainability:

- Use meaningful variable and function names: Choose descriptive names for variables and functions that accurately represent their purpose. This makes the code more understandable for yourself and others who may read or work on the code in the future.
- Keep control flow statements concise: Avoid writing overly complex conditions or nested control flow statements. Break down complex logic into smaller, more manageable pieces. This improves code readability and reduces the likelihood of introducing errors.
- Use comments to explain complex control flow: If you have intricate control flow logic, consider adding comments to explain the reasoning behind the code. This helps other developers understand the purpose and behavior of the code.
- Test different scenarios: Write test cases to verify that your control flow statements are working as expected. Test both the expected outcomes and edge cases to ensure your code handles various scenarios correctly.
- Follow coding style conventions: Adhere to coding style guidelines to maintain

consistency and make the code easier to read. Consistent indentation, proper spacing, and the use of braces are essential for clarity and avoiding potential mistakes.

By following these best practices, you can write control flow statements that are clear, maintainable, and robust. Understanding how to effectively use control flow in your programs is a crucial skill in becoming a proficient C++ programmer. In the next section, we will explore functions, which provide a way to encapsulate reusable code and enhance the modular structure of your programs.

2.6 FUNCTIONS

In C++, a function is a self-contained block of code that performs a specific task. Functions allow you to encapsulate reusable code and improve the modular structure of your programs. You can define your own functions or use predefined functions provided by libraries.

Function Syntax

The syntax for defining a function in C++ is as follows:

```
return_type function_name(parameter_list) {
    // Function body
    // Code statements
    // Return statement (if applicable)
}
```

Let's break down the components of a function:

- **return_type**: This specifies the data type of the value that the function returns, if any. It can be any valid C++ data type, such as `int`, `double`, `bool`, or `void` (if the function doesn't return a value).
- **function_name**: This is the name of the function. Choose a descriptive name that reflects the purpose of the function. Follow naming conventions, such as using lowercase letters and underscores for multi-word names.
- **parameter_list**: This is a list of input parameters (also known as arguments) that the function accepts. Parameters allow you to pass values into the function for processing. If the function doesn't require any parameters, the parameter list can be left empty or contain the `void` keyword.
- **Function body**: This is the block of code enclosed within curly braces `{}` that defines the actions performed by the function.
- **Code statements**: These are the individual statements that make up the function's logic. They are executed sequentially when the function is called.
- **Return statement**: If the function has a return type other than `void`, it must include a `return` statement to specify the value to be returned. The return statement also exits the function and transfers control back to the calling code.

Example Program: Calculating the Area of a Rectangle

Let's write a complete program in C++ that demonstrates the use of functions to calculate the area of a rectangle. We'll define a function called `calculateArea` that accepts the length and width of the rectangle as parameters and returns the calculated area.

```cpp
#include <iostream>

// Function to calculate the area of a rectangle
double calculateArea(double length, double width) {
    double area = length * width;
```

```
    return area;
}

int main() {
    double length, width;

    // Prompt the user for input
    std::cout << "Enter the length of the rectangle: ";
    std::cin >> length;

    std::cout << "Enter the width of the rectangle: ";
    std::cin >> width;

    // Calculate the area using the function
    double rectangleArea = calculateArea(length, width);

    // Display the result
    std::cout << "The area of the rectangle is: " << rectangleArea << std::endl;

    return 0;
}
```

Now, let's analyze the program line by line:
- Line 1: The `#include <iostream>` directive is used to include the necessary input/output stream library.
- Line 4: The function `calculateArea` is defined with a return type of `double`. It takes two parameters: `length` and `width`.
- Line 5: The function body begins with an opening curly brace `{`.
- Line 6: A variable `area` is declared to store the calculated area.
- Line 7: The area is calculated by multiplying `length` and `width`.
- Line 8: The calculated `area` value is returned using the `return` statement.
- Line 11: The `main` function is defined as the entry point of the program.
- Line 13-14: Variables `length` and `width` are declared to store user input.
- Line 17-18: The user is prompted to enter the length and width of the rectangle using `std::cout` for output and `std::cin` for input.
- Line 21: The `calculateArea` function is called with `length` and `width` as arguments, and the result is assigned to the variable `rectangleArea`.
- Line 24: The calculated area is displayed to the user using `std::cout`.
- Line 27: The `main` function returns 0 to indicate successful program execution.

By encapsulating the calculation logic within the `calculateArea` function, we achieve code reusability and improve the readability of the main program logic. Functions allow us to modularize our code and promote efficient program development.

In the next chapter, we will explore more advanced topics in C++ programming, including object-oriented programming and class structures.

2.7 C++ PROGRAMMING WITH VISUAL STUDIO CODE

Visual Studio Code (VS Code) is a widely used, open-source integrated development environment (IDE) that offers robust features and extensibility for various programming languages, including C++. It provides a streamlined and efficient environment for writing, debugging, and managing C++ code. In this section, we'll explore how to set up and use Visual Studio Code for C++ programming, covering essential features and workflows.

2.7.1 INSTALLING VISUAL STUDIO CODE

To get started with C++ programming using Visual Studio Code, follow these steps to install the necessary components:

1. **Install Visual Studio Code:** Download and install Visual Studio Code from the official website (https://code.visualstudio.com/). Choose the version appropriate for your operating system.

2. **Install Extensions:** Visual Studio Code's power comes from its extensions. Install the following extensions to enhance your C++ programming experience:
   - **C/C++ Extension:** This extension provides essential features such as code completion, debugging, and IntelliSense for C++ programming.
   - **CMake Tools Extension:** If you're using CMake for your C++ projects, this extension offers CMake integration within Visual Studio Code.

3. **Install a C++ Compiler:** To compile and run C++ code, you need a C++ compiler. Depending on your platform, you can install compilers like GCC (GNU Compiler Collection) or Clang.

2.7.2 CREATING A C++ PROJECT

Visual Studio Code makes it convenient to create and manage C++ projects. Here's how you can create a simple C++ project:

1. **Create a New Folder:** Create a new folder for your C++ project. Open this folder in Visual Studio Code.

2. **Create a Source File:** Inside the project folder, create a new C++ source file (e.g., `main.cpp`). You can use the built-in terminal within Visual Studio Code to create files and folders.

3. **Write Code:** Write your C++ code in the source file. You can take advantage of features like code highlighting, IntelliSense, and code formatting provided by the C/C++ extension.

2.7.3 BUILDING AND RUNNING C++ CODE

Visual Studio Code simplifies the process of building and running C++ code. Here's how you can build and execute your C++ program:

1. **Configure Build Tasks:** Open your project folder in Visual Studio Code and create a `tasks.json` file. Configure build tasks to compile and build your C++ program using the chosen compiler (e.g., GCC or Clang).

2. **Build the Code:** Use the integrated terminal to run the build task you configured. This will compile your C++ code and generate the executable.

3. **Run the Program:** Once the build is successful, you can run the generated executable directly from the terminal within Visual Studio Code.

2.7.4 DEBUGGING C++ CODE

Visual Studio Code offers powerful debugging capabilities for C++ programming. To debug your C++ program:

1. **Set Breakpoints:** Open your source file and set breakpoints at desired locations in your code.

2. **Configure Debugging:** Create a `launch.json` file in your project folder. Configure the debugging settings, specifying the executable file and any required arguments.

3. **Start Debugging:** Use the debugging interface in Visual Studio Code to start debugging your C++ program. You can step through the code, inspect variables, and analyze program behavior.

2.7.5 ADVANCED FEATURES AND CUSTOMIZATION

Visual Studio Code provides a wide range of advanced features and customization options to enhance your C++ programming workflow. You can explore and utilize features such as version control integration, code snippets, task automation, and more. Additionally, you can install various extensions from the VS Code marketplace to tailor the IDE to your specific needs.

In conclusion, Visual Studio Code is a versatile and efficient IDE for C++ programming. By following the steps outlined in this section, you can set up a productive environment for writing, building, debugging, and managing your C++ projects with ease.

2.8 CONCLUSION

As we conclude this chapter on C++ programming, I hope you've enjoyed diving into the fundamentals of the language. From understanding the syntax and control flow to exploring data types, operators, arrays, pointers, and functions, you've taken significant strides on your programming journey.

You've learned how to write clean and efficient code, using control flow statements to make decisions and repeat actions. You've grasped the importance of organizing your code into functions, making it modular and reusable. With each example and exercise, you've honed your skills and gained confidence in your ability to tackle programming challenges.

Remember, programming is an art, and mastering it requires patience, practice, and a never-ending thirst for knowledge. Embrace the joy of coding, and let your creativity soar as you explore the vast possibilities of C++.

As you move forward, keep challenging yourself, pushing the boundaries of your understanding, and seeking opportunities to apply your newfound knowledge. Embrace the mistakes and learn from them, for they are the stepping stones to growth.

So, take a moment to appreciate how far you've come. Celebrate your accomplishments, no matter how small they may seem. You are now equipped with the foundational knowledge of C++, and the world of programming awaits your creative touch.

In the next chapter, we will embark on a captivating journey into object-oriented programming, where we will unlock the power of classes, inheritance, and polymorphism. Get ready to elevate your programming skills to new heights!

Stay passionate, stay curious, and keep coding with your heart. The possibilities are endless, and your potential knows no bounds. Happy programming!

3 TOP-DOWN DESIGN

Welcome to Chapter 3 of our journey into **Advanced Programming with C++**! In this chapter, we will explore the powerful concept of **Top-Down Design** - a fundamental approach that enables us to tackle complex problems and create well-structured and maintainable code.

Top-Down Design is a problem-solving methodology that involves breaking down a large problem into smaller, more manageable sub-problems. By approaching the problem from a high-level perspective and gradually refining the solution, we can create a structured roadmap that leads to an efficient and elegant code implementation.

Throughout this chapter, we will delve into the following key sections, each accompanied by examples to solidify your understanding:

1. **Problem Decomposition and Modularization**
   - Understand the importance of breaking down problems into smaller modules
   - Identify appropriate functions and modules for code organization
   - Follow modular design guidelines to ensure code flexibility and reusability

2. **Stepwise Refinement**
   - Grasp the concept of refining high-level concepts into detailed and coherent steps
   - Learn techniques to ensure clarity and maintainability in stepwise refinement
   - Apply stepwise refinement to tackle real-world programming challenges

3. **Algorithm Design and Pseudocode**
   - Explore the foundations of algorithm design and problem-solving approaches
   - Translate complex algorithms into *pseudocode*, a human-readable representation of code
   - Use pseudocode as a powerful tool for planning and discussing algorithms

As a C++ teacher, my goal is to equip you with the essential skills and methodologies to approach programming challenges with confidence and creativity. Embrace the concepts of top-down design, and you will find yourself efficiently designing solutions, fostering code reusability, and crafting elegant and effective code.

Let's embark on this exciting journey into the world of Top-Down Design in C++ and unleash your full potential as an advanced programmer!

3.1 PROBLEM DECOMPOSITION AND MODULARIZATION

In the world of programming, tackling large and complex problems can be daunting. However, with the technique of *Problem Decomposition and Modularization*, we can break down these challenges into smaller, more manageable parts. Let's dive in and explore this fundamental approach!

3.1.1 UNDERSTANDING THE IMPORTANCE OF DECOMPOSITION

Decomposition is the process of dividing a large problem into smaller, independent sub-problems, or modules. It allows us to focus on solving each sub-problem individually, which often leads to clearer and more maintainable code.

Consider a scenario where you need to create a program to manage a library. Instead of trying to implement the entire system at once, decomposition allows you to identify individual tasks, such as adding new books, searching for books, or handling book rentals. Each task becomes a separate module, making it easier to understand and modify specific functionalities.

Example: Decomposition in Library Management

Suppose we want to decompose the library management program into three modules:

1. **Adding New Books**: A module responsible for adding new books to the library's database.
2. **Searching for Books**: A module that allows users to search for books based on different criteria.
3. **Book Rentals**: A module to handle the rental and return of books.

By decomposing the problem, we can focus on each module's implementation independently, making the development process more manageable and less prone to errors.

3.1.2 IDENTIFYING MODULES AND FUNCTIONS

Once we understand the significance of decomposition, the next step is to identify the individual *modules* and *functions* that will make up our program. Modules represent distinct components, while functions are self-contained blocks of code that perform specific tasks.

Example: Identifying Modules and Functions

For our library management program, we can identify the following modules and functions:

1. **Module: Book Database**
   - Function: `addBook()`
   - Function: `searchBook()`
   - Function: `updateBook()`
2. **Module: User Interface**
   - Function: `displayMenu()`
   - Function: `getUserChoice()`
   - Function: `showBookDetails()`
3. **Module: Book Rental**
   - Function: `rentBook()`
   - Function: `returnBook()`
   - Function: `checkAvailability()`

By identifying these modules and their corresponding functions, we can focus on writing clear and concise code for each task, making our program more organized and easier to maintain.

3.1.3 MODULAR DESIGN GUIDELINES

When creating modules and functions, it is essential to follow certain *Modular Design Guidelines* to ensure that our code remains robust and extensible:

1. **Single Responsibility Principle**: Each module and function should have a clear and distinct purpose, focusing on accomplishing a single task.
2. **Information Hiding**: Modules should encapsulate their internal workings, exposing only necessary interfaces to other parts of the program. This improves code isolation and reduces dependencies.
3. **Reusability**: Aim to write modules and functions that can be reused in different parts of the program or even in other projects.
4. **Consistency**: Maintain a consistent naming convention and coding style across all modules and functions for improved readability.

By adhering to these guidelines, we create modular code that enhances code organization, fosters code reuse, and simplifies future modifications and expansions.

In summary, *Problem Decomposition and Modularization* is a vital technique in advanced C++ programming. Breaking down complex problems into smaller modules and functions leads to clearer code, better maintainability, and increased code reuse. Embrace this approach, and you'll find yourself crafting elegant and efficient solutions to challenging programming tasks.

3.2 STEPWISE REFINEMENT

In the process of **Stepwise Refinement**, we take a high-level view of a problem and break it down into smaller, more manageable steps. This approach helps us develop a clear and systematic plan to solve the problem, ensuring that each step is well-defined and coherent.

3.2.1 OVERVIEW OF STEPWISE REFINEMENT

Stepwise Refinement is like solving a puzzle - you start with the big picture, then gradually focus on smaller pieces until you complete the entire picture. Similarly, in programming, we start by understanding the problem at a high level, and then we refine our approach into smaller, detailed steps.

Let's illustrate this with a simple example:

Example: Printing the Sum of Two Numbers

Suppose we want to create a program that calculates and prints the sum of two numbers. We can use stepwise refinement to outline the solution:

1. **High-Level Approach:**
   - Input the two numbers from the user.
   - Calculate the sum of the two numbers.
   - Display the result.
2. **Detailed Steps:** a. Input the first number and store it in a variable, let's call it *num1*. b. Input the second number and store it in another variable, let's call it *num2*. c. Add *num1* and *num2* together, and store the result in a variable, let's call it *sum*. d. Display the value of *sum* as the output.

3.2.2 REFINING HIGH-LEVEL CONCEPTS INTO DETAILED STEPS

In the detailed steps, each high-level concept is broken down into specific actions or instructions. We specify precisely what needs to be done at each stage. This approach makes our code more manageable and easier to implement.

Example: Calculating the Area of a Rectangle

Consider another example: calculating the area of a rectangle.

1. **High-Level Approach:**
   - Input the length and width of the rectangle.
   - Calculate the area.
   - Display the result.
2. **Detailed Steps:** a. Input the length of the rectangle and store it in a variable, say *length*. b. Input the width of the rectangle and store it in another variable, say *width*. c. Calculate the area by multiplying *length* and *width*, and store the result in a variable, say *area*. d. Display the value of *area* as the output.

3.2.3 ENSURING CLARITY AND COHERENCE IN STEPWISE REFINEMENT

To ensure clarity and coherence in stepwise refinement, we must be precise in our descriptions and ensure that each step logically follows the previous one. Our steps should be concise and easy to understand, so anyone reading our code can grasp the solution without confusion.

Stepwise refinement enables us to tackle complex problems by approaching them systematically, making it a powerful technique for building sophisticated programs. By breaking down problems into manageable steps, we can confidently implement our solutions and produce clear, coherent, and efficient code. Embrace the process of stepwise refinement, and you'll find that programming becomes a more enjoyable and rewarding experience.

3.3 ALGORITHM DESIGN

Welcome to the fascinating world of **Algorithm Design**! In this section, we will explore the art of crafting step-by-step instructions to solve problems efficiently and effectively. Algorithms are at the core of every program, guiding the computer to perform tasks with precision and speed.

3.3.1 INTRODUCTION TO ALGORITHM DESIGN

Algorithm Design involves devising a clear and logical plan to solve a problem or perform a specific task. Think of algorithms as recipes - a set of instructions that lead to a desired outcome. As programmers, we need to design algorithms that are not only correct but also optimized for performance.

To illustrate the importance of algorithms, let's consider a classic problem: finding the maximum value in a list of numbers. There are various ways to approach this problem, and we'll explore different algorithms to demonstrate their efficiency.

3.3.2 PROBLEM SOLVING APPROACHES AND STRATEGIES

Solving a problem with an algorithm requires choosing the right approach and strategy. Here are two common problem-solving approaches:

1. **Brute Force Approach**: This approach involves trying all possible solutions to find the correct one. While simple, it may not be efficient for large datasets.

Example: Finding the Maximum Value

For a list of numbers {5, 9, 2, 1, 7}, the brute force approach would involve checking each number to find the maximum, which in this case is 9.

2. **Optimized Approach**: This approach utilizes specific techniques and insights to arrive at the solution more efficiently.

Example: Finding the Maximum Value using an Optimized Approach

For the same list of numbers {5, 9, 2, 1, 7}, an optimized approach would involve comparing each number as we iterate through the list, efficiently keeping track of the maximum value encountered. This results in finding the maximum value (9) with fewer operations, making it more efficient than the brute force approach.

3.3.3 TRANSLATING ALGORITHMS INTO PSEUDOCODE

Pseudocode is a human-readable representation of an algorithm. It uses informal, high-level descriptions to outline the logic of the algorithm without getting into the specifics of a particular programming language.

Example: Pseudocode for Finding the Maximum Value

Here's a pseudocode representation of an optimized algorithm to find the maximum value in a list of numbers:

```
Function findMax(numbers)
  maxVal = numbers[0]  // Initialize maxVal with the first element
  For each num in numbers
    If num > maxVal
       maxVal = num
  End For
  Return maxVal
End Function
```

In this pseudocode, we define a function called `findMax` that takes a list of `numbers` as input. We initialize `maxVal` with the first element of the list and then iterate through the list, comparing each element with the current maximum value, and updating `maxVal` if a larger value is found. Finally, the function returns the maximum value.

Algorithm design is a powerful skill that empowers you to solve complex problems with precision and elegance. As you delve deeper into the world of C++ programming, honing your algorithm design skills will enable you to create efficient and robust solutions to a wide range of challenges. Embrace the art of algorithms, and you'll unlock the true potential of your programming journey. Happy coding!

4 UNDERSTANDING OBJECTS AND CLASSES

Welcome to the exciting world of **Object-Oriented Programming (OOP)**! In this section, we will embark on a journey to understand the core concepts of OOP - *Objects* and *Classes*. These fundamental concepts form the backbone of modern programming, allowing us to model real-world entities in our code and build powerful and scalable applications.

4.1 INTRODUCTION TO OBJECT-ORIENTED PROGRAMMING (OOP)

Object-Oriented Programming is a programming paradigm that revolves around the idea of organizing code into objects, each representing a unique entity with its own characteristics and behavior. OOP enables us to think and design programs in a way that closely mimics real-world interactions.

At the heart of OOP are four key principles:

1. **Encapsulation**: Encapsulation refers to the bundling of data (attributes) and methods (functions) that operate on that data within a single unit called an *object*. It hides the internal implementation details and exposes only relevant interfaces for interaction with the object.

2. **Abstraction**: Abstraction allows us to focus on the essential features of an object while hiding unnecessary details. It simplifies complex systems by providing a clear and concise representation.

3. **Inheritance**: Inheritance allows us to create new classes based on existing classes, inheriting their attributes and behaviors. It promotes code reuse and hierarchical organization.

4. **Polymorphism**: Polymorphism allows objects of different classes to be treated as objects of a common base class. This flexibility allows us to write code that works seamlessly with a variety of objects.

4.1.1 OBJECTS: THE BUILDING BLOCKS OF OOP

An *object* is a concrete instance of a class, representing a specific entity with its own state and behavior. It combines data (attributes) and methods (functions) that operate on that data, encapsulated within a single unit.

Example: Creating a Class and an Object

Let's consider a simple example of a class representing a *Circle*:

```
class Circle {
public:
    double radius;
```

```cpp
    double calculateArea() {
        return 3.14 * radius * radius;
    }
};

int main() {
    Circle myCircle; // Creating an object of the Circle class
    myCircle.radius = 5.0;

    double area = myCircle.calculateArea();
    cout << "Area of the circle: " << area << endl;

    return 0;
}
```

In this example, we define a class called `Circle` with a public attribute `radius` and a method `calculateArea()`. We then create an object `myCircle` from the `Circle` class and set its radius to 5.0. We call the `calculateArea()` method on `myCircle` to compute the area of the circle and display the result.

4.1.2 CLASSES: BLUEPRINT FOR OBJECTS

A *class* serves as a blueprint or template for creating objects. It defines the structure and behavior that the objects belonging to the class will exhibit. It encapsulates the attributes and methods that the objects will possess.

Example: Defining a Class for a Book

```cpp
class Book {
public:
    string title;
    string author;
    int year;
};
```

In this example, we define a class called **Book** with three attributes - `title`, `author`, and `year`. The class acts as a blueprint for creating individual **Book** objects, each having its own values for the attributes.

4.1.3 CREATING OBJECTS FROM CLASSES

To create an object from a class, we declare a variable of the class type. This variable becomes an instance of the class, representing a unique object.

Example: Creating Multiple Book Objects

```cpp
int main() {
    Book book1;
    book1.title = "The Alchemist";
    book1.author = "Paulo Coelho";
```

```
    book1.year = 1988;

    Book book2;
    book2.title = "To Kill a Mockingbird";
    book2.author = "Harper Lee";
    book2.year = 1960;

    // Code to use the book objects goes here...

    return 0;
}
```

In this example, we create two **Book** objects - `book1` and `book2`. Each object represents a unique book with its own values for the `title`, `author`, and `year` attributes.

Understanding objects and classes is the foundation of object-oriented programming. By creating and manipulating objects, we can design powerful, flexible, and organized code. Embrace the world of OOP, and you'll unlock the potential to create sophisticated and elegant C++ programs.

4.2 ENCAPSULATION AND DATA HIDING

In the world of Object-Oriented Programming (OOP), *Encapsulation* and *Data Hiding* are powerful concepts that play a crucial role in designing robust and secure code. They ensure that the internal details of an object are hidden from external access, providing a well-defined interface for interacting with the object.

4.2.1 ENCAPSULATION: KEEPING DATA AND BEHAVIOR TOGETHER

Encapsulation is the process of bundling data (attributes) and methods (functions) that operate on that data within a single unit called an *object*. It allows us to combine related data and behavior together, effectively organizing the code and promoting code reusability.

By encapsulating data and behavior, we prevent direct access to an object's internal details from outside the object. Instead, external interactions with the object are limited to a well-defined set of methods, which ensures controlled and consistent manipulation of the object's state.

Example: Encapsulation in a Bank Account

```
class BankAccount {
private:
    double balance; // Encapsulated attribute

public:
    // Encapsulated methods
    void deposit(double amount) {
        balance += amount;
    }

    void withdraw(double amount) {
        if (balance >= amount) {
            balance -= amount;
        } else {
```

```
        cout << "Insufficient funds!" << endl;
    }
}

double getBalance() {
    return balance;
}
};
```

In this example, we define a **BankAccount** class with an encapsulated **balance** attribute. We provide methods (**deposit** and **withdraw**) to manipulate the balance, and the **getBalance** method allows external access to the account's balance.

4.2.2 ACCESS MODIFIERS: CONTROLLING DATA VISIBILITY

In C++, access modifiers are keywords that determine the visibility and accessibility of class members (attributes and methods) from outside the class.

There are three access modifiers:

1. **Public**: Members declared as public are accessible from anywhere in the program, including outside the class.

2. **Private**: Members declared as private are only accessible from within the class. They are hidden from outside access.

3. **Protected**: Members declared as protected are accessible from within the class and its derived classes. We won't cover protected members in this section, but they are useful in inheritance scenarios.

By using access modifiers, we can control the visibility and ensure the encapsulation of our class's attributes and methods.

Example: Access Modifiers in a Student Class

```
class Student {
public:
    string name; // Public attribute
    int age;     // Public attribute

private:
    int rollNumber; // Private attribute
};
```

In this example, **name** and **age** are public attributes, which means they can be accessed and modified directly from outside the **Student** class. However, **rollNumber** is a private attribute, so it can only be accessed and modified from within the **Student** class.

4.2.3 GETTERS AND SETTERS: SAFELY ACCESSING AND MODIFYING DATA

To ensure controlled access to private attributes, we use *getters* and *setters*. Getters provide read-only access to the attribute, while setters allow controlled modification.

Example: Using Getters and Setters for Roll Number

```
class Student {
```

```
private:
    int rollNumber; // Private attribute

public:
    // Getter for rollNumber
    int getRollNumber() {
        return rollNumber;
    }

    // Setter for rollNumber
    void setRollNumber(int newRollNumber) {
        if (newRollNumber > 0) {
            rollNumber = newRollNumber;
        } else {
            cout << "Invalid roll number!" << endl;
        }
    }
};
```

In this example, we define `getRollNumber()` to provide external access to the `rollNumber` attribute, and `setRollNumber()` allows controlled modification of the `rollNumber` attribute by checking if the input is valid.

Encapsulation and data hiding are crucial in developing secure and maintainable code. By controlling access to class members and providing well-defined interfaces through getters and setters, we ensure that our objects remain in a consistent and valid state. Embrace encapsulation and data hiding to design elegant and robust C++ programs.

4.3 BENEFITS OF OBJECT-ORIENTED PROGRAMMING

Object-Oriented Programming (OOP) is a powerful paradigm that revolutionized the way we approach software development. It brings a host of advantages over traditional procedural programming, making it the preferred choice for building complex and scalable applications.

4.3.1 ADVANTAGES OF OOP OVER PROCEDURAL PROGRAMMING

In OOP, programs are organized around objects that represent real-world entities. This approach offers several key advantages over procedural programming:

1. **Modularity**: OOP promotes modular code design, where functionalities are encapsulated within objects. This modular approach makes the code easier to understand, maintain, and update.

2. **Code Reusability**: OOP allows you to create reusable classes and objects. You can easily reuse existing code in new projects, reducing development time and effort.

3. **Data Encapsulation**: With encapsulation, the internal details of objects are hidden from external access. This enhances security and prevents unintended modification of data.

4. **Code Organization**: OOP encourages a hierarchical organization of code through classes and inheritance, making it easier to manage and navigate large projects.

4.3.2 CODE REUSABILITY: CREATING MODULAR AND MAINTAINABLE CODE

One of the key benefits of OOP is code reusability. By creating reusable classes and objects, you can save time and effort in developing new applications.

Example: Reusable Class for Mathematical Operations

Let's consider a reusable class that performs basic mathematical operations:

```cpp
class MathOperations {
public:
    int add(int a, int b) {
        return a + b;
    }

    int multiply(int a, int b) {
        return a * b;
    }
};
```

With this class, you can perform addition and multiplication in multiple projects without rewriting the same code.

4.3.3 INHERITANCE: BUILDING HIERARCHICAL AND EXTENSIBLE CODE

Inheritance is a powerful OOP concept that allows you to create new classes based on existing ones. It enables code reuse and promotes a hierarchical organization of classes.

Example: Inheritance in Animal Classes

```cpp
class Animal {
public:
    void makeSound() {
        cout << "Animal makes a sound." << endl;
    }
};


class Dog : public Animal {
public:
    void makeSound() {
        cout << "Dog barks." << endl;
    }
};


class Cat : public Animal {
public:
    void makeSound() {
        cout << "Cat meows." << endl;
    }
};
```

In this example, Dog and Cat are derived classes of the base class Animal. They inherit the `makeSound()` method from the base class and override it to provide specific behavior.

4.3.4 POLYMORPHISM: PROMOTING FLEXIBILITY AND SCALABILITY

Polymorphism allows objects of different classes to be treated as objects of a common base class. It promotes flexibility and scalability in your code.

Example: Polymorphism with Shape Classes

```cpp
class Shape {
public:
    virtual void draw() {
        cout << "Drawing a shape." << endl;
    }
};

class Circle : public Shape {
public:
    void draw() override {
        cout << "Drawing a circle." << endl;
    }
};

class Square : public Shape {
public:
    void draw() override {
        cout << "Drawing a square." << endl;
    }
};
```

In this example, `Circle` and `Square` are derived classes of the base class `Shape`. By using polymorphism, you can treat any shape object as a `Shape`, making it easier to work with diverse shapes in your application.

By leveraging the benefits of OOP - code reusability, data encapsulation, inheritance, and polymorphism - you can build sophisticated and scalable applications. OOP empowers you to create elegant and maintainable code, making it an essential skill for any aspiring C++ programmer. Embrace the power of OOP and unlock the full potential of your programming journey.

4.4 EXAMPLE: BUILDING A LIBRARY MANAGEMENT SYSTEM

Let's put all the concepts we've learned in Chapter 4 into practice by building a simple Library Management System using C++. In this example, we'll create classes to represent books and library users, demonstrate encapsulation, use inheritance, and showcase polymorphism.

Step 1: Define the Book Class

```cpp
#include <iostream>
#include <string>
using namespace std;
```

```cpp
class Book {
private:
    string title;
    string author;
    int year;

public:
    Book(string _title, string _author, int _year) : title(_title), author(_author),
year(_year) {}

    void displayInfo() {
        cout << "Title: " << title << endl;
        cout << "Author: " << author << endl;
        cout << "Year: " << year << endl;
    }
};
```

In this class, we have three private attributes - `title`, `author`, and `year` - representing the book's information. The constructor is used to initialize these attributes. We also have a public method `displayInfo()` to display the book's information.

Step 2: Define the User Class

```cpp
class User {
private:
    string name;
    int age;

public:
    User(string _name, int _age) : name(_name), age(_age) {}

    void displayInfo() {
        cout << "Name: " << name << endl;
        cout << "Age: " << age << endl;
    }
};
```

In this class, we have two private attributes - `name` and `age` - representing the user's information. The constructor is used to initialize these attributes. We also have a public method `displayInfo()` to display the user's information.

Step 3: Define the Student Class

```cpp
class Student : public User {
private:
    int rollNumber;
```

```cpp
public:
    Student(string _name, int _age, int _rollNumber) : User(_name, _age),
rollNumber(_rollNumber) {}

    void displayInfo() {
        User::displayInfo();
        cout << "Roll Number: " << rollNumber << endl;
    }
};
```

In this class, we have a private attribute `rollNumber` and a constructor to initialize it. The `Student` class inherits from the `User` class, allowing us to reuse the `User` class's attributes and methods. We override the `displayInfo()` method to include the student's roll number.

Step 4: Implementing the Library Management System

```cpp
int main() {
    // Create books
    Book book1("The Alchemist", "Paulo Coelho", 1988);
    Book book2("To Kill a Mockingbird", "Harper Lee", 1960);

    // Create users
    User user1("John Doe", 25);
    Student student1("Alice Smith", 20, 12345);

    // Display book and user information
    cout << "Book 1 Information:" << endl;
    book1.displayInfo();

    cout << "\nBook 2 Information:" << endl;
    book2.displayInfo();

    cout << "\nUser 1 Information:" << endl;
    user1.displayInfo();

    cout << "\nStudent 1 Information:" << endl;
    student1.displayInfo();

    return 0;
}
```

In the `main()` function, we create instances of the `Book`, `User`, and `Student` classes and display their information using the `displayInfo()` method. Since the `Student` class inherits from the `User` class, we can use polymorphism to treat a `Student` object as a `User` object.

Output:

```
Book 1 Information:
Title: The Alchemist
Author: Paulo Coelho
Year: 1988

Book 2 Information:
Title: To Kill a Mockingbird
Author: Harper Lee
Year: 1960

User 1 Information:
Name: John Doe
Age: 25

Student 1 Information:
Name: Alice Smith
Age: 20
Roll Number: 12345
```

In this example, we've demonstrated the concepts of encapsulation, inheritance, and polymorphism in a simple Library Management System. By using object-oriented programming, we've organized the code into classes, provided reusability, and made the code more manageable. This is just a glimpse of what OOP can achieve. As you explore further, you'll find that OOP is a powerful and elegant paradigm that can be applied to build complex and sophisticated C++ applications.

5 BASIC STRUCTURES OF OBJECT-ORIENTED PROGRAMMING: OBJECTS AND CONSTRUCTORS

In C++, objects are instances of classes, representing real-world entities with their own attributes and behaviors. To create an object, we use the concept of instantiation, which involves allocating memory and initializing the object's data. In this section, we will explore the process of creating objects and initializing their data in C++.

5.1 CREATING OBJECTS AND INITIALIZING DATA

5.1.1 INTRODUCTION TO OBJECT CREATION

In C++, *object creation* is a fundamental concept in object-oriented programming. Objects are instances of classes, and they represent real-world entities with their own attributes and behaviors. The process of creating an object involves allocating memory for the object and initializing its data members. In C++, we use the concept of *instantiation* to create objects from classes.

Creating Objects:

To create an object, we follow the syntax of the class and use the new keyword to allocate memory dynamically. However, in C++, we often prefer to create objects using automatic memory allocation, without explicitly using new. This is achieved by creating objects on the *stack*.

Example: Creating a Simple Class

```cpp
#include <iostream>
using namespace std;

class Person {
public:
    string name;
    int age;
};

int main() {
    // Creating objects of the Person class
    Person person1;
```

```
    person1.name = "John";
    person1.age = 30;

    Person person2;
    person2.name = "Alice";
    person2.age = 25;

    // Displaying object data
    cout << "Person 1: Name - " << person1.name << ", Age - " << person1.age << endl;
    cout << "Person 2: Name - " << person2.name << ", Age - " << person2.age << endl;

    return 0;
}
```

In this example, we define a `Person` class with two attributes - `name` and `age`. Inside the `main()` function, we create two `Person` objects - `person1` and `person2`. We then set the values of their attributes and display the data.

Output:

```
Person 1: Name - John, Age - 30
Person 2: Name - Alice, Age - 25
```

Initializing Data:

In C++, you can initialize an object's data at the time of creation using *constructors*. A constructor is a special member function that gets called automatically when an object is created. It is responsible for initializing the object's data members.

Example: Initializing Data with Constructors

```cpp
#include <iostream>
using namespace std;

class Circle {
public:
    double radius;

    // Constructor to initialize the radius
    Circle(double r) : radius(r) {}

    double calculateArea() {
        return 3.14 * radius * radius;
    }
};

int main() {
    // Creating a Circle object and initializing the radius
```

```
    Circle circle1(5.0);
    Circle circle2(3.0);

    // Displaying the areas of the circles
    cout << "Area of Circle 1: " << circle1.calculateArea() << endl;
    cout << "Area of Circle 2: " << circle2.calculateArea() << endl;

    return 0;
}
```

In this example, we define a `Circle` class with a `radius` attribute. We also define a constructor for the `Circle` class that takes a `double` parameter `r` and initializes the `radius` with the provided value.

In the constructor, there is a colon `:` followed by `radius(r)`. This is called a **member initializer list**. It is a way to initialize the member variable `radius` with the value provided as the argument `r`. The member initializer list syntax is used to specify how member variables should be initialized.

By using the member initializer list, the `radius` member variable of the `Circle` object is directly set to the value of `r` during the object's creation, ensuring that the circle object starts with the specified radius without needing to use assignment inside the constructor body.

When we create `circle1` and `circle2`, we pass the radius values (5.0 and 3.0, respectively) to the constructor, and the constructor sets the `radius` attribute accordingly.

Output:

```
Area of Circle 1: 78.5
Area of Circle 2: 28.26
```

Creating objects and initializing their data are essential concepts in object-oriented programming. By understanding these concepts, you can create powerful and flexible code that models real-world entities efficiently. As you continue your journey in C++, remember that objects are the building blocks of OOP, and their proper creation and initialization are crucial for writing effective and maintainable code.

5.1.2 INSTANTIATING OBJECTS

In C++, *instantiating objects* is the process of creating instances of classes, commonly referred to as objects. Objects are the tangible representation of the abstract blueprint defined by a class. They allow us to work with data and perform actions defined in the class. Instantiation is a crucial step in object-oriented programming as it allows us to bring the class to life and use its functionalities.

Creating Objects:

To instantiate an object, we use the class name followed by parentheses `()` to call the constructor. The constructor is a special member function that gets executed automatically when the object is created. It is responsible for initializing the object's data members and setting up the object.

Example: Creating and Instantiating a Simple Class

```
#include <iostream>
using namespace std;

class Car {
public:
    string make;
```

```
    string model;
    int year;

    // Constructor to initialize car details
    Car(string _make, string _model, int _year) : make(_make), model(_model), year(_year) {}
};

int main() {
    // Instantiating objects of the Car class
    Car car1("Toyota", "Corolla", 2022);
    Car car2("Honda", "Civic", 2021);

    // Displaying car details
    cout << "Car 1: " << car1.make << " " << car1.model << " (" << car1.year << ")" << endl;
    cout << "Car 2: " << car2.make << " " << car2.model << " (" << car2.year << ")" << endl;

    return 0;
}
```

In this example, we define a Car class with three attributes - make, model, and year. We also define a constructor that takes three parameters to initialize the car details. In the main() function, we instantiate two objects - car1 and car2 - of the Car class by calling the constructor with the appropriate arguments. Each object is initialized with its specific details.

Output:

```
Car 1: Toyota Corolla (2022)
Car 2: Honda Civic (2021)
```

Automatic Memory Allocation:

In the example above, the objects car1 and car2 were created using automatic memory allocation. When the program enters the main() function, memory is automatically allocated for these objects on the stack. This means that when the objects go out of scope, their memory is automatically deallocated.

Dynamic Memory Allocation:

Alternatively, you can create objects using dynamic memory allocation with the new keyword. This approach allows you to control the object's lifetime explicitly and is commonly used when you need objects with a longer lifespan, beyond the scope of a particular function.

Example: Dynamic Memory Allocation

```
#include <iostream>
using namespace std;

class Person {
public:
    string name;
    int age;
```

```
};

int main() {
    // Creating a Person object using dynamic memory allocation
    Person* person = new Person;
    person->name = "Alice";
    person->age = 25;

    // Displaying person details
    cout << "Person: " << person->name << ", Age: " << person->age << endl;

    // Deallocating memory to avoid memory leaks
    delete person;

    return 0;
}
```

In this example, we create a **Person** object using dynamic memory allocation with the **new** keyword. We access the object's attributes using the arrow operator **->** since **person** is a pointer to the object. After using the object, we must explicitly deallocate the memory using the **delete** keyword to prevent memory leaks.

Instantiating objects in C++ allows you to bring your classes to life and work with real data. Whether you use automatic or dynamic memory allocation depends on the object's scope and lifespan. Understanding how to create and manage objects is essential for building robust and flexible C++ programs.

5.1.3 INITIALIZING OBJECT DATA

In C++, *initializing object data* is the process of setting the initial values of an object's attributes at the time of its creation. When we create an object, it is essential to provide meaningful initial values to ensure the object is in a valid and usable state. This initialization is typically done using constructors, special member functions of a class responsible for initializing the object's data members.

Using Constructors for Initialization:

Constructors are invoked automatically when an object is created. They play a vital role in setting up the object's initial state. By defining constructors in a class, we can ensure that the object's attributes are initialized to desired values. Constructors can have parameters to accept input values, allowing us to customize the initialization process.

Example: Initializing Object Data using Constructors

```
#include <iostream>
using namespace std;

class Point {
private:
    int x;
    int y;
```

```cpp
public:
    // Default constructor to set attributes to zero
    Point() : x(0), y(0) {}

    // Parameterized constructor to set attributes based on input values
    Point(int _x, int _y) : x(_x), y(_y) {}

    void displayCoordinates() {
        cout << "X: " << x << ", Y: " << y << endl;
    }
};

int main() {
    // Creating Point objects and initializing their data
    Point origin;        // Using the default constructor
    Point point(3, 5);   // Using the parameterized constructor

    // Displaying coordinates of the points
    cout << "Origin Point: ";
    origin.displayCoordinates();

    cout << "Custom Point: ";
    point.displayCoordinates();

    return 0;
}
```

In this example, we define a **Point** class with two attributes - **x** and **y**, representing the coordinates. We provide two constructors: a default constructor that sets both attributes to zero and a parameterized constructor that takes two arguments and sets the attributes accordingly.

When we create the **origin** object using the default constructor, its attributes are automatically set to zero. When we create the **point** object using the parameterized constructor and pass the values 3 and 5, its attributes are initialized with these values.

Output:
```
Origin Point: X: 0, Y: 0
Custom Point: X: 3, Y: 5
```
Initializer Lists:

In more complex classes with multiple attributes, initializing each attribute separately can be tedious. In such cases, we can use *initializer lists* to set the initial values of the attributes directly inside the constructor's definition.

Example: Using Initializer List

```cpp
#include <iostream>
using namespace std;
```

```cpp
class Rectangle {
private:
    int length;
    int width;

public:
    Rectangle(int _length, int _width) : length(_length), width(_width) {}

    void displayArea() {
        cout << "Area: " << length * width << endl;
    }
};

int main() {
    // Creating a Rectangle object and initializing its data using an initializer list
    Rectangle rectangle(4, 6);

    // Displaying the area of the rectangle
    rectangle.displayArea();

    return 0;
}
```

In this example, we define a `Rectangle` class with two attributes - `length` and `width`. We use an initializer list inside the constructor definition to set the initial values of these attributes directly.

When we create the `rectangle` object with the values 4 and 6, the constructor initializes its `length` and `width` attributes using the initializer list.

Output:

```
Area: 24
```

Initializing object data ensures that objects are created in a valid state and ready to be used. Constructors are powerful tools for customizing object initialization, making C++ classes more versatile and flexible. By understanding how to initialize object data, you can create robust and well-organized C++ programs.

5.1.4 OBJECT LIFETIME AND SCOPE

In C++, *object lifetime* refers to the period during which an object exists in memory. It begins when the object is created and ends when it is destroyed. Understanding the object's lifetime is essential for efficient memory management and avoiding memory leaks.

Object Scope:

The *scope* of an object refers to the portion of the code where the object is visible and accessible. In C++, objects created inside a block of code have *local scope*, meaning they are only accessible within that block. When the block ends, the objects declared within it are automatically destroyed, and their memory is deallocated.

Example: Object Scope

```cpp
#include <iostream>
using namespace std;

void functionA() {
    int localVar = 10; // Local variable with local scope

    cout << "Inside functionA: " << localVar << endl;
}

int main() {
    int mainVar = 20; // Local variable with local scope

    cout << "Inside main: " << mainVar << endl;

    functionA();

    // cout << "Outside functionA: " << localVar << endl; // Error: localVar is not in scope
here

    return 0;
}
```

In this example, we have two variables: `mainVar` declared inside the `main()` function and `localVar` declared inside `functionA()`. Each variable has its own scope - `mainVar` is accessible within the `main()` function, while `localVar` is accessible only within `functionA()`. If we try to access `localVar` outside `functionA()`, it will result in a compilation error since it is not in scope.

Object Lifetime:

The lifetime of an object refers to the period during which the object exists in memory, and its resources are allocated and deallocated appropriately. In C++, objects can have different lifetimes based on how they are created and what scope they belong to. Understanding the object's lifetime is essential for proper memory management and resource utilization in C++ programs.

Stack-Allocated Objects: Objects created on the stack have a lifetime limited to the scope in which they are declared. When the scope ends, such as when the function or block of code in which the object is declared completes execution, the object is automatically destroyed, and its memory is deallocated. This process is facilitated by the object's destructor.

Destructor: A destructor is a special member function in C++ that is automatically called when an object goes out of scope or is explicitly deleted. Its purpose is to release any resources that were allocated during the object's lifetime. Destructors have the same name as the class, preceded by a tilde ~, and they don't take any arguments or return any values.

Syntax of a Destructor:

```cpp
class ClassName {
public:
    // Constructor
    ClassName() {
```

```
        // Constructor code
    }

    // Destructor
    ~ClassName() {
        // Destructor code
    }

    // Other member functions and variables
};
```

Example: Object Lifetime on Stack

```cpp
#include <iostream>
using namespace std;

class Counter {
public:
    Counter() {
        cout << "Object created!" << endl;
    }

    ~Counter() {
        cout << "Object destroyed!" << endl;
    }
};

int main() {
    cout << "Before block" << endl;
    {
        Counter counter1; // Object created with local scope
    }
    cout << "After block" << endl;

    return 0;
}
```

In this example, we define a `Counter` class with a constructor and a destructor. The constructor displays a message when an object is created, and the destructor displays a message when an object is destroyed.

Inside the `main()` function, we create a `counter1` object within a block of code. When the block ends, the object's scope is over, and it is automatically destroyed, triggering the destructor message.

Output:

```
Before block
Object created!
```

```
Object destroyed!
After block
```

Understanding the object's lifetime and scope is crucial for proper memory management in C++. By creating objects with appropriate scope and using dynamic memory allocation wisely, you can ensure efficient utilization of memory resources and build robust C++ programs.

5.2 CONSTRUCTORS AND THEIR ROLE IN OBJECT CREATION

In C++, *constructors* are special member functions of a class that play a fundamental role in object creation. They are automatically called when an object is instantiated, allowing us to initialize the object's data members and prepare it for use. Constructors ensure that objects are created in a valid and consistent state, ready to perform their designated tasks.

Understanding Constructors:

The primary purpose of a constructor is to initialize the attributes of an object when it is created. It enables us to set default values or take specific input parameters to customize the object's initialization.

Constructor Syntax and Rules:

- A constructor has the same name as the class and no return type, not even **void**.
- The constructor is invoked automatically when an object is created, using the class name followed by parentheses ( ).
- If no constructor is defined in the class, C++ provides a default constructor that takes no arguments and does nothing. However, when you define your own constructor, the default constructor is no longer implicitly available.
- A class can have multiple constructors with different parameter lists, which is known as *constructor overloading.*

Example: Constructors Syntax and Rules

```cpp
#include <iostream>
using namespace std;

class Student {
public:
    string name;
    int age;

    // Default constructor
    Student() {
        cout << "Default constructor called." << endl;
    }

    // Parameterized constructor
    Student(string _name, int _age) {
        name = _name;
        age = _age;
        cout << "Parameterized constructor called." << endl;
    }
};
```

```
int main() {
    // Using the default constructor
    Student student1;

    // Using the parameterized constructor
    Student student2("Alice", 22);

    return 0;
}
```

In this example, we define a **Student** class with two constructors - a default constructor and a parameterized constructor. The default constructor displays a message when called, while the parameterized constructor takes two arguments to initialize the **name** and **age** attributes.

Output:

```
Default constructor called.
Parameterized constructor called.
```

The Default Constructor:

If you do not provide any constructor for a class, C++ automatically generates a default constructor. However, once you define your own constructor(s), the default constructor is no longer implicitly available. If you still wish to use the default constructor, you must explicitly define it in your class.

Example: Using the Default Constructor

```
#include <iostream>
using namespace std;

class Book {
public:
    string title;
    string author;

    // Using the default constructor
    Book() = default;
};

int main() {
    // Creating a Book object using the default constructor
    Book book;

    return 0;
}
```

In this example, we explicitly define the default constructor using the `= default` syntax. Now, we can use the default constructor to create a **Book** object without any arguments.

Constructors Overloading:

C++ allows you to create multiple constructors in a class with different parameter lists. This is known as *constructor overloading.* Overloaded constructors provide flexibility, enabling you to create objects in various ways, depending on the provided arguments.

Example: Constructor Overloading

```cpp
#include <iostream>
using namespace std;

class Rectangle {
private:
    int length;
    int width;

public:
    // Default constructor
    Rectangle() {
        length = 0;
        width = 0;
    }

    // Constructor with one argument to create a square
    Rectangle(int side) {
        length = side;
        width = side;
    }

    // Constructor with two arguments to create a rectangle
    Rectangle(int _length, int _width) {
        length = _length;
        width = _width;
    }

    void displayDimensions() {
        cout << "Length: " << length << ", Width: " << width << endl;
    }
};

int main() {
    Rectangle square;            // Using the default constructor
    Rectangle rectangle(4);      // Using the constructor with one argument
    Rectangle custom(6, 8);      // Using the constructor with two arguments

    // Displaying the dimensions of the shapes
    cout << "Square: ";
```

```
    square.displayDimensions();

    cout << "Rectangle: ";
    rectangle.displayDimensions();

    cout << "Custom Shape: ";
    custom.displayDimensions();

    return 0;
}
```

In this example, we define a `Rectangle` class with three constructors - a default constructor, a constructor that creates a square, and a constructor that creates a rectangle. Depending on the number and types of arguments provided during object creation, the corresponding constructor is called.

Output:

```
Square: Length: 0, Width: 0
Rectangle: Length: 4, Width: 4
Custom Shape: Length: 6, Width: 8
```

Constructors play a crucial role in object-oriented programming, ensuring objects are properly initialized for their tasks. By understanding constructor syntax and leveraging constructor overloading, you can create flexible and well-structured C++ classes.

5.3 DEFAULT CONSTRUCTORS AND PARAMETERIZED CONSTRUCTORS

In C++, constructors are essential for initializing objects when they are created. Constructors can be categorized into two main types: *default constructors* and *parameterized constructors*. Each type serves a specific purpose and provides flexibility in object initialization.

5.3.1 THE DEFAULT CONSTRUCTOR:

A *default constructor* is a constructor that takes no arguments. If you do not define any constructor in your class, C++ automatically generates a default constructor for you. The default constructor initializes the object's attributes to default values, which typically means no initialization at all.

Example: Default Constructor

```
#include <iostream>
using namespace std;

class Rectangle {
private:
    int length;
    int width;

public:
    // Default constructor (Automatically generated if not defined)
    Rectangle() {
        length = 0;
```

```
        width = 0;
    }

    void displayDimensions() {
        cout << "Length: " << length << ", Width: " << width << endl;
    }
};

int main() {
    // Creating a Rectangle object using the default constructor
    Rectangle rectangle;

    // Displaying the dimensions of the rectangle
    rectangle.displayDimensions();

    return 0;
}
```

In this example, we define a `Rectangle` class with a default constructor. When we create the `rectangle` object, the default constructor automatically initializes its `length` and `width` attributes to zero.

Output:

```
Length: 0, Width: 0
```

5.3.2 PARAMETERIZED CONSTRUCTORS

Parameterized constructors are constructors that take one or more arguments. Unlike the default constructor, which provides default values, parameterized constructors allow us to customize the object's initialization by providing specific values during object creation.

Example: Parameterized Constructor

```
#include <iostream>
using namespace std;

class Circle {
private:
    double radius;

public:
    // Parameterized constructor
    Circle(double _radius) {
        radius = _radius;
    }

    double calculateArea() {
```

```
        return 3.14 * radius * radius;
    }
};

int main() {
    // Creating a Circle object using the parameterized constructor
    Circle circle1(5.0);

    // Displaying the area of the circle
    cout << "Area of the Circle: " << circle1.calculateArea() << endl;

    return 0;
}
```

In this example, we define a `Circle` class with a parameterized constructor that takes a `double` argument `_radius`. When we create the `circle1` object, we provide the value `5.0` as an argument to the constructor, initializing the `radius` attribute with that value.

Output:

```
Area of the Circle: 78.5
```

5.3.3 BENEFITS OF PARAMETERIZED CONSTRUCTORS:

Parameterized constructors provide several benefits:
- They allow us to create objects with specific initial values, enabling customization and flexibility.
- They reduce the need for separate setter functions to modify object attributes after creation, promoting encapsulation.
- They streamline the object creation process by initializing the object directly during instantiation.

5.4 EXAMPLE: WORKING WITH POINTERS AND CONSTRUCTORS

In this example, we will review the concepts covered in Chapter 5: *Basic Structures of Object-Oriented Programming: Objects and Constructors*. We will create a simple C++ program that demonstrates the use of pointers, constructors, and object initialization.

Scenario:

Suppose we want to create a program to manage students' information. Each student has a name, age, and a unique ID. We will use constructors and pointers to achieve this.

Code:

```
#include <iostream>
using namespace std;

class Student {
private:
    string name;
    int age;
    int studentID;
```

```cpp
public:
    // Parameterized constructor
    Student(string _name, int _age, int _studentID) {
        name = _name;
        age = _age;
        studentID = _studentID;
    }

    // Display student information
    void displayInfo() {
        cout << "Student ID: " << studentID << endl;
        cout << "Name: " << name << endl;
        cout << "Age: " << age << endl;
    }
};

int main() {
    // Creating student objects using pointers and constructors
    Student* student1 = new Student("Alice", 20, 1001);
    Student* student2 = new Student("Bob", 22, 1002);

    // Displaying student information using pointers and object members
    cout << "Student 1 Information:" << endl;
    student1->displayInfo();
    cout << endl;

    cout << "Student 2 Information:" << endl;
    student2->displayInfo();
    cout << endl;

    // Deleting the dynamically allocated objects to free memory
    delete student1;
    delete student2;

    return 0;
}
```

Explanation:

1. We define a `Student` class with private attributes `name`, `age`, and `studentID`. These attributes store information about the student.

2. The `Student` class has a parameterized constructor that takes the student's name, age, and student ID as arguments. Inside the constructor, we initialize the attributes using the passed arguments.

3. We define a member function `displayInfo()` that prints the student's information (ID, name, and age) to the console.

4. In the `main()` function, we demonstrate object creation using pointers and constructors. We create two student objects dynamically using the `new` keyword, which returns a pointer to the newly allocated memory.

5. We use the arrow operator `->` to access the member functions of the student objects using the pointers.

6. After displaying the student information, we free the dynamically allocated memory using the `delete` keyword to avoid memory leaks.

Output:

The output of the program will be:

```
Student 1 Information:
Student ID: 1001
Name: Alice
Age: 20

Student 2 Information:
Student ID: 1002
Name: Bob
Age: 22
```

Summary:

In this example, we showcased the concepts of constructors, and object initialization in C++. Using pointers, we dynamically allocated memory for the student objects and accessed their member functions. Constructors helped us initialize the objects with specific attributes, making the code concise and efficient. By understanding these fundamental concepts, you can create more complex and versatile programs in C++.

6 INHERITANCE AND POLYMORPHISM

Welcome to Chapter 6 of our book on advanced programming in C++. In this chapter, we will explore the powerful concepts of *inheritance* and *polymorphism*. Inheritance is a fundamental feature of object-oriented programming (OOP) that allows us to create new classes based on existing ones, promoting code reuse and structuring our code hierarchically. Polymorphism, on the other hand, allows objects of different classes to be treated uniformly, enhancing flexibility and extensibility in our programs.

Through comprehensive explanations and real-world examples, we will delve into the various aspects of inheritance and polymorphism, providing you with a solid understanding of these essential concepts in C++.

Let's dive in and explore the fascinating world of inheritance and polymorphism in C++!

6.1 INTRODUCTION TO INHERITANCE

Inheritance is a fundamental concept in object-oriented programming (OOP) that enables the creation of new classes based on existing classes. It allows us to model relationships between classes, promote code reuse, and build a hierarchical structure in our programs. Inheritance is one of the key pillars of OOP, along with encapsulation and polymorphism.

6.1.1 THE CONCEPT OF INHERITANCE:

At its core, inheritance represents an "is-a" relationship between classes. In other words, a derived class (also known as a *subclass* or *child class*) inherits the properties and behaviors of a base class (also known as a *superclass* or *parent class*). This means that the derived class not only acquires the data members and member functions of the base class but can also extend or modify them as needed.

Example:

Let's consider an example of a simple geometric shape hierarchy. We have a base class called **Shape**, which represents the common properties and behaviors of all shapes. We will then create derived classes **Circle** and **Rectangle**, which inherit from the **Shape** class:

```cpp
#include <iostream>
using namespace std;

// Base class: Shape
class Shape {
public:
    void displayShapeType() {
        cout << "I am a generic shape." << endl;
```

```
    }
};

// Derived class: Circle
class Circle : public Shape {
public:
    void displayShapeType() {
        cout << "I am a circle." << endl;
    }
};

// Derived class: Rectangle
class Rectangle : public Shape {
public:
    void displayShapeType() {
        cout << "I am a rectangle." << endl;
    }
};

int main() {
    Shape genericShape;
    Circle circle;
    Rectangle rectangle;

    genericShape.displayShapeType();
    circle.displayShapeType();
    rectangle.displayShapeType();

    return 0;
}
```

Output:

```
I am a generic shape.
I am a circle.
I am a rectangle.
```

Explanation:

In the above example, we have a base class `Shape` with a member function `displayShapeType()`, which prints a generic message about being a shape. We then create two derived classes, `Circle` and `Rectangle`, each having their own `displayShapeType()` function.

By using inheritance, the `Circle` and `Rectangle` classes inherit the `displayShapeType()` function from the `Shape` class. When we create objects of the derived classes and call the `displayShapeType()` function, each object correctly identifies its shape type.

6.1.2 BASE AND DERIVED CLASSES:

Inheritance introduces a hierarchical relationship between classes. The class from which other classes are derived is called the *base class*, and the classes that inherit from the base class are known as *derived classes*. A derived class can have multiple base classes, leading to multiple inheritance.

6.1.3 ACCESS CONTROL IN INHERITANCE:

Access control in inheritance determines how the members (data members and member functions) of the base class can be accessed by the derived class. C++ offers three types of access specifiers for inheritance:

1. **Public Inheritance (*default*):** When a class inherits publicly from a base class, all public members of the base class become public members of the derived class, and all protected members of the base class become protected members of the derived class. Private members of the base class remain inaccessible to the derived class.

2. **Protected Inheritance:** When a class inherits protectedly from a base class, all members of the base class become protected members of the derived class. Both public and private members of the base class remain inaccessible to objects of the derived class.

3. **Private Inheritance:** When a class inherits privately from a base class, all members of the base class become private members of the derived class. Both public and protected members of the base class remain inaccessible to objects of the derived class.

Example:

Consider the following example of access control in inheritance:

```cpp
#include <iostream>
using namespace std;

// Base class: Shape
class Shape {
public:
    int publicVar;
protected:
    int protectedVar;
private:
    int privateVar;
};

// Derived class: Circle (public inheritance)
class Circle : public Shape {
public:
    void accessBaseMembers() {
        publicVar = 1;       // Accessible (public member of base class)
        protectedVar = 2;    // Accessible (protected member of base class)
        // privateVar = 3;    // Not accessible (private member of base class)
    }
};

// Derived class: Rectangle (private inheritance)
class Rectangle : private Shape {
```

```cpp
public:
    void accessBaseMembers() {
        publicVar = 1;        // Accessible (public member of base class)
        protectedVar = 2;     // Accessible (protected member of base class)
        // privateVar = 3;    // Not accessible (private member of base class)
    }
};

int main() {
    Circle circle;
    Rectangle rectangle;

    circle.publicVar = 1;       // Accessible (public member of base class)
    // circle.protectedVar = 2; // Not accessible (protected member of base class)
    // circle.privateVar = 3;   // Not accessible (private member of base class)

    // rectangle.publicVar = 1;     // Not accessible (private inheritance)
    // rectangle.protectedVar = 2;  // Not accessible (private inheritance)
    // rectangle.privateVar = 3;    // Not accessible (private inheritance)

    return 0;
}
```

Explanation:

In this example, we have a base class **Shape** with public, protected, and private data members. We then create two derived classes, **Circle** and **Rectangle**. The **Circle** class inherits publicly from the **Shape** class, and the **Rectangle** class inherits privately from the **Shape** class.

For the **Circle** class, the **publicVar** and **protectedVar** members of the base class are accessible, while the **privateVar** member remains inaccessible due to its private nature.

For the **Rectangle** class, all members of the base class become private members of the derived class. This means that neither **publicVar**, **protectedVar**, nor **privateVar** is accessible from outside the **Rectangle** class.

Summary:

Inheritance is a powerful concept that allows us to build complex class hierarchies and reuse code effectively. We can create derived classes based on existing classes, enabling us to model real-world relationships and design flexible and maintainable software solutions. Understanding access control in inheritance is crucial for managing member visibility and ensuring the proper encapsulation of data and behavior in our classes.

In the upcoming sections, we will explore the concepts of single and multiple inheritance, polymorphism, abstract classes, and interfaces. Let's continue our journey into the exciting world of C++ programming!

6.2 SINGLE INHERITANCE AND MULTIPLE INHERITANCE

Inheritance allows a class to derive properties and behaviors from another class, known as the base class. When a class inherits from a single base class, it is called *single inheritance*. On the other hand, when a class inherits from multiple base classes, it is referred to as *multiple inheritance*.

6.2.1 SINGLE INHERITANCE

In single inheritance, a class can inherit from only one base class. This is the most common form of inheritance, where the derived class gains access to the members of the single base class. Single inheritance allows us to establish a simple and straightforward class hierarchy.

Example:

```cpp
#include <iostream>
using namespace std;

// Base class: Vehicle
class Vehicle {
public:
    void displayType() {
        cout << "I am a generic vehicle." << endl;
    }
};

// Derived class: Car (single inheritance from Vehicle)
class Car : public Vehicle {
public:
    void displayType() {
        cout << "I am a car." << endl;
    }
};

int main() {
    Vehicle genericVehicle;
    Car myCar;

    genericVehicle.displayType();
    myCar.displayType();

    return 0;
}
```

Output:

```
I am a generic vehicle.
I am a car.
```

Explanation:

In the above example, we have a base class **Vehicle** with a member function **displayType()**, which prints a generic message about being a vehicle. We then create a derived class **Car**, which inherits from the **Vehicle** class.

By using single inheritance, the **Car** class inherits the **displayType()** function from the **Vehicle** class. When we create objects of both classes and call the **displayType()** function, each object correctly identifies its type.

6.2.2 MULTIPLE INHERITANCE

Multiple inheritance allows a class to inherit from multiple base classes. This enables a class to combine the properties and behaviors of multiple classes. However, multiple inheritance can lead to ambiguity if two or more base classes have members with the same name. In such cases, explicit scope resolution is required to access the correct member.

Example:

```cpp
#include <iostream>
using namespace std;

// Base class: Animal
class Animal {
public:
    void displayType() {
        cout << "I am an animal." << endl;
    }
};

// Base class: Vehicle
class Vehicle {
public:
    void displayType() {
        cout << "I am a vehicle." << endl;
    }
};

// Derived class: FlyingCar (multiple inheritance from Animal and Vehicle)
class FlyingCar : public Animal, public Vehicle {
public:
    void displayType() {
        cout << "I am a flying car." << endl;
    }
};

int main() {
    Animal genericAnimal;
    Vehicle genericVehicle;
    FlyingCar myFlyingCar;

    genericAnimal.displayType();
    genericVehicle.displayType();
```

```
    myFlyingCar.displayType();

    return 0;
}
```

Output:

```
I am an animal.
I am a vehicle.
I am a flying car.
```

Explanation:

In this example, we have two base classes, `Animal` and `Vehicle`, each with a member function `displayType()`. We then create a derived class `FlyingCar`, which inherits from both `Animal` and `Vehicle` classes using multiple inheritance.

As a result, the `FlyingCar` class gains access to the `displayType()` functions of both base classes. When we create objects of all three classes and call the `displayType()` function, each object correctly identifies its type.

Summary:

Inheritance in C++ provides the flexibility to create class hierarchies and reuse code effectively. With single inheritance, a class can inherit from a single base class, while multiple inheritance allows a class to inherit from multiple base classes, combining their properties and behaviors. When using multiple inheritance, it is essential to handle potential ambiguities that may arise due to the presence of identical member names in different base classes. By understanding the distinctions between single and multiple inheritance, you can design your class hierarchies efficiently and leverage the full power of OOP in C++.

6.3 POLYMORPHISM

Polymorphism is a fundamental concept in object-oriented programming that allows objects of different classes to be treated as objects of a common base class. This enables a single interface to represent multiple forms or behaviors. Polymorphism can be achieved through two approaches: static polymorphism, which involves function overloading, and dynamic polymorphism, which relies on virtual functions.

6.3.1 UNDERSTANDING POLYMORPHISM:

Polymorphism allows you to write flexible and extensible code by abstracting common functionalities into a base class and providing specific implementations in derived classes. This way, you can create a collection of objects that share a common interface, allowing you to treat them uniformly while calling specific behaviors.

Example:

```cpp
#include <iostream>
using namespace std;

// Base class: Shape
class Shape {
public:
    // Virtual function to calculate area (to be overridden by derived classes)
    virtual double calculateArea() const {
        return 0.0;
    }
};
```

```cpp
// Derived class: Rectangle (inherits from Shape)
class Rectangle : public Shape {
private:
    double width;
    double height;

public:
    Rectangle(double w, double h) : width(w), height(h) {}

    // Override the virtual function to calculate area for Rectangle
    double calculateArea() const override {
        return width * height;
    }
};

// Derived class: Circle (inherits from Shape)
class Circle : public Shape {
private:
    double radius;

public:
    Circle(double r) : radius(r) {}

    // Override the virtual function to calculate area for Circle
    double calculateArea() const override {
        return 3.14159 * radius * radius;
    }
};

int main() {
    Rectangle rectangle(4.0, 5.0);
    Circle circle(3.0);

    // An array of Shape pointers that can hold objects of Rectangle and Circle
    Shape* shapes[] = {&rectangle, &circle};

    // Calculate and display the areas of the shapes using polymorphism
    for (const auto& shape : shapes) {
        cout << "Area: " << shape->calculateArea() << endl;
    }
```

```
    return 0;
}
```

Output:

```
Area: 20
Area: 28.2743
```

Explanation:

In the example above, we have a base class **Shape**, which contains a virtual function `calculateArea()`. The `calculateArea()` function is declared as virtual, allowing it to be overridden by derived classes. We then create two derived classes, `Rectangle` and `Circle`, both inheriting from the **Shape** class.

By using dynamic polymorphism, we can treat objects of both `Rectangle` and `Circle` classes as objects of the base class **Shape**. This allows us to create an array of **Shape** pointers that can hold objects of `Rectangle` and `Circle`. During the loop, we call the `calculateArea()` function on each shape, and the correct version of the function from the respective class is executed, displaying the areas of the shapes.

The `const` keyword in these member functions serves as a promise to not modify the state of the object on which these functions are called. It is part of the concept of const-correctness, which allows the programmer to indicate which member functions are allowed to be called on a `const` object. When a member function is declared as `const`, it means it can be called on both mutable and `const` instances of the class, but it can only access and return values without modifying any data members of the class.

6.3.2 STATIC POLYMORPHISM: FUNCTION OVERLOADING:

Static polymorphism, also known as compile-time polymorphism, is achieved through function overloading. It allows a function to perform different operations based on the number or types of arguments it receives.

Example:

```cpp
#include <iostream>
using namespace std;

// Function to add integers
int add(int a, int b) {
    return a + b;
}

// Function to add doubles
double add(double a, double b) {
    return a + b;
}

int main() {
    int num1 = 5, num2 = 10;
    double doubleNum1 = 2.5, doubleNum2 = 3.7;

    cout << "Sum of integers: " << add(num1, num2) << endl;
```

```
        cout << "Sum of doubles: " << add(doubleNum1, doubleNum2) << endl;

    return 0;
}
```

Output:

```
Sum of integers: 15
Sum of doubles: 6.2
```

Explanation:

In the example above, we have two functions named **add**, one that takes two **int** arguments and another that takes two **double** arguments. The function overloading technique allows us to use the same function name for different types of inputs.

During the function call, the compiler determines which version of the **add** function to invoke based on the argument types. This is resolved at compile-time, hence the name "static polymorphism."

6.3.3 DYNAMIC POLYMORPHISM: VIRTUAL FUNCTIONS:

Dynamic polymorphism, also known as runtime polymorphism, is achieved through virtual functions. Virtual functions allow the selection of the appropriate function implementation based on the actual object type at runtime.

Example:

```cpp
#include <iostream>
using namespace std;

// Base class: Animal
class Animal {
public:
    // Virtual function to produce the animal sound (to be overridden by derived classes)
    virtual void makeSound() const {
        cout << "Some generic sound" << endl;
    }
};

// Derived class: Cat (inherits from Animal)
class Cat : public Animal {
public:
    void makeSound() const override {
        cout << "Meow!" << endl;
    }
};

// Derived class: Dog (inherits from Animal)
class Dog : public Animal {
public:
```

```cpp
    void makeSound() const override {
        cout << "Woof!" << endl;
    }
};

int main() {
    Animal* animals[] = {new Cat(), new Dog()};

    // Produce the animal sounds using polymorphism
    for (const auto& animal : animals) {
        animal->makeSound();
    }

    // Free the allocated memory
    for (const auto& animal : animals) {
        delete animal;
    }

    return 0;
}
```

Output:
```
Meow!
Woof!
```

Explanation:

In this example, we have a base class **Animal** with a virtual function **makeSound()**. We then create two derived classes, **Cat** and **Dog**, both inheriting from the **Animal** class.

Using dynamic polymorphism, we can create an array of **Animal** pointers that hold objects of **Cat** and **Dog**. During the loop, we call the **makeSound()** function on each animal, and the correct version of the function from the respective class is executed, producing the corresponding animal sound.

Summary:

Polymorphism is a powerful feature in C++ that allows objects to be treated uniformly, irrespective of their specific types. Dynamic polymorphism achieved through virtual functions enables runtime selection of the correct function implementation, while static polymorphism through function overloading allows compile-time selection based on argument types. Understanding and applying polymorphism appropriately in your programs can lead to more maintainable and flexible code, making your applications more adaptable to future changes.

6.4 ABSTRACT CLASSES AND INTERFACES

6.4.1 ABSTRACT CLASSES

An abstract class in C++ is a class that cannot be instantiated, meaning you cannot create objects directly from it. It serves as a blueprint for other classes and often contains one or more pure virtual functions. A pure virtual function is a virtual function that has no implementation in the abstract class. Any derived class inheriting from an abstract class must provide implementations for all the pure virtual functions.

Example:

```cpp
#include <iostream>
using namespace std;

// Abstract class: Shape
class Shape {
public:
    // Pure virtual function for calculating area
    virtual double calculateArea() const = 0;
};

// Derived class: Circle (inherits from Shape)
class Circle : public Shape {
private:
    double radius;

public:
    Circle(double r) : radius(r) {}

    // Implementing the pure virtual function for Circle
    double calculateArea() const override {
        return 3.14159 * radius * radius;
    }
};

// Derived class: Rectangle (inherits from Shape)
class Rectangle : public Shape {
private:
    double width;
    double height;

public:
    Rectangle(double w, double h) : width(w), height(h) {}

    // Implementing the pure virtual function for Rectangle
    double calculateArea() const override {
        return width * height;
    }
};

int main() {
    Circle circle(3.0);
    Rectangle rectangle(4.0, 5.0);
```

```cpp
// An array of Shape pointers that can hold objects of Circle and Rectangle
Shape* shapes[] = {&circle, &rectangle};

// Calculate and display the areas using polymorphism
for (const auto& shape : shapes) {
    cout << "Area: " << shape->calculateArea() << endl;
}

return 0;
}
```

Output:

```
Area: 28.2743
Area: 20
```

Explanation:

In this example, we have an abstract class **Shape**, which contains a pure virtual function `calculateArea()`. The **Shape** class cannot be instantiated directly due to the presence of the pure virtual function.

We then create two derived classes, `Circle` and `Rectangle`, both inheriting from the **Shape** class. Each derived class implements the `calculateArea()` function according to its specific formula for calculating the area.

The **Shape*** array can hold pointers to both `Circle` and `Rectangle` objects. During the loop, we call the `calculateArea()` function on each shape, and the appropriate version of the function is executed based on the actual object type. The correct implementations of the `calculateArea()` functions from the derived classes are called, and the areas of the shapes are calculated and displayed.

6.4.2 PURE VIRTUAL FUNCTIONS:

A pure virtual function is declared using the syntax `virtual returnType functionName() = 0;` in the base class. It provides a way to define a function's interface in the base class while delegating its implementation to the derived classes.

6.4.3 INTERFACES:

In C++, an interface is a class that consists entirely of pure virtual functions. It serves as a contract, specifying a set of functions that derived classes must implement. Interfaces allow classes with different hierarchies to share a common set of functionalities.

Example:

```cpp
#include <iostream>
using namespace std;

// Interface: Printable
class Printable {
public:
    // Pure virtual function for printing details
    virtual void printDetails() const = 0;
```

```cpp
};

// Derived class: Book (inherits from Printable)
class Book : public Printable {
private:
    string title;
    string author;

public:
    Book(const string& t, const string& a) : title(t), author(a) {}

    // Implementing the pure virtual function for Book
    void printDetails() const override {
        cout << "Book Title: " << title << ", Author: " << author << endl;
    }
};

// Derived class: Person (inherits from Printable)
class Person : public Printable {
private:
    string name;
    int age;

public:
    Person(const string& n, int a) : name(n), age(a) {}

    // Implementing the pure virtual function for Person
    void printDetails() const override {
        cout << "Person Name: " << name << ", Age: " << age << endl;
    }
};

int main() {
    Book book("The Great Gatsby", "F. Scott Fitzgerald");
    Person person("John Doe", 30);

    // An array of Printable pointers that can hold objects of Book and Person
    Printable* printableObjects[] = {&book, &person};

    // Print details using polymorphism
    for (const auto& printable : printableObjects) {
        printable->printDetails();
```

```
    }

    return 0;
}
```

Output:

```
Book Title: The Great Gatsby, Author: F. Scott Fitzgerald
Person Name: John Doe, Age: 30
```

Explanation:

In this example, we have an interface `Printable`, which consists of a pure virtual function `printDetails()`. The `Printable` class serves as a contract that specifies the behavior of the `printDetails()` function.

We then create two classes, **Book** and **Person**, both inheriting from the `Printable` interface. Each class implements the `printDetails()` function according to its specific details to be printed.

The `Printable*` array can hold pointers to both **Book** and **Person** objects. During the loop, we call the `printDetails()` function on each object, and the appropriate version of the function is executed based on the actual object type. The correct implementations of the `printDetails()` functions from the derived classes are called, and the details of the books and persons are printed.

Summary:

Abstract classes and interfaces play an essential role in object-oriented programming, allowing for the creation of a common interface for a group of classes. Abstract classes with pure virtual functions define an interface that derived classes must implement, while interfaces consist entirely of pure virtual functions and define a contract that derived classes must follow. Utilizing abstract classes and interfaces helps achieve consistency and modularity in your code, making it easier to maintain and extend the functionality of your C++ programs.

6.5 THE 'FINAL' KEYWORD AND PREVENTING INHERITANCE

6.5.1 THE 'FINAL' KEYWORD

In C++, the `final` keyword is used to prevent further inheritance from a class or to make a virtual function non-overridable in derived classes. When a class is marked as `final`, it cannot be used as a base class, and no other class can inherit from it.

Example:

```cpp
#include <iostream>
using namespace std;

// Base class: Vehicle (marked as final)
class Vehicle final {
public:
    void displayInfo() const {
        cout << "This is a vehicle." << endl;
    }
};

// Derived class: Car (attempting to inherit from a final class, which is not allowed)
```

```
class Car : public Vehicle {
};

int main() {
    Vehicle vehicle;
    vehicle.displayInfo();

    // Uncomment the code below to see the error
    // Car car;

    return 0;
}
```

Explanation:

In this example, we have a `Vehicle` class marked as `final`, which means it cannot be inherited from by any other class. The `Vehicle` class has a member function `displayInfo()`.

We then attempt to create a derived class `Car` that inherits from the `Vehicle` class. However, since the `Vehicle` class is marked as `final`, the attempt to inherit from it results in a compilation error. The error message will indicate that inheritance from a `final` class is not allowed.

6.5.2 PREVENTING INHERITANCE FOR VIRTUAL FUNCTIONS:

The `final` keyword can also be used with virtual functions to prevent them from being overridden in derived classes. When a virtual function is marked as `final`, any attempt to override it in a derived class will result in a compilation error.

Example:

```
#include <iostream>
using namespace std;

// Base class: Shape
class Shape {
public:
    virtual void displayInfo() const {
        cout << "This is a shape." << endl;
    }

    // Marking the virtual function as 'final' to prevent overriding
    virtual void calculateArea() const final {
        cout << "Area calculation method for shapes." << endl;
    }
};

// Derived class: Circle
class Circle : public Shape {
public:
```

```
    // Uncomment the code below to see the error
    // void calculateArea() const override {
    //     cout << "Area calculation method for circles." << endl;
    // }
};

int main() {
    Circle circle;
    circle.displayInfo();
    circle.calculateArea();

    return 0;
}
```

Explanation:

In this example, we have a **Shape** class with a virtual function **calculateArea()**. We mark this virtual function as **final**, indicating that it cannot be overridden in any derived class.

We then create a derived class **Circle** that attempts to override the **calculateArea()** function. However, since the **calculateArea()** function in the **Shape** class is marked as **final**, the attempt to override it in the **Circle** class will result in a compilation error.

Summary:

The **final** keyword is a powerful tool in C++ that allows you to prevent inheritance from a class or prevent virtual functions from being overridden in derived classes. Marking a class or virtual function as **final** can help enforce design decisions and protect certain functionalities from being modified or extended in unintended ways. However, it should be used with care, as it restricts the flexibility of the code and should only be applied when necessary to maintain the integrity and structure of the program.

6.6 SUMMARY AND BEST PRACTICES

In this chapter, we explored the powerful concepts of inheritance and polymorphism in C++. Let's summarize the key points and discuss some best practices for using these features effectively in your code.

Summary:

- Inheritance is a fundamental object-oriented programming concept that allows a new class (derived class) to inherit properties and behaviors from an existing class (base class). It promotes code reuse and enhances the maintainability and extensibility of the codebase.
- Derived classes inherit all the non-private members (data members and member functions) of the base class. This includes constructors, destructors, and other member functions.
- The access control specifiers (**public**, **protected**, and **private**) in C++ play a crucial role in controlling the visibility of members in derived classes. **public** members are accessible by any code, while **protected** members are accessible by derived classes and **private** members are only accessible within the base class.
- Single inheritance involves deriving a class from only one base class, while multiple inheritance allows a class to inherit from multiple base classes. Multiple inheritance can lead to the "diamond problem" if two or more base classes have the same member names, which can be resolved using virtual inheritance.
- Polymorphism is the ability of a class to take on multiple forms. In C++, polymorphism is achieved through function overloading and virtual functions.
- Function overloading allows multiple functions with the same name but different parameter lists

to coexist in a class. The appropriate function is called based on the number or type of arguments passed to it.

- Virtual functions enable dynamic polymorphism. They are declared in the base class with the `virtual` keyword and can be overridden in derived classes. The correct version of the function is determined at runtime based on the actual type of the object.
- Abstract classes are classes that cannot be instantiated and contain at least one pure virtual function. They serve as a blueprint for derived classes and provide a common interface for a group of related classes.
- Pure virtual functions have no implementation in the base class and must be overridden in derived classes.
- Interfaces in C++ are implemented using abstract classes with all pure virtual functions, providing a contract that derived classes must adhere to.
- The `final` keyword is used to prevent further inheritance from a class or to make a virtual function non-overridable in derived classes.

Best Practices:

- Use inheritance when you have a clear hierarchical relationship between classes and when code reuse and organization are essential.
- Prefer single inheritance over multiple inheritance to avoid potential complications like the diamond problem.
- Make use of access control specifiers (`public`, `protected`, and `private`) to maintain encapsulation and prevent unintended access to class members.
- Be cautious when using function overloading to avoid ambiguous function calls.
- Declare functions in base classes as virtual if you intend to override them in derived classes to achieve dynamic polymorphism.
- Use abstract classes and interfaces to define a common interface for a group of related classes and enforce a contract on derived classes.
- Consider using the `final` keyword when you want to prevent further inheritance or protect important virtual functions from being overridden.
- Always follow good design principles and consider the overall architecture of your code when using inheritance and polymorphism.

By understanding and effectively utilizing inheritance and polymorphism, you can write more maintainable, flexible, and scalable code in your C++ programs. Embrace these powerful concepts to take your object-oriented programming skills to the next level.

6.7 EXAMPLE: ATM SIMULATION

In this practical example, we will simulate the basic operations of an ATM (Automated Teller Machine) using C++ to demonstrate the concepts of inheritance and polymorphism. We will create a simple ATM system that supports multiple account types and allows users to withdraw, deposit, and check their account balance.

6.7.1 ATM CLASS HIERARCHY

To represent different account types and their operations, we will create a class hierarchy with a base class called `Account` and two derived classes, `SavingsAccount` and `CheckingAccount`. The base class `Account` will define common functionalities like account number and balance, while the derived classes will specialize in their respective account types.

6.7.2 IMPLEMENTING THE ATM CLASSES

Let's start by implementing the `Account` base class:

```cpp
#include <iostream>
using namespace std;

class Account {
protected:
    int accountNumber;
    double balance;

public:
    Account(int accNumber, double initialBalance) : accountNumber(accNumber),
balance(initialBalance) {}

    virtual void deposit(double amount) {
        balance += amount;
        cout << "Deposited $" << amount << " to account " << accountNumber << endl;
    }

    virtual void withdraw(double amount) {
        if (balance >= amount) {
            balance -= amount;
            cout << "Withdrew $" << amount << " from account " << accountNumber << endl;
        } else {
            cout << "Insufficient balance for account " << accountNumber << endl;
        }
    }

    virtual void displayBalance() const {
        cout << "Account " << accountNumber << " has a balance of $" << balance << endl;
    }

    virtual ~Account() {}
};
```

Next, we will implement the derived classes `SavingsAccount` and `CheckingAccount`, which inherit from the `Account` base class:

```cpp
class SavingsAccount : public Account {
    double interestRate;

public:
    SavingsAccount(int accNumber, double initialBalance, double rate)
        : Account(accNumber, initialBalance), interestRate(rate) {}
```

```cpp
    void applyInterest() {
        balance += balance * interestRate;
        cout << "Applied interest to account " << accountNumber << ". New balance: $" <<
balance << endl;
    }
};


class CheckingAccount : public Account {
    double overdraftLimit;

public:
    CheckingAccount(int accNumber, double initialBalance, double limit)
        : Account(accNumber, initialBalance), overdraftLimit(limit) {}

    void withdraw(double amount) override {
        if (balance + overdraftLimit >= amount) {
            balance -= amount;
            cout << "Withdrew $" << amount << " from account " << accountNumber << endl;
        } else {
            cout << "Insufficient funds. Overdraft limit exceeded for account " <<
accountNumber << endl;
        }
    }
};
```

6.7.3 USING THE ATM CLASSES:

Now, let's create an example main program to test our ATM simulation:

```cpp
int main() {
    Account* account1 = new SavingsAccount(1001, 5000.0, 0.05);
    Account* account2 = new CheckingAccount(2001, 3000.0, 1000.0);

    account1->deposit(1000.0);
    account2->deposit(2000.0);

    account1->displayBalance();
    account2->displayBalance();

    account1->withdraw(2000.0);
    account2->withdraw(4000.0);

    account1->displayBalance();
    account2->displayBalance();
```

```
    delete account1;
    delete account2;

    return 0;
}
```

Output:

```
Deposited $1000 to account 1001
Deposited $2000 to account 2001
Account 1001 has a balance of $6000
Account 2001 has a balance of $5000
Withdrew $2000 from account 1001
Insufficient funds. Overdraft limit exceeded for account 2001
Account 1001 has a balance of $4000
Account 2001 has a balance of $5000
```

Explanation:

In the above example, we created instances of **SavingsAccount** and **CheckingAccount** derived from the **Account** base class. We demonstrated dynamic polymorphism by using pointers to the base class **Account** to handle different account types interchangeably.

We used the **virtual** keyword in the base class to declare virtual functions, which were overridden in the derived classes to achieve dynamic polymorphism. The **virtual** keyword enables the compiler to choose the correct version of the function based on the actual object type during runtime.

By utilizing inheritance and polymorphism, we achieved code reusability and flexibility, making it easier to manage different account types within our ATM simulation.

6.7.4 CONCLUSION

In this practical example, we demonstrated how inheritance and polymorphism can be used in C++ to create an ATM simulation with multiple account types. By using the concept of inheritance, we were able to create a hierarchy of classes, and with polymorphism, we could handle different account types using a common interface. This allowed us to build a flexible and extensible ATM system. Understanding inheritance and polymorphism is crucial for developing complex and efficient C++ programs that can be easily maintained and expanded.

7 MEMORY MANAGEMENT - AN INTRODUCTION TO DYNAMIC DATA STRUCTURES

Memory management is a critical aspect of programming that involves the allocation and deallocation of memory resources for storing data. In this chapter, we will delve into the world of dynamic data structures and explore how they can be used to efficiently manage memory during program execution.

7.1 DYNAMIC MEMORY ALLOCATION AND DEALLOCATION

Program memory structure includes essential components:

- **Text (Code) Segment:**
  The text segment, also known as the code segment, contains compiled machine code instructions executed by the CPU. It's typically read-only to prevent unintended modifications during runtime.
- **Stack:**
  The stack is a memory region for local variables, function call data, and management. It follows a Last-In-First-Out (LIFO) order, with the most recent function's data at the top, removed when the function exits.
- **Heap:**
  The heap is a dynamic memory area for data that outlives a function's scope. It's used for dynamic memory allocation, such as creating objects or structures at runtime using `new` or `malloc`. Proper heap memory management prevents memory leaks and fragmentation.

Usually, dynamic memory refers to heap memory. Effective memory management is crucial, especially for adaptable data structures. Dynamic memory allocation enables requesting memory during runtime for data structure creation and resizing. Deallocation releases memory, preventing leaks and optimizing usage.

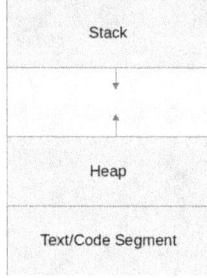

7.1.1 UNDERSTANDING DYNAMIC MEMORY ALLOCATION

In C++, dynamic memory allocation is achieved using the **new** operator. This operator allows us to request memory from the heap, which is a region of memory reserved for dynamic memory allocation. When we create objects or arrays using **new**, memory is allocated at runtime, and we are provided with a pointer to the allocated memory. This pointer allows us to access and use the allocated memory during the program's execution.

Here's an example of dynamic memory allocation:

```cpp
#include <iostream>

int main() {
    // Dynamically allocate an integer variable
    int* dynamicInteger = new int;

    // Assign a value to the dynamically allocated variable
    *dynamicInteger = 42;

    // Print the value of the dynamically allocated variable
    std::cout << "Value of dynamicInteger: " << *dynamicInteger << std::endl;

    // Deallocate the dynamically allocated memory
    delete dynamicInteger;

    return 0;
}
```

In this example, we use **new** to allocate memory for an integer variable `dynamicInteger`. We then assign a value to it and print the value. Finally, we deallocate the memory using the `delete` operator to free up the memory for reuse.

7.1.2 ALLOCATING MEMORY WITH **NEW** AND DEALLOCATION WITH **DELETE**

As mentioned earlier, dynamic memory allocation is done using the **new** operator, while memory deallocation is achieved using the `delete` operator. It is essential to remember that memory allocated with **new** should always be deallocated with `delete` to prevent memory leaks.

Here's a more complex example that demonstrates dynamic memory allocation and deallocation for an array of integers:

```cpp
#include <iostream>

int main() {
    // Dynamically allocate an array of integers
    int size = 5;
    int* dynamicArray = new int[size];

    // Assign values to the dynamically allocated array
    for (int i = 0; i < size; i++) {
        dynamicArray[i] = i * 10;
```

```
    }

    // Print the values of the dynamically allocated array
    std::cout << "Values of dynamicArray: ";
    for (int i = 0; i < size; i++) {
        std::cout << dynamicArray[i] << " ";
    }
    std::cout << std::endl;

    // Deallocate the dynamically allocated memory
    delete[] dynamicArray;

    return 0;
}
```

In this example, we use **new** to allocate memory for an array of integers **dynamicArray**. We then assign values to each element of the array and print its contents. Finally, we use **delete[]** to deallocate the memory for the array.

7.1.3 MEMORY LEAKS AND HOW TO AVOID THEM

A memory leak occurs when memory that is no longer needed is not deallocated, resulting in wasted memory and potential program instability. To avoid memory leaks, it is crucial to ensure that every memory allocation using **new** is matched with a corresponding deallocation using **delete**. Additionally, it is essential to avoid losing track of allocated memory, as this can lead to inaccessible memory and leaks.

One common practice to prevent memory leaks is to use smart pointers, such as **std::unique_ptr** and **std::shared_ptr**, provided by the C++ Standard Library. Smart pointers manage memory automatically and ensure that memory is deallocated when it is no longer needed, reducing the risk of memory leaks in your code.

```
#include <iostream>
#include <memory>

int main() {
    // Using std::unique_ptr for dynamic memory allocation
    std::unique_ptr<int> dynamicInt = std::make_unique<int>(42);

    // Print the value of the dynamically allocated variable
    std::cout << "Value of dynamicInt: " << *dynamicInt << std::endl;

    // No explicit deallocation needed, memory is automatically released
    return 0;
}
```

In this example, we use **std::unique_ptr** to automatically manage the memory for the dynamically allocated integer. When `dynamicInt` goes out of scope, the memory will be automatically deallocated, preventing memory leaks.

By following best practices, using smart pointers, and being mindful of memory allocation and deallocation, you can effectively manage memory in your C++ programs and create more robust and efficient code.

7.2 POINTERS AND REFERENCES

Pointers and references are fundamental concepts in C++ that allow us to work with memory addresses and access data indirectly. They play a crucial role in memory management, dynamic data structures, and other advanced programming concepts. Understanding pointers and references is essential for efficient memory usage and effective programming.

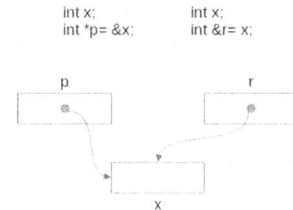

7.2.1 INTRODUCTION TO POINTERS

Pointers are variables that store memory addresses. They allow us to indirectly access and manipulate data stored at that address. Pointers are denoted by using the asterisk (*) symbol in their declaration.

Let's consider a simple example to understand pointers:

```cpp
#include <iostream>

int main() {
    int number = 10; // Declare an integer variable 'number'
    int* pointer;    // Declare a pointer to an integer

    pointer = &number; // Assign the address of 'number' to 'pointer'

    // Print the value of 'number' and the address it is stored in
    std::cout << "Value of 'number': " << number << std::endl;
    std::cout << "Address of 'number': " << &number << std::endl;

    // Print the value of the pointer (address of 'number')
    std::cout << "Value of 'pointer': " << pointer << std::endl;

    // To access the value stored at the address pointed by 'pointer', we use the dereference
operator (*)
    std::cout << "Value at the address pointed by 'pointer': " << *pointer << std::endl;
```

```
        return 0;
}
```

Output:

```
Value of 'number': 10
Address of 'number': 0x7ffeedb14d64 (memory address may vary)
Value of 'pointer': 0x7ffeedb14d64 (memory address may vary)
Value at the address pointed by 'pointer': 10
```

In this example, we declare an integer variable number and a pointer pointer. We assign the address of number to pointer using the address-of operator (&). We then print the value of number, the address of number, the value of pointer (which is the memory address), and the value at the address pointed by pointer using the dereference operator (*).

7.2.2 WORKING WITH POINTERS: ACCESSING AND MODIFYING DATA

Pointers allow us to access and modify data indirectly by using the dereference operator (*). When we dereference a pointer, we obtain the value stored at the memory address it points to. We can then read or modify that value.

Let's see how to use pointers to modify the value of a variable:

```cpp
#include <iostream>

int main() {
    int number = 5; // Declare and initialize an integer variable 'number'
    int* pointer;   // Declare a pointer to an integer

    pointer = &number; // Assign the address of 'number' to 'pointer'

    // Print the initial value of 'number'
    std::cout << "Initial value of 'number': " << number << std::endl;

    // Modify the value of 'number' through the pointer
    *pointer = 20;

    // Print the modified value of 'number'
    std::cout << "Modified value of 'number': " << number << std::endl;

    return 0;
}
```

Output:

```
Initial value of 'number': 5
Modified value of 'number': 20
```

In this example, we use a pointer `pointer` to modify the value of the variable `number`. By dereferencing the pointer and assigning a new value to it (`*pointer = 20`), we modify the value stored at the memory address pointed to by `pointer`.

7.2.3 POINTER ARITHMETIC AND POINTER ARITHMETIC ERRORS

Pointers in C++ support arithmetic operations such as addition and subtraction. When we perform arithmetic on pointers, the result depends on the size of the data type the pointer points to. For instance, if the pointer points to an integer, adding 1 to the pointer will move it to the next memory location for an integer (usually 4 bytes on a 32-bit system).

Here's an example of pointer arithmetic:

```cpp
#include <iostream>

int main() {
    int numbers[5] = {10, 20, 30, 40, 50}; // Declare and initialize an integer array
    int* pointer = numbers;                 // Assign the address of the first element to
'pointer'

    // Print the elements of the array using pointer arithmetic
    for (int i = 0; i < 5; i++) {
        std::cout << "Element " << i << ": " << *(pointer + i) << std::endl;
    }

    return 0;
}
```

Output:

```
Element 0: 10
Element 1: 20
Element 2: 30
Element 3: 40
Element 4: 50
```

In this example, we have an integer array `numbers`, and we use a pointer `pointer` to access the elements of the array using pointer arithmetic. The expression `*(pointer + i)` gives us the value of the i-th element of the array.

However, it's crucial to use pointer arithmetic with caution. Incorrect use of pointers, such as accessing invalid memory addresses, can lead to **undefined behavior** or runtime errors. For example, dereferencing an uninitialized or a null pointer can result in a crash or unpredictable behavior.

7.2.4 REFERENCES: AN ALTERNATIVE TO POINTERS

References provide an alternative way to work with memory addresses without the need for pointer arithmetic. A reference is like an alias for an existing variable, allowing us to access the variable directly without using pointers and dereferencing.

Let's explore how to use references:

```
#include <iostream>

int main() {
    int number = 10; // Declare and initialize an integer variable 'number'
    int& refNumber = number; // Declare a reference to 'number'

    // Print the initial value of 'number'
    std::cout << "Initial value of 'number': " << number << std::endl;

    // Modify the value of 'number' through the reference
    refNumber = 20;

    // Print the modified value of 'number'
    std::cout << "Modified value of 'number': " << number << std::endl;

    return 0;
}
```

Output:

```
Initial value of 'number': 10
Modified value of 'number': 20
```

In this example, we declare an integer variable number and a reference refNumber to number. We can directly modify the value of number through the reference refNumber, eliminating the need for pointer dereferencing.

Unlike pointers, references cannot be reassigned to point to a different memory location once initialized. Once a reference is bound to a variable, it stays bound to that variable throughout its lifetime. This characteristic makes references safer to use than pointers in certain scenarios.

Overall, pointers and references are essential concepts in C++ that enable us to work with memory addresses and manage dynamic data structures effectively. Understanding the differences between pointers and references and using them appropriately will help you write more efficient and reliable C++ code.

7.3 LINKED LISTS

In this section, we will explore the concept of **Linked Lists** as an essential data structure in C++. A linked list is a dynamic data structure that consists of a sequence of elements, called nodes, each containing a value and a reference (or pointer) to the next node in the list. Linked lists are useful for efficient insertion and deletion of elements, and they can dynamically grow or shrink based on the application's needs.

7.3.1 UNDERSTANDING LINKED LISTS

A linked list is a collection of nodes where each node points to the next node in the list. The last node points to a special value, usually null, indicating the end of the list. Unlike arrays, linked lists do not require contiguous memory allocation, making them suitable for dynamic memory management.

Let's define the structure of a simple singly linked list node:

```
struct Node {
```

```
    int data;        // Value of the node
    Node* next;      // Pointer to the next node
};
```

In this example, Node is a user-defined structure representing a node in the linked list. It contains an integer data field to store the value and a pointer next that points to the next node in the list.

Note: A **struct** is a user-defined data type that groups together variables of different data types under a single name. It is similar to a class in that it can contain data members and member functions, but unlike a class, its members are public by default.

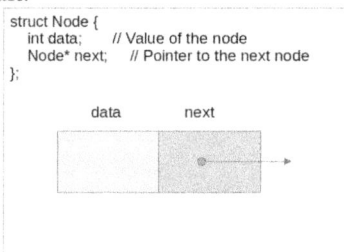

7.3.2 SINGLY LINKED LISTS: IMPLEMENTATION AND OPERATIONS

A **singly linked list** is a type of linked list where each node only points to the next node. It does not have a reference to the previous node. Singly linked lists are relatively simple to implement and are commonly used.

Let's implement a simple singly linked list with basic operations like inserting a node at the beginning and traversing the list:

```cpp
#include <iostream>

struct Node {
    int data;
    Node* next;
};

class SinglyLinkedList {
private:
    Node* head; // Pointer to the first node in the list

public:
    SinglyLinkedList() : head(nullptr) {}

    // Function to insert a new node at the beginning of the list
    void insertAtBeginning(int value) {
        Node* newNode = new Node;
        newNode->data = value;
        newNode->next = head;
        head = newNode;
    }
```

```cpp
    // Function to traverse and print the elements of the list
    void traverse() {
        Node* current = head;
        while (current != nullptr) {
            std::cout << current->data << " ";
            current = current->next;
        }
        std::cout << std::endl;
    }
};

int main() {
    SinglyLinkedList myList;

    myList.insertAtBeginning(10);
    myList.insertAtBeginning(20);
    myList.insertAtBeginning(30);

    myList.traverse(); // Output: 30 20 10

    return 0;
}
```

In this example, we define a class `SinglyLinkedList` that contains a private member `head`, which is a pointer to the first node in the linked list. The class provides two functions: `insertAtBeginning()` to insert a new node at the beginning of the list and `traverse()` to print the elements of the list.

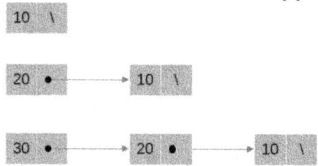

7.3.3 DOUBLY LINKED LISTS: IMPLEMENTATION AND ADVANTAGES

A **doubly linked list** is another type of linked list in which each node points both to the next node and the previous node. This bidirectional linking provides efficient traversal in both directions but requires extra memory for the previous node reference.

Let's implement a simple doubly linked list with basic operations like inserting a node at the beginning and traversing the list:

```cpp
#include <iostream>
```

```cpp
struct Node {
    int data;
    Node* prev; // Pointer to the previous node
    Node* next; // Pointer to the next node
};

class DoublyLinkedList {
private:
    Node* head; // Pointer to the first node in the list

public:
    DoublyLinkedList() : head(nullptr) {}

    // Function to insert a new node at the beginning of the list
    void insertAtBeginning(int value) {
        Node* newNode = new Node;
        newNode->data = value;
        newNode->prev = nullptr;
        newNode->next = head;

        if (head != nullptr) {
            head->prev = newNode;
        }

        head = newNode;
    }

    // Function to traverse and print the elements of the list
    void traverse() {
        Node* current = head;
        while (current != nullptr) {
            std::cout << current->data << " ";
            current = current->next;
        }
        std::cout << std::endl;
    }
};

int main() {
    DoublyLinkedList myList;

    myList.insertAtBeginning(10);
```

```
    myList.insertAtBeginning(20);
    myList.insertAtBeginning(30);

    myList.traverse(); // Output: 30 20 10

    return 0;
}
```

In this example, we define a class **DoublyLinkedList** that contains a private member **head**, which is a pointer to the first node in the linked list. The class provides two functions: **insertAtBeginning()** to insert a new node at the beginning of the list and **traverse()** to print the elements of the list.

prev	Data	next
●		●

7.3.4 CIRCULAR LINKED LISTS: IMPLEMENTATION AND APPLICATIONS

A **circular linked list** is a variation of linked lists where the last node points back to the first node instead of having a null reference. This creates a loop, making it easier to traverse the entire list without reaching the end. Circular linked lists are useful in certain applications, such as scheduling algorithms.

Let's implement a simple circular linked list with basic operations like inserting a node at the beginning and traversing the list:

```
#include <iostream>

struct Node {
    int data;
    Node* next; // Pointer to the next node
};

class CircularLinkedList {
private:
    Node* head; // Pointer to the first node in the list

public:
    CircularLinkedList() : head(nullptr) {}

    // Function to insert a new node at the beginning of the list
    void insertAtBeginning(int value) {
        Node* newNode = new Node;
        newNode->data = value;
```

```cpp
        if (head == nullptr) {
            head = newNode;
            newNode->next = newNode; // Point back to itself
        } else {
            newNode->next = head->next;
            head->next = newNode;
        }
    }

    // Function to traverse and print the elements of the list
    void traverse() {
        if (head == nullptr) {
            return;
        }

        Node* current = head;
        do {
            std::cout << current->data << " ";
            current = current->next;
        } while (current != head);

        std::cout << std::endl;
    }
};

int main() {
    CircularLinkedList myList;

    myList.insertAtBeginning(10);
    myList.insertAtBeginning(20);
    myList.insertAtBeginning(30);

    myList.traverse(); // Output: 30 20 10

    return 0;
}
```

In this example, we define a class `CircularLinkedList` that contains a private member `head`, which is a pointer to the first node in the linked list. The class provides two functions: `insertAtBeginning()` to insert a new node at the beginning of the list and `traverse()` to print the elements of the list in a circular manner.

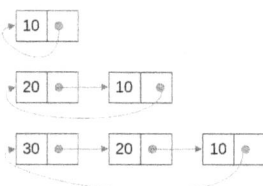

Linked lists, stacks, and queues are fundamental dynamic data structures used in various applications, from managing memory to solving complex problems efficiently. Understanding these data structures and their implementations will strengthen your C++ programming skills and enable you to tackle a wide range of programming challenges.

7.4 STACKS

In this section, we will delve into the concept of **Stacks** as an essential data structure in C++. A stack is a linear data structure that follows the Last In, First Out (LIFO) principle, meaning that the last element added to the stack will be the first one to be removed. Stacks are widely used in programming for various applications, including function calls, expression evaluation, and managing memory during program execution.

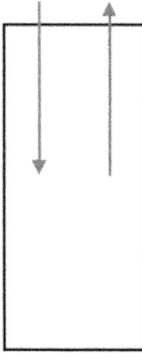

7.4.1 INTRODUCTION TO STACKS

A **stack** can be visualized as a collection of elements arranged in a sequential manner, where the addition of elements (called pushing) and the removal of elements (called popping) occur from the same end, known as the top of the stack. The last element added becomes the top element, and the first element added is the bottom element.

Stacks can be thought of as a stack of plates in a cafeteria. You can only place a plate on the top of the stack or remove a plate from the top, not from the middle or bottom.

7.4.2 IMPLEMENTING STACKS: ARRAY-BASED AND LINKED LIST-BASED

There are various ways to implement a stack, but two common methods are **array-based** and **linked list-based** implementations.

Array-based implementation:

In an array-based implementation, a fixed-size array is used to store the stack elements. The top of the stack is represented by an index pointing to the last inserted element. When an element is pushed onto the stack, it is added at the top index. Similarly, when an element is popped, it is removed from the top index.

Let's see a simple example of an array-based stack:

```
#include <iostream>
```

```cpp
const int MAX_SIZE = 5; // Maximum number of elements in the stack

class ArrayStack {
private:
    int stack[MAX_SIZE];
    int top; // Index of the top element

public:
    ArrayStack() : top(-1) {}

    bool isEmpty() const {
        return top == -1;
    }

    bool isFull() const {
        return top == MAX_SIZE - 1;
    }

    void push(int value) {
        if (!isFull()) {
            stack[++top] = value;
        } else {
            std::cout << "Stack is full. Cannot push element: " << value << std::endl;
        }
    }

    void pop() {
        if (!isEmpty()) {
            --top;
        } else {
            std::cout << "Stack is empty. Cannot pop." << std::endl;
        }
    }

    int peek() const {
        if (!isEmpty()) {
            return stack[top];
        } else {
            std::cout << "Stack is empty. Cannot peek." << std::endl;
            return -1;
        }
    }
}
```

```
};

int main() {
    ArrayStack myStack;

    myStack.push(10);
    myStack.push(20);
    myStack.push(30);

    std::cout << "Top element: " << myStack.peek() << std::endl; // Output: 30

    myStack.pop();

    std::cout << "Top element after popping: " << myStack.peek() << std::endl; // Output: 20

    return 0;
}
```

In this example, we define a class **ArrayStack** with a private integer array **stack** to store the elements and an integer variable **top** to keep track of the top index. The class provides functions for pushing, popping, and peeking the elements in the stack.

Linked list-based implementation:

In a linked list-based implementation, a dynamically allocated linked list is used to represent the stack. Each node in the linked list contains the data element and a pointer to the next node (similar to the singly linked list implementation we discussed earlier).

Let's see a simple example of a linked list-based stack:

```
#include <iostream>

struct Node {
    int data;
    Node* next;
};

class LinkedListStack {
private:
    Node* top; // Pointer to the top node of the stack

public:
    LinkedListStack() : top(nullptr) {}

    bool isEmpty() const {
        return top == nullptr;
```

```cpp
    }

    void push(int value) {
        Node* newNode = new Node;
        newNode->data = value;
        newNode->next = top;
        top = newNode;
    }

    void pop() {
        if (!isEmpty()) {
            Node* temp = top;
            top = top->next;
            delete temp;
        } else {
            std::cout << "Stack is empty. Cannot pop." << std::endl;
        }
    }

    int peek() const {
        if (!isEmpty()) {
            return top->data;
        } else {
            std::cout << "Stack is empty. Cannot peek." << std::endl;
            return -1;
        }
    }
};

int main() {
    LinkedListStack myStack;

    myStack.push(10);
    myStack.push(20);
    myStack.push(30);

    std::cout << "Top element: " << myStack.peek() << std::endl; // Output: 30

    myStack.pop();

    std::cout << "Top element after popping: " << myStack.peek() << std::endl; // Output: 20
```

```
    return 0;
}
```

In this example, we define a class `LinkedListStack` that contains a private member `top`, which is a pointer to the top node of the linked list. The class provides functions for pushing, popping, and peeking the elements in the stack.

7.4.3 STACK OPERATIONS: PUSH, POP, AND PEEK

As mentioned earlier, the stack supports three fundamental operations:
1. **Push**: Inserting an element onto the top of the stack.
2. **Pop**: Removing the top element from the stack.
3. **Peek**: Viewing the top element without removing it.

The examples provided above demonstrate the implementation of these stack operations for both array-based and linked list-based stacks.

7.4.4 APPLICATIONS OF STACKS IN PROBLEM SOLVING

Stacks find extensive applications in problem-solving scenarios. Some common applications of stacks include:

- **Expression Evaluation**: Stacks can be used to evaluate arithmetic expressions involving parentheses, brackets, and operators.
- **Function Calls**: Stacks are crucial for managing function calls and maintaining the execution context of functions.
- **Undo/Redo Operations**: Stacks can be used to implement undo/redo functionality in applications.
- **Backtracking Algorithms**: In algorithms like Depth-First Search (DFS), stacks are used to keep track of the search path.
- **Memory Management**: Stacks play a role in managing memory during program execution.

Understanding and mastering stack data structures will empower you to tackle various programming challenges effectively. Proper use of stacks can lead to more efficient and organized code, enhancing your programming skills in C++.

7.5 QUEUES

In this section, we will explore the concept of **Queues**, another fundamental data structure in C++. A queue is a linear data structure that follows the First In, First Out (FIFO) principle. It means that the element added first will be the first one to be removed from the queue. Queues are widely used in programming for various applications, such as managing tasks, data processing, and breadth-first search algorithms.

7.5.1 UNDERSTANDING QUEUES

A **queue** can be visualized as a collection of elements arranged in a sequential manner, where the addition of elements (called enqueue) occurs at the rear, and the removal of elements (called dequeue) occurs from the front. This behavior is analogous to people waiting in a queue at a ticket counter, where the first person to join the queue is the first one to get the ticket and leave the queue.

7.5.2 IMPLEMENTING QUEUES: ARRAY-BASED AND LINKED LIST-BASED

Like stacks, queues can also be implemented using different approaches, including **array-based** and **linked list-based** implementations.

Array-based implementation:

In an array-based implementation, a fixed-size array is used to store the queue elements. Two indices, front and rear, are used to keep track of the front and rear positions of the queue, respectively.

Let's see a simple example of an array-based queue:

```cpp
#include <iostream>

const int MAX_SIZE = 5; // Maximum number of elements in the queue

class ArrayQueue {
private:
    int queue[MAX_SIZE];
    int front;
    int rear;

public:
    ArrayQueue() : front(-1), rear(-1) {}

    bool isEmpty() const {
        return front == -1 && rear == -1;
    }

    bool isFull() const {
        return (rear + 1) % MAX_SIZE == front;
    }

    void enqueue(int value) {
        if (!isFull()) {
            if (isEmpty()) {
                front = 0;
            }
            rear = (rear + 1) % MAX_SIZE;
            queue[rear] = value;
        } else {
            std::cout << "Queue is full. Cannot enqueue element: " << value << std::endl;
        }
    }

    void dequeue() {
```

```cpp
        if (!isEmpty()) {
            if (front == rear) {
                front = rear = -1;
            } else {
                front = (front + 1) % MAX_SIZE;
            }
        } else {
            std::cout << "Queue is empty. Cannot dequeue." << std::endl;
        }
    }

    int peek() const {
        if (!isEmpty()) {
            return queue[front];
        } else {
            std::cout << "Queue is empty. Cannot peek." << std::endl;
            return -1;
        }
    }
};

int main() {
    ArrayQueue myQueue;

    myQueue.enqueue(10);
    myQueue.enqueue(20);
    myQueue.enqueue(30);

    std::cout << "Front element: " << myQueue.peek() << std::endl; // Output: 10

    myQueue.dequeue();

    std::cout << "Front element after dequeue: " << myQueue.peek() << std::endl; // Output: 20

    return 0;
}
```

In this example, we define a class ArrayQueue with a private integer array queue to store the elements, and integers front and rear to keep track of the front and rear indices. The class provides functions for enqueueing, dequeueing, and peeking the elements in the queue.

Linked list-based implementation:

In a linked list-based implementation, a dynamically allocated linked list is used to represent the queue. Each node in the linked list contains the data element and a pointer to the next node.

Let's see a simple example of a linked list-based queue:

```cpp
#include <iostream>

struct Node {
    int data;
    Node* next;
};

class LinkedListQueue {
private:
    Node* front;
    Node* rear;

public:
    LinkedListQueue() : front(nullptr), rear(nullptr) {}

    bool isEmpty() const {
        return front == nullptr;
    }

    void enqueue(int value) {
        Node* newNode = new Node;
        newNode->data = value;
        newNode->next = nullptr;

        if (isEmpty()) {
            front = rear = newNode;
        } else {
            rear->next = newNode;
            rear = newNode;
        }
    }

    void dequeue() {
        if (!isEmpty()) {
            Node* temp = front;
            front = front->next;
            delete temp;
```

```cpp
            if (front == nullptr) {
                rear = nullptr;
            }
        } else {
            std::cout << "Queue is empty. Cannot dequeue." << std::endl;
        }
    }

    int peek() const {
        if (!isEmpty()) {
            return front->data;
        } else {
            std::cout << "Queue is empty. Cannot peek." << std::endl;
            return -1;
        }
    }
};

int main() {
    LinkedListQueue myQueue;

    myQueue.enqueue(10);
    myQueue.enqueue(20);
    myQueue.enqueue(30);

    std::cout << "Front element: " << myQueue.peek() << std::endl; // Output: 10

    myQueue.dequeue();

    std::cout << "Front element after dequeue: " << myQueue.peek() << std::endl; // Output: 20

    return 0;
}
```

In this example, we define a class `LinkedListQueue` that contains two pointers, `front` and `rear`, pointing to the front and rear nodes of the linked list, respectively. The class provides functions for enqueueing, dequeueing, and peeking the elements in the queue.

7.5.3 QUEUE OPERATIONS: ENQUEUE AND DEQUEUE

As mentioned earlier, a queue supports two fundamental operations:

    1. **Enqueue**: Inserting an element at the rear of the queue.

2. **Dequeue**: Removing the element from the front of the queue.

The examples provided above demonstrate the implementation of these queue operations for both array-based and linked list-based queues.

7.5.4 APPLICATIONS OF QUEUES IN DATA PROCESSING

Queues find widespread applications in data processing scenarios. Some common applications of queues include:

- **Task Scheduling**: Queues are used to schedule and manage tasks in a multitasking environment.
- **Print Spooling**: Queues are employed in print spoolers to manage print jobs.
- **Breadth-First Search (BFS)**: Queues are used in BFS algorithms for graph traversal.
- **Simulation and Modeling**: Queues are used to simulate real-world scenarios and processes.

Understanding the concept of queues and their implementations will enhance your ability to handle various programming tasks effectively. Proper utilization of queues can lead to efficient and well-organized code, elevating your C++ programming skills.

7.6 SUMMARY AND BEST PRACTICES

In this chapter, we explored various fundamental concepts related to memory management and dynamic data structures in C++. Understanding these concepts is crucial for writing efficient and robust programs that can handle data dynamically during runtime. Let's summarize the key points discussed in each section and explore some best practices to follow when working with dynamic data structures.

7.1 Dynamic Memory Allocation and Deallocation

- Dynamic memory allocation allows us to create data structures whose size can be determined at runtime, providing flexibility in memory usage.
- The `new` operator is used to allocate memory on the heap, and the `delete` operator is used to deallocate memory to prevent memory leaks.
- Memory leaks occur when dynamically allocated memory is not deallocated properly, leading to the loss of available memory in the program.
- To avoid memory leaks, always ensure to deallocate dynamically allocated memory using `delete` when it is no longer needed.

7.2 Pointers and References

- Pointers are variables that store memory addresses and are powerful tools for working with dynamic data structures.
- Dereferencing a pointer allows us to access the data it points to.
- Pointer arithmetic allows us to navigate through arrays and dynamic data structures efficiently.
- Care should be taken to avoid pointer arithmetic errors, such as accessing memory outside the allocated region.
- References are aliases to existing variables and provide a convenient and safe way to work with data without the complexities of pointers.

7.3 Linked Lists

- Linked lists are dynamic data structures where each element (node) contains both data and a reference to the next node in the sequence.
- Singly linked lists allow traversal in one direction, while doubly linked lists allow traversal in both directions.
- Circular linked lists connect the last node with the first, forming a loop.
- Linked lists are useful when the number of elements is unknown or can change during runtime.

7.4 Stacks

- Stacks are data structures that follow the Last In, First Out (LIFO) principle, making them suitable for tasks like function call management and expression evaluation.
- Stacks can be implemented using arrays or linked lists, depending on the requirements of the

program.

7.5 Queues

- Queues are data structures that follow the First In, First Out (FIFO) principle, making them ideal for scenarios like task scheduling and BFS traversal.
- Queues can also be implemented using arrays or linked lists, based on the application's specific needs.

Best Practices

1. **Memory Management**: Always ensure to deallocate dynamically allocated memory using `delete` when it is no longer needed. Adopting smart pointers like `std::unique_ptr` and `std::shared_ptr` can help manage memory automatically and reduce memory-related issues.

2. **Pointers and References**: Prefer using references when possible to avoid pointer arithmetic errors and potential memory issues. Use pointers responsibly and initialize them properly to avoid accessing uninitialized memory.

3. **Choosing Data Structures**: Select the appropriate data structure (arrays, linked lists, stacks, or queues) based on the specific requirements of your program. Consider the data size, insertions, deletions, and traversal operations when making a choice.

4. **Testing and Debugging**: Thoroughly test your code, especially when working with dynamic data structures, to identify and fix potential bugs and memory-related issues. Utilize debugging tools to inspect and validate your program's memory usage.

5. **Code Readability**: Write clear and well-documented code to improve code readability and maintainability. Using meaningful variable and function names helps others understand your code easily.

In conclusion, mastering memory management and dynamic data structures is essential for C++ programmers to develop efficient and reliable programs. By understanding and applying the concepts covered in this chapter, you can build robust applications and become a more proficient C++ developer.

7.7 ADVANCED OPERATIONS ON LINKED LISTS: SEARCHING, SORTING, MERGING, AND SPLITTING

In addition to the fundamental operations covered in the previous sections, linked lists offer a versatile set of operations that can be applied to solve various problems efficiently. In this section, we will explore some common additional operations on linked lists, including searching, sorting, merging, and splitting.

7.7.1 SEARCHING IN A LINKED LIST

Searching for a specific element in a linked list involves traversing the list and comparing the target value with each node's data. If a match is found, we return the node containing the element; otherwise, we continue searching until we reach the end of the list (or the element is not found).

Example: Searching for an element in a singly linked list

Let's consider a singly linked list of integers and write a function to search for a given value in the list.

```
#include <iostream>

struct Node {
    int data;
    Node* next;
};

Node* searchElement(Node* head, int target) {
    Node* current = head;
```

```cpp
    while (current != nullptr) {
        if (current->data == target) {
            return current;
        }
        current = current->next;
    }
    return nullptr; // Element not found
}

int main() {
    // Create a sample linked list: 1 -> 2 -> 3 -> 4 -> 5
    Node* head = new Node{1, nullptr};
    head->next = new Node{2, nullptr};
    head->next->next = new Node{3, nullptr};
    head->next->next->next = new Node{4, nullptr};
    head->next->next->next->next = new Node{5, nullptr};

    int target = 3;
    Node* result = searchElement(head, target);

    if (result) {
        std::cout << "Element " << target << " found in the linked list." << std::endl;
    } else {
        std::cout << "Element " << target << " not found in the linked list." << std::endl;
    }

    // Don't forget to free the allocated memory to avoid memory leaks.
    while (head) {
        Node* temp = head;
        head = head->next;
        delete temp;
    }
    return 0;
}
```

7.7.2 SORTING A LINKED LIST USING INSERTION SORT

Insertion Sort is a popular algorithm for sorting linked lists. Unlike other sorting algorithms like Merge Sort, Insertion Sort constructs the final sorted list one element at a time by inserting elements into their correct positions. It is particularly well-suited for linked lists due to its efficient way of inserting elements without the need for additional memory allocation.

Algorithm for Insertion Sort:
1. Create a new sorted linked list (result) with a dummy head node.
2. Traverse the original linked list, and for each node in the original list: a. Save the next node in a

temporary pointer, as it will be detached from the original list during insertion. b. Find the appropriate position in the sorted list to insert the current node. This involves traversing the sorted list until the correct position is found, considering the data values in ascending or descending order. c. Insert the current node into the sorted list at the found position. d. Repeat steps (a) to (c) until all nodes in the original list are processed.

3. Update the head of the original list to point to the next node after the dummy head node of the sorted list.

4. Delete the dummy head node of the sorted list.

Example: Sorting a singly linked list using Insertion Sort

Let's modify the previous example and implement Insertion Sort to sort a singly linked list of integers.

```cpp
#include <iostream>

struct Node {
    int data;
    Node* next;

    Node(int value) : data(value), next(nullptr) {}
};

// Function to perform Insertion Sort on a linked list
Node* insertionSort(Node* head) {
    Node* result = new Node(0); // Dummy head for the sorted list
    Node* current = head;
    Node* nextNode = nullptr;

    while (current != nullptr) {
        nextNode = current->next;
        Node* sortedCurrent = result;

        // Find the appropriate position to insert the current node in the sorted list
        while (sortedCurrent->next != nullptr && sortedCurrent->next->data < current->data) {
            sortedCurrent = sortedCurrent->next;
        }

        // Insert the current node into the sorted list
        current->next = sortedCurrent->next;
        sortedCurrent->next = current;

        current = nextNode;
    }
```

```cpp
    Node* sortedHead = result->next;
    delete result; // Delete the dummy head

    return sortedHead;
}


// Utility function to insert a new node at the end of the linked list
void insertEnd(Node*& head, int value) {
    Node* newNode = new Node(value);
    if (head == nullptr) {
        head = newNode;
    } else {
        Node* current = head;
        while (current->next != nullptr) {
            current = current->next;
        }
        current->next = newNode;
    }
}


// Utility function to print the linked list
void printList(Node* head) {
    Node* current = head;
    while (current != nullptr) {
        std::cout << current->data << " -> ";
        current = current->next;
    }
    std::cout << "nullptr" << std::endl;
}

int main() {
    // Create a sample linked list: 4 -> 2 -> 1 -> 5 -> 3
    Node* head = nullptr;
    insertEnd(head, 4);
    insertEnd(head, 2);
    insertEnd(head, 1);
    insertEnd(head, 5);
    insertEnd(head, 3);

    std::cout << "Original linked list: ";
    printList(head);
```

```
    // Sort the linked list using Insertion Sort
    head = insertionSort(head);

    std::cout << "Sorted linked list: ";
    printList(head);

    // Don't forget to free the allocated memory to avoid memory leaks.
    while (head) {
        Node* temp = head;
        head = head->next;
        delete temp;
    }
    return 0;
}
```

In this example, we introduce the `insertionSort` function that performs the Insertion Sort algorithm on the linked list. The `result` node acts as a dummy head for the sorted list. We traverse the original linked list and insert each node into the correct position in the sorted list. Finally, we update the head of the original list to point to the sorted list, and we delete the dummy head node.

After running the code, you will see the original linked list `4 -> 2 -> 1 -> 5 -> 3` and the sorted linked list `1 -> 2 -> 3 -> 4 -> 5`, demonstrating the effectiveness of Insertion Sort for sorting linked lists.

7.7.3 MERGING LINKED LISTS

Merging two linked lists involves combining them into a single linked list while maintaining the sorted order if the individual lists are already sorted. This operation is commonly used when working with smaller sorted lists to produce a larger sorted list.

Example: Merging two sorted singly linked lists

Let's consider two sorted singly linked lists and merge them into a single sorted list.

```
#include <iostream>

struct Node {
    int data;
    Node* next;

    Node(int value) : data(value), next(nullptr) {}
};

// Function to merge two sorted linked lists
Node* mergeLists(Node* left, Node* right) {
    if (left == nullptr) return right;
    if (right == nullptr) return left;
```

```cpp
    Node* result = nullptr;
    if (left->data <= right->data) {
        result = left;
        result->next = mergeLists(left->next, right);
    } else {
        result = right;
        result->next = mergeLists(left, right->next);
    }

    return result;
}

// Utility function to insert a new node at the end of the linked list
void insertEnd(Node*& head, int value) {
    Node* newNode = new Node(value);
    if (head == nullptr) {
        head = newNode;
    } else {
        Node* current = head;
        while (current->next != nullptr) {
            current = current->next;
        }
        current->next = newNode;
    }
}

// Utility function to print the linked list
void printList(Node* head) {
    Node* current = head;
    while (current != nullptr) {
        std::cout << current->data << " -> ";
        current = current->next;
    }
    std::cout << "nullptr" << std::endl;
}

int main() {
    // Create two sorted linked lists: 1 -> 3 -> 5 and 2 -> 4 -> 6
    Node* list1 = nullptr;
    insertEnd(list1, 1);
    insertEnd(list1, 3);
    insertEnd(list1, 5);
```

```cpp
Node* list2 = nullptr;
insertEnd(list2, 2);
insertEnd(list2, 4);
insertEnd(list2, 6);

std::cout << "First sorted linked list: ";
printList(list1);

std::cout << "Second sorted linked list: ";
printList(list2);

// Merge the two sorted linked lists
Node* mergedList = mergeLists(list1, list2);

std::cout << "Merged sorted linked list: ";
printList(mergedList);

// Don't forget to free the allocated memory to avoid memory leaks.
while (mergedList) {
    Node* temp = mergedList;
    mergedList = mergedList->next;
    delete temp;
}
return 0;
}
```

In this example, we first define a **Node** struct representing the nodes of the linked list. The **mergeLists** function is reused from the previous example, as it efficiently merges two sorted linked lists. The **insertEnd** function is used to insert new elements at the end of the linked list. We create two sorted linked lists, **list1** and **list2**, and then merge them into a single sorted linked list **mergedList**. Finally, we print the original linked lists, as well as the merged sorted linked list.

After running the code, you will see the first sorted linked list 1 -> 3 -> 5, the second sorted linked list 2 -> 4 -> 6, and the merged sorted linked list 1 -> 2 -> 3 -> 4 -> 5 -> 6. The **mergeLists** function ensures that the elements are merged in ascending order to maintain the sorted property.

7.7.4 SPLITTING A LINKED LIST

Splitting a linked list means dividing it into two separate lists. This operation is useful when we need to process different parts of the linked list separately.

Example: Splitting a singly linked list at a given element

In this example, we'll split a singly linked list into two parts at a specific element.

```cpp
#include <iostream>
```

```cpp
struct Node {
    int data;
    Node* next;

    Node(int value) : data(value), next(nullptr) {}
};

// Function to split a linked list into two parts at a specific element
void splitLinkedList(Node* head, int splitValue, Node*& left, Node*& right) {
    Node* current = head;
    Node* prev = nullptr;

    while (current != nullptr) {
        if (current->data == splitValue) {
            left = head;
            right = current->next;
            if (prev != nullptr) {
                prev->next = nullptr; // Disconnect the left part
            }
            break;
        }
        prev = current;
        current = current->next;
    }
}

// Utility function to insert a new node at the end of the linked list
void insertEnd(Node*& head, int value) {
    Node* newNode = new Node(value);
    if (head == nullptr) {
        head = newNode;
    } else {
        Node* current = head;
        while (current->next != nullptr) {
            current = current->next;
        }
        current->next = newNode;
    }
}

// Utility function to print the linked list
```

```cpp
void printList(Node* head) {
    Node* current = head;
    while (current != nullptr) {
        std::cout << current->data << " -> ";
        current = current->next;
    }
    std::cout << "nullptr" << std::endl;
}

int main() {
    // Create a sample linked list: 1 -> 3 -> 5 -> 2 -> 4 -> 6
    Node* head = nullptr;
    insertEnd(head, 1);
    insertEnd(head, 3);
    insertEnd(head, 5);
    insertEnd(head, 2);
    insertEnd(head, 4);
    insertEnd(head, 6);

    std::cout << "Original linked list: ";
    printList(head);

    int splitValue = 2;
    Node* leftList = nullptr;
    Node* rightList = nullptr;
    splitLinkedList(head, splitValue, leftList, rightList);

    std::cout << "Left part of the linked list (before " << splitValue << "): ";
    printList(leftList);

    std::cout << "Right part of the linked list (including and after " << splitValue << "): ";
    printList(rightList);

    // Don't forget to free the allocated memory to avoid memory leaks.
    while (head) {
        Node* temp = head;
        head = head->next;
        delete temp;
    }
    return 0;
}
```

In this code illustration, we begin by defining a Node struct to represent individual nodes within a linked list. Each Node contains an integer value and a pointer to the next node.

The splitLinkedList function plays a crucial role. It accepts the head of a linked list and a designated value (splitValue) as parameters. By executing this function, the original linked list is partitioned into two distinct linked lists: left and right. This partitioning is based on the occurrence of the provided splitValue. Nodes with values before the splitValue are included in the left list, while nodes with values equal to or after the splitValue are included in the right list. Notably, any connections between the two parts are severed.

For insertion of new elements at the end of the linked list, the insertEnd function is employed. The sample linked list is created with values 1, 3, 5, 2, 4, and 6.

Upon invoking the splitLinkedList function with a splitValue of 2, the original linked list is effectively split into two segments: the leftList, containing elements 1, 3, and 5, and the rightList, containing elements 2, 4, and 6.

Upon execution of the code, the output will display three linked lists. The original linked list is presented as 1 -> 3 -> 5 -> 2 -> 4 -> 6. The left portion of the linked list, denoted as elements occurring prior to the splitValue (in this case, 2), is depicted as 1 -> 3 -> 5. Similarly, the right portion, encompassing elements including and after the splitValue, is illustrated as 2 -> 4 -> 6.

This practical example underscores the utility of the splitLinkedList function in effectively dividing a linked list at a specific element, providing the capability to process distinct segments of the list separately. Moreover, it serves as a reminder to manage memory appropriately by deallocating memory using the delete operator to prevent memory leaks.

8 GENERIC PROGRAMMING

Welcome to Chapter 8 of our book on advanced programming in C++. In this chapter, we will delve into the powerful world of "Generic Programming." Generic programming is a programming paradigm that allows us to write flexible and reusable code by using templates. Templates enable us to create functions and classes that can work with different data types, providing a high level of abstraction and code flexibility.

8.1 INTRODUCTION TO TEMPLATES

In this section, we will embark on a journey to explore the world of templates in C++. **Templates** are a powerful feature that enables us to write generic code, allowing functions and classes to work with different data types. This flexibility empowers programmers to create versatile and reusable code, making templates a fundamental aspect of modern C++ programming.

8.1.1 UNDERSTANDING GENERIC PROGRAMMING

At the heart of templates lies the concept of **generic programming**. This programming paradigm focuses on writing code that can operate on a wide range of data types, without duplicating the implementation for each type. Instead of writing separate functions or classes for different data types, templates allow us to define generic structures that adapt to the specific type at compile-time.

Let's begin with a simple example of a **generic function** that can add two numbers of any data type:

```cpp
#include <iostream>

// Generic function to add two values of any type
template <typename T>
T add(T a, T b) {
    return a + b;
}

int main() {
    int sum1 = add(5, 10);
    double sum2 = add(3.14, 2.71);
    std::cout << "Sum 1: " << sum1 << std::endl;
```

```
    std::cout << "Sum 2: " << sum2 << std::endl;
    return 0;
}
```

In this example, we define a generic function **add** using a template. The keyword `template` indicates that we are defining a template, and `<typename T>` is the template parameter, which represents an arbitrary data type. The function takes two arguments of type T, and it returns the sum of these arguments.

By using the **add** function, we can perform addition for different data types, such as `int` and `double`, without writing separate functions for each type. This is the essence of generic programming with templates.

8.1.2 TEMPLATE FUNCTIONS AND CLASSES

Templates are not limited to just functions; we can also create **generic classes** that can handle various data types. The syntax for template classes is similar to template functions.

Let's take a look at a generic class example, where we create a simple **Stack** that can store elements of any data type:

```cpp
#include <iostream>
#include <vector>

// Generic Stack class using template
template <typename T>
class Stack {
private:
    std::vector<T> elements;

public:
    void push(T value) {
        elements.push_back(value);
    }

    void pop() {
        if (!elements.empty()) {
            elements.pop_back();
        }
    }

    T top() const {
        if (!elements.empty()) {
            return elements.back();
        }
        throw std::runtime_error("Stack is empty.");
    }
```

```cpp
    bool empty() const {
        return elements.empty();
    }
};

int main() {
    Stack<int> intStack;
    intStack.push(10);
    intStack.push(20);
    intStack.push(30);

    Stack<std::string> stringStack;
    stringStack.push("Hello");
    stringStack.push("World");

    std::cout << "Int Stack Top: " << intStack.top() << std::endl;
    std::cout << "String Stack Top: " << stringStack.top() << std::endl;

    return 0;
}
```

In this example, we create a generic `Stack` class using a template. The class can be instantiated for any data type `T`. We use the standard `std::vector` to store the elements in the stack. The methods `push`, `pop`, `top`, and `empty` work seamlessly with any data type due to the generic nature of the template class.

8.1.3 TEMPLATE PARAMETERS AND ARGUMENTS

In C++, templates can have both **type parameters** and **non-type parameters**. Type parameters represent data types, and non-type parameters represent values that are not types. Both types of parameters can be used in both functions and classes.

Let's illustrate the concept of template parameters and arguments with an example of a generic function to find the minimum of two values:

```cpp
#include <iostream>

// Generic function to find the minimum of two values
template <typename T>
T minimum(T a, T b) {
    return (a < b) ? a : b;
}

int main() {
```

```
int minInt = minimum(10, 5);
double minDouble = minimum(3.14, 2.71);

std::cout << "Minimum Integer: " << minInt << std::endl;
std::cout << "Minimum Double: " << minDouble << std::endl;

return 0;
}
```

In this example, we define a generic function `minimum` with a type parameter `T`. The function takes two arguments of type `T` and returns the minimum of the two. When calling the `minimum` function, the compiler automatically deduces the appropriate data type based on the arguments passed.

The `?:` operator, also known as the ternary conditional operator, is a shorthand way to express simple conditional expressions in C++. It takes three operands and returns the second operand if the first operand (the condition) evaluates to true, otherwise, it returns the third operand.

The syntax of the `?:` operator is as follows:

```
condition ? expression1 : expression2;
```

Here, `condition` is the expression that is evaluated for its truth value. If `condition` is true, `expression1` is evaluated and becomes the value of the entire `?:` expression. If `condition` is false, `expression2` is evaluated and becomes the value of the `?:` expression.

Additionally, we can have non-type template parameters that represent values, such as integers or enumerations. Non-type template parameters are known at compile-time and can be used to configure classes or functions accordingly.

Understanding template parameters and arguments is essential for effectively utilizing templates and writing flexible and generic code in C++. By mastering the power of templates, you will become proficient in generic programming, enhancing the maintainability and reusability of your C++ code.

8.2 CREATING GENERIC CLASSES AND FUNCTIONS

In the previous section, we got introduced to the basics of templates and how they enable us to write generic code in C++. Now, let's dive deeper into creating **generic classes** and **functions** using templates. With the power of templates, we can design flexible and versatile structures that can work with various data types, making our code more efficient and maintainable.

8.2.1 IMPLEMENTING GENERIC FUNCTIONS

Let's start by exploring how to implement generic functions. We've already seen examples of generic functions in the Introduction to Templates section. However, let's reinforce the concept with another example of a generic function that can find the maximum of two values:

```
#include <iostream>

// Generic function to find the maximum of two values
template <typename T>
T maximum(T a, T b) {
    return (a > b) ? a : b;
}
```

```cpp
int main() {
    int maxInt = maximum(10, 5);
    double maxDouble = maximum(3.14, 2.71);

    std::cout << "Maximum Integer: " << maxInt << std::endl;
    std::cout << "Maximum Double: " << maxDouble << std::endl;

    return 0;
}
```

In this example, we define a generic function **maximum** using a template. The function takes two arguments of type **T** and returns the maximum of the two. The **typename** keyword before **T** indicates that **T** is a type parameter. The compiler deduces the data type based on the arguments we pass when calling the function.

8.2.2 CREATING GENERIC CLASSES

Now, let's move on to creating **generic classes** using templates. Generic classes are similar to generic functions, but they allow us to design entire classes that can handle different data types efficiently.

Consider a simple example of a generic class called **Pair**, which can hold a pair of values of any data type:

```cpp
#include <iostream>

// Generic Pair class using template
template <typename T1, typename T2>
class Pair {
private:
    T1 first;
    T2 second;

public:
    Pair(T1 f, T2 s) : first(f), second(s) {}

    T1 getFirst() const {
        return first;
    }

    T2 getSecond() const {
        return second;
    }
};
```

```cpp
int main() {
    Pair<int, double> myPair(10, 3.14);
    std::cout << "First: " << myPair.getFirst() << ", Second: " << myPair.getSecond() <<
std::endl;

    Pair<std::string, bool> anotherPair("Hello", true);
    std::cout << "First: " << anotherPair.getFirst() << ", Second: " <<
anotherPair.getSecond() << std::endl;

    return 0;
}
```

In this example, we define a generic **Pair** class using templates with two type parameters **T1** and **T2**. The class can be instantiated for any data types we specify. The constructor of the class takes two arguments of type **T1** and **T2**, and the member functions **getFirst** and **getSecond** return the stored values accordingly.

8.2.3 TEMPLATE SPECIALIZATION

Sometimes, we might need to provide specialized implementations for specific data types within a generic class or function. This is achieved through **template specialization**. Template specialization allows us to override the generic implementation with a custom one for a particular data type.

Let's illustrate template specialization with an example of a generic **show** function that prints a message for various data types:

```cpp
#include <iostream>

// Generic show function
template <typename T>
void show(T value) {
    std::cout << "Generic Show: " << value << std::endl;
}

// Template specialization for std::string
template <>
void show<std::string>(std::string value) {
    std::cout << "Special Show for Strings: " << value << std::endl;
}

int main() {
    show(10);
    show(3.14);
```

```
    show("Hello, World!");

    return 0;
}
```

In this example, we define a generic **show** function using a template. The function prints the value of any data type passed to it. However, we provide a template specialization for **std::string**, which overrides the generic implementation. When the **show** function is called with a **std::string**, the specialized version is executed instead.

By creating generic classes and functions with templates and utilizing template specialization when needed, we can harness the full potential of generic programming in C++. The ability to write code that works with multiple data types enhances code reusability and maintainability, making templates an essential tool for advanced C++ programming.

8.3 BENEFITS AND LIMITATIONS OF GENERIC PROGRAMMING

As we delve deeper into **generic programming** with templates in C++, it's essential to understand the advantages and limitations of this powerful programming paradigm.

8.3.1 ADVANTAGES OF TEMPLATES

Templates offer several significant advantages that make them a valuable tool in modern C++ programming:

1. Code Reusability: Templates allow us to write generic functions and classes that work with various data types. This results in code that can be reused across different parts of the program, reducing redundant implementations.

2. Maintainability: By using templates, we can create a single, flexible piece of code that handles multiple data types. This leads to more maintainable codebases since changes and improvements can be made in one place instead of scattered throughout the code.

3. Performance Optimization: Templates generate specialized code for each data type at compile time. This allows the compiler to perform type-specific optimizations, leading to better performance compared to runtime polymorphism.

4. Type Safety: Template parameters are strongly typed. This means that the compiler enforces type checking, preventing us from passing incompatible data types to generic functions or classes.

8.3.2 CODE REUSABILITY AND MAINTAINABILITY

Code reusability and **maintainability** are perhaps the most compelling advantages of generic programming. Instead of writing separate implementations for different data types, we can create a single generic implementation that adapts to varying data types.

Let's revisit the example of a generic **Pair** class that we introduced earlier:

```
#include <iostream>

// Generic Pair class using template
template <typename T1, typename T2>
class Pair {
private:
    T1 first;
```

```
    T2 second;

public:
    Pair(T1 f, T2 s) : first(f), second(s) {}

    T1 getFirst() const {
        return first;
    }

    T2 getSecond() const {
        return second;
    }
};

int main() {
    Pair<int, double> myPair(10, 3.14);
    std::cout << "First: " << myPair.getFirst() << ", Second: " << myPair.getSecond() <<
std::endl;

    Pair<std::string, bool> anotherPair("Hello", true);
    std::cout << "First: " << anotherPair.getFirst() << ", Second: " <<
anotherPair.getSecond() << std::endl;

    return 0;
}
```

In this example, we create a generic `Pair` class that can store pairs of values of any data type. The class is defined using templates, with two type parameters `T1` and `T2`. By doing so, we achieve code reusability since this single `Pair` class can be used with various data types, such as `int`, `double`, `std::string`, or even user-defined types.

8.3.3 OVERHEAD AND CODE BLOAT

While templates bring a lot of benefits, they can also introduce some **overhead** and **code bloat**. Since templates generate specialized code for each data type, using numerous templates with different data types can lead to an increase in the size of the compiled binary (code bloat).

For example, if we create a generic container class to store any data type, the compiled binary will contain separate code for each data type used with that container. This can lead to larger executable files.

However, C++ compilers are equipped with various optimization techniques to mitigate this issue. For example, they can perform **template instantiation optimization** to remove unused or unnecessary template instantiations from the final binary.

8.3.4 COMPILER ERRORS AND TEMPLATE METAPROGRAMMING

One of the challenges of working with templates is dealing with **compiler errors**. Template errors can be more complex to interpret than regular errors since they involve template instantiation and substitution during the compilation process.

In some cases, you might encounter lengthy error messages when working with complex templates. Learning to read and understand these error messages becomes crucial to fixing issues in generic code.

Additionally, **template metaprogramming** involves using templates to perform computations and decisions during compile-time. While this technique is powerful, it can be challenging for beginners due to its complex nature.

To summarize, generic programming with templates offers significant advantages in terms of code reusability, maintainability, and performance optimization. However, it can also lead to code bloat and more complex error messages, especially when working with complex templates or template metaprogramming. Proper understanding of template best practices and compiler optimizations can help mitigate potential drawbacks and harness the full power of generic programming in C++.

8.4 BEST PRACTICES FOR GENERIC PROGRAMMING

Writing efficient and flexible template code requires following certain best practices. These practices help ensure that your code is not only correct but also easy to understand and maintain. In this section, we will explore some essential best practices for **generic programming** with templates in C++.

8.4.1 WRITING EFFICIENT AND FLEXIBLE TEMPLATE CODE

When designing generic functions or classes, it's crucial to consider performance and flexibility. Here are some tips to write efficient and flexible template code:

1. Use References for Large Objects: When working with large objects like `std::vector` or user-defined classes, prefer passing them by reference to avoid unnecessary copies.

```cpp
template <typename T>
void printVector(const std::vector<T>& vec) {
    for (const auto& item : vec) {
        std::cout << item << " ";
    }
}
```

2. Utilize `const` Correctness: Use `const` where appropriate to indicate that the function or class won't modify the input data.

```cpp
template <typename T>
T findMax(const std::vector<T>& vec) {
    if (vec.empty()) {
        throw std::invalid_argument("Empty vector");
    }

    T maxVal = vec[0];
    for (const auto& item : vec) {
        if (item > maxVal) {
            maxVal = item;
        }
    }
```

```
    return maxVal;
}
```

3. Limit Use of Template Specialization: While template specialization can be useful in certain scenarios, avoid overusing it, as it can lead to code duplication and maintenance challenges.

4. Avoid Excessive Template Nesting: Limit the level of nesting in your template code to enhance readability and maintainability.

5. Provide Clear Error Messages: When a template-related error occurs, the error messages can be complex. To aid debugging, provide clear and informative error messages by using static assertions and `static_assert`.

8.4.2 MINIMIZING CODE DUPLICATION

Generic programming is all about code reusability. To achieve this, minimize code duplication by creating generic components that can be used across different parts of your codebase.

For example, let's create a function to find the minimum of two values, which works with different data types using a template:

```
template <typename T>
T min(T a, T b) {
    return (a < b) ? a : b;
}
```

Now, this `min` function can be used with various data types, such as `int`, `double`, `float`, and even custom types that support the comparison operator (`<`).

```
int main() {
    int x = 10, y = 5;
    std::cout << "Minimum: " << min(x, y) << std::endl;

    double a = 3.14, b = 2.71;
    std::cout << "Minimum: " << min(a, b) << std::endl;

    return 0;
}
```

8.4.3 UNDERSTANDING SFINAE (SUBSTITUTION FAILURE IS NOT AN ERROR)

SFINAE is an acronym for "Substitution Failure Is Not An Error." It is a fundamental principle in C++ templates that allows the compiler to continue compiling code even if a substitution (template instantiation) fails.

This principle is commonly used to enable or disable certain template overloads based on specific conditions.

```
template <typename T>
struct HasSizeMethod {
private:
    template <typename U>
    static auto test(int) -> decltype(std::declval<U>().size(), std::true_type{});

    template <typename U>
    static auto test(...) -> std::false_type;

public:
    static constexpr bool value = decltype(test<T>(0))::value;
};
```

In this example, we create a `HasSizeMethod` struct that determines whether a given type `T` has a member function named `size()`. It uses SFINAE with the `test` functions to check if the substitution (calling `size()`) succeeds.

8.4.4 PROPER USE OF TYPE TRAITS

Type traits are a powerful tool in C++ templates that provide information about types at compile-time. Use type traits to enable conditional behavior based on type properties.

For example, the `std::is_integral` type trait determines whether a type is an integral type:

```
template <typename T>
void processNumber(T num) {
    if (std::is_integral<T>::value) {
        std::cout << "Integer type" << std::endl;
    } else {
        std::cout << "Non-integer type" << std::endl;
    }
}
```

By using type traits, you can tailor your generic functions or classes to handle different types differently based on their properties.

By following these best practices, you can write efficient, maintainable, and flexible template code that takes full advantage of generic programming in C++. These guidelines will help you harness the true power of templates and make your codebase more robust and reusable.

8.5 EXAMPLE

Let's illustrate the power of **generic programming** in C++ with a practical example. In this example, we'll create a generic class called `Pair`, which can store a pair of values of any data type. The class will demonstrate the flexibility and reusability achieved through templates.

8.5.1 IMPLEMENTING THE **PAIR** CLASS

To create a generic `Pair` class, we'll define a template class with two type parameters, `T1` and `T2`. These parameters will allow us to store values of any data type in the pair.

```cpp
template <typename T1, typename T2>
class Pair {
public:
    Pair(T1 first, T2 second) : first_(first), second_(second) {}

    T1 getFirst() const { return first_; }
    T2 getSecond() const { return second_; }

private:
    T1 first_;
    T2 second_;
};
```

In the above code, we defined a **Pair** class template with two data members **first_** and **second_**. The constructor takes two arguments of type **T1** and **T2**, respectively, and initializes the data members with these values.

8.5.2 USING THE **PAIR** CLASS

Now that we have the generic **Pair** class, let's use it to create pairs of different data types:

```cpp
int main() {
    // Create a pair of integers
    Pair<int, int> intPair(1, 2);
    std::cout << "First: " << intPair.getFirst() << ", Second: " << intPair.getSecond() <<
std::endl;

    // Create a pair of doubles
    Pair<double, double> doublePair(3.14, 2.71);
    std::cout << "First: " << doublePair.getFirst() << ", Second: " << doublePair.getSecond()
<< std::endl;

    // Create a pair of strings
    Pair<std::string, std::string> stringPair("Hello", "World");
    std::cout << "First: " << stringPair.getFirst() << ", Second: " << stringPair.getSecond()
<< std::endl;

    return 0;
}
```

In the `main` function, we created three pairs: one for integers, one for doubles, and one for strings. Thanks to the generic `Pair` class, we were able to create pairs of different data types without writing separate classes for each type.

8.5.3 TEMPLATE SPECIALIZATION

The generic `Pair` class we defined is quite versatile, but what if we want to perform specific operations for a particular data type? We can achieve this using **template specialization**.

Let's specialize the `Pair` class for a pair of `int` values, and add a function that returns their sum:

```cpp
template <>
class Pair<int, int> {
public:
    Pair(int first, int second) : first_(first), second_(second) {}

    int getFirst() const { return first_; }
    int getSecond() const { return second_; }

    int sum() const { return first_ + second_; }

private:
    int first_;
    int second_;
};
```

Now, when we create a `Pair` of `int` values, we can use the `sum` function:

```cpp
int main() {
    Pair<int, int> intPair(3, 5);
    std::cout << "First: " << intPair.getFirst() << ", Second: " << intPair.getSecond() <<
std::endl;
    std::cout << "Sum: " << intPair.sum() << std::endl;

    return 0;
}
```

By specializing the `Pair` class for `int`, we were able to add a specific behavior to the class for a particular data type, demonstrating the power of template specialization.

8.5.4 CONCLUSION

In this example, we explored the concept of generic programming in C++ using templates. We created a versatile `Pair` class that can store pairs of different data types, and we even demonstrated how to specialize the class for specific types to provide specialized behavior.

Generic programming with templates is a powerful technique that allows you to write reusable, efficient, and flexible code that can work with various data types. By leveraging templates, you can make your C++ programs more generic and easier to maintain.

9 HANDLING ERRORS AND EXCEPTIONS

Errors are an inevitable part of programming, and they can occur for various reasons, such as invalid user input, resource unavailability, or unexpected behavior. In C++, we have mechanisms to handle these errors gracefully, allowing our programs to recover from exceptional situations and continue executing smoothly. This chapter will introduce you to the world of exception handling, a powerful feature that enables us to manage errors effectively.

9.1 EXCEPTION HANDLING MECHANISMS

Errors are an inevitable part of software development, and handling them effectively is crucial to writing robust and reliable programs. Exception handling is a powerful mechanism in C++ that allows us to manage errors in a structured and controlled manner. In this section, we will explore the fundamental concepts of exception handling and how it enables us to gracefully handle exceptional situations.

9.1.1 UNDERSTANDING EXCEPTIONS

An exception is an object that represents an error or an exceptional situation that occurs during the execution of a program. Instead of terminating the program abruptly when an error occurs, C++ allows us to throw an exception when exceptional circumstances arise. When an exception is thrown, the normal flow of program execution is disrupted, and the control is transferred to a designated block of code responsible for handling the exception.

The concept of exception handling is based on three fundamental operations:

1. **Throwing Exceptions:** When an error condition is detected, we can create an exception object and throw it using the **throw** keyword. This indicates that an exceptional situation has occurred and needs to be handled.

2. **Catching Exceptions:** We use **catch** blocks to handle exceptions that are thrown by other parts of the code. A **catch** block is responsible for catching and processing a specific type of exception.

3. **Rethrowing Exceptions:** In some situations, we may want to handle an exception at one level of the program and then rethrow it to be caught and handled at a higher level.

9.1.2 THROWING EXCEPTIONS

To throw an exception, we use the **throw** keyword followed by an exception object. The exception object can be of any data type, including built-in types, user-defined classes, or standard library classes. When an exception is thrown, the program searches for an appropriate **catch** block that can handle the exception.

Let's look at a simple example of throwing an exception:

```
#include <iostream>
```

```cpp
void divide(int numerator, int denominator) {
    if (denominator == 0) {
        throw std::runtime_error("Division by zero is not allowed.");
    }
    std::cout << "Result: " << numerator / denominator << std::endl;
}

int main() {
    try {
        divide(10, 2);
        divide(7, 0); // This will throw an exception
        divide(15, 3);
    } catch (std::exception& ex) {
        std::cerr << "Exception caught: " << ex.what() << std::endl;
    }
    return 0;
}
```

In this example, the **divide** function takes two integers as arguments and calculates their division. If the denominator is zero, we throw a **std::runtime_error** exception with the message "Division by zero is not allowed." In the **main** function, we call **divide** three times, and the second call will throw an exception due to division by zero. The thrown exception is caught in the **catch** block, and the error message is printed to the standard error stream.

9.1.3 CATCHING EXCEPTIONS

Catching exceptions is done using **catch** blocks. A **catch** block follows the **try** block that contains the code that might throw an exception. It specifies the type of exception it can handle in parentheses, which allows the program to match the thrown exception's type with the catch block.

```cpp
#include <iostream>

void divide(int numerator, int denominator) {
    if (denominator == 0) {
        throw std::runtime_error("Division by zero is not allowed.");
    }
    std::cout << "Result: " << numerator / denominator << std::endl;
}

int main() {
    try {
        divide(10, 2);
```

```
        divide(7, 0); // This will throw an exception
        divide(15, 3);
    } catch (const std::runtime_error& ex) {
        std::cerr << "Exception caught: " << ex.what() << std::endl;
    }
    return 0;
}
```

In this modified example, the **catch** block specifies **const std::runtime_error&** as the parameter, indicating that it can handle exceptions of type **std::runtime_error**. When the second call to **divide** throws an exception, it is caught by this **catch** block, and the error message is printed.

9.1.4 RETHROWING EXCEPTIONS

In some cases, we may want to catch an exception in one part of the program and then rethrow it to be caught and handled at a higher level. This is useful when we want to perform some local handling of the exception but still allow the program's upper levels to be aware of the exceptional situation.

```
#include <iostream>

void someFunction() {
    try {
        // ... some code that throws an exception ...
    } catch (std::exception& ex) {
        std::cerr << "Exception caught in someFunction: " << ex.what() << std::endl;
        throw; // Rethrow the exception
    }
}

int main() {
    try {
        someFunction();
    } catch (std::exception& ex) {
        std::cerr << "Exception caught in main: " << ex.what() << std::endl;
    }
    return 0;
}
```

In this example, the **someFunction** catches an exception and then rethrows it using **throw;** without any argument. This causes the exception to propagate up the call stack to the **main** function, where it is caught and handled again.

9.1.5 EXCEPTION CLASS HIERARCHY

C++ provides a hierarchy of exception classes to organize different types of exceptions. At the top of this hierarchy is the **std::exception** class, which serves as the base class for all standard exceptions. Each standard exception is derived from **std::exception**, and they provide more specific error information.

```cpp
#include <iostream>
#include <stdexcept>

void divide(int numerator, int denominator) {
    if (denominator == 0) {
        throw std::runtime_error("Division by zero is not allowed.");
    }
    std::cout << "Result: " << numerator / denominator << std::endl;
}

int main() {
    try {
        divide(10, 2);
        divide(7, 0); // This will throw an exception
        divide(15, 3);
    } catch (const std::exception& ex) {
        std::cerr << "Exception caught: " << ex.what() << std::endl;
    }
    return 0;
}
```

In this example, we use **std::runtime_error**, which is derived from **std::exception**, to throw an exception. We catch it using a **const std::exception&** parameter in the catch block, allowing us to handle both **std::exception** and its derived classes.

Exception handling provides a powerful mechanism to manage errors and exceptional situations in C++. Understanding the basics of exception handling is essential for writing reliable and maintainable code. In the next section, we will explore more advanced topics related to try-catch blocks and exception propagation.

9.2 TRY-CATCH BLOCKS AND EXCEPTION PROPAGATION

In the previous section, we learned about the basics of exception handling and how to use **try**, **catch**, and **throw** to manage exceptional situations. In this section, we will explore more advanced concepts related to try-catch blocks and how exceptions propagate through different parts of the program.

9.2.1 USING TRY-CATCH BLOCKS

A **try-catch** block is used to catch exceptions that may be thrown in the **try** block. The **try** block contains the code that might throw an exception, and the **catch** block specifies the type of exception it can handle. If an exception is thrown in the **try** block, the program immediately jumps to the appropriate **catch** block that matches the type of the thrown exception.

The syntax of a **try-catch** block is as follows:

```cpp
try {
    // code that might throw an exception
```

```
} catch (ExceptionType1& ex1) {
    // exception handling for ExceptionType1
} catch (ExceptionType2& ex2) {
    // exception handling for ExceptionType2
} catch (...) {
    // generic exception handling for any other type of exception
}
```

Let's look at an example:

```
#include <iostream>

int divide(int numerator, int denominator) {
    if (denominator == 0) {
        throw std::runtime_error("Division by zero is not allowed.");
    }
    return numerator / denominator;
}

int main() {
    try {
        int result = divide(10, 2);
        std::cout << "Result: " << result << std::endl;

        result = divide(7, 0); // This will throw an exception
        std::cout << "Result: " << result << std::endl; // This line will not be executed
    } catch (const std::exception& ex) {
        std::cerr << "Exception caught: " << ex.what() << std::endl;
    }
    return 0;
}
```

In this example, the **divide** function calculates the division of two integers. When the denominator is zero, it throws a **std::runtime_error** exception. The **try** block in the **main** function calls **divide** twice. The first call with valid inputs successfully executes, and the result is printed. However, the second call with a denominator of zero throws an exception, and the control is transferred to the **catch** block, printing the error message.

9.2.2 HANDLING MULTIPLE EXCEPTIONS

In some scenarios, multiple types of exceptions might be thrown in the **try** block. We can use multiple **catch** blocks to handle different types of exceptions separately.

```cpp
#include <iostream>

void processNumber(int num) {
    if (num < 0) {
        throw std::invalid_argument("Negative numbers are not allowed.");
    } else if (num == 0) {
        throw std::out_of_range("Number cannot be zero.");
    }
    std::cout << "Processed number: " << num << std::endl;
}

int main() {
    try {
        processNumber(10);
        processNumber(-5); // This will throw an invalid_argument exception
        processNumber(0);  // This will throw an out_of_range exception
    } catch (const std::invalid_argument& ex) {
        std::cerr << "Invalid argument: " << ex.what() << std::endl;
    } catch (const std::out_of_range& ex) {
        std::cerr << "Out of range: " << ex.what() << std::endl;
    } catch (const std::exception& ex) {
        std::cerr << "Exception caught: " << ex.what() << std::endl;
    }
    return 0;
}
```

In this example, the **processNumber** function takes an integer as an argument and performs some processing on it. It throws an **std::invalid_argument** exception for negative numbers and an **std::out_of_range** exception for zero. The **main** function calls **processNumber** three times with different inputs, and each time an exception is thrown, it is caught by the appropriate **catch** block.

9.2.3 NESTED TRY-CATCH BLOCKS

C++ allows nested **try-catch** blocks, where an outer **try** block contains an inner **try** block. If an exception is thrown in the inner **try** block, the program searches for a matching **catch** block within the inner **try** block. If none is found, it continues searching in the outer **try** block and so on until a matching **catch** block is found or the exception is not caught, resulting in program termination.

```cpp
#include <iostream>

void processNumber(int num) {
    if (num < 0) {
        throw std::invalid_argument("Negative numbers are not allowed.");
```

```
    }
    std::cout << "Processed number: " << num << std::endl;
}

int main() {
    try {
        try {
            processNumber(-5);
        } catch (const std::invalid_argument& ex) {
            std::cerr << "Inner catch: " << ex.what() << std::endl;
            throw; // Rethrow the exception
        }
    } catch (const std::invalid_argument& ex) {
        std::cerr << "Outer catch: " << ex.what() << std::endl;
    }
    return 0;
}
```

In this example, the **processNumber** function throws an **std::invalid_argument** exception for negative numbers. In the **main** function, we have a nested **try-catch** block. When **processNumber(-5)** is called, it throws an exception, which is caught in the inner **catch** block. The inner **catch** block rethrows the exception using **throw;**, and it is caught by the outer **catch** block.

9.2.4 EXCEPTION PROPAGATION

When an exception is thrown in a function and is not caught within that function, it propagates up the call stack until it is caught by an appropriate **catch** block or until it reaches the **main** function. If an exception is not caught at all, the program terminates.

```
#include <iostream>

void processNumber(int num) {
    if (num < 0) {
        throw std::invalid_argument("Negative numbers are not allowed.");
    }
    std::cout << "Processed number: " << num << std::endl;
}

void processNumbers() {
    try {
        processNumber(10);
        processNumber(-5); // This will throw an exception
        processNumber(20); // This line will not be executed
```

```
    } catch (const std::exception& ex) {
        std::cerr << "Exception caught in processNumbers(): " << ex.what() << std::endl;
    }
}

int main() {
    try {
        processNumbers();
    } catch (const std::exception& ex) {
        std::cerr << "Exception caught in main(): " << ex.what() << std::endl;
    }
    return 0;
}
```

In this example, the **processNumbers** function calls **processNumber** three times. The first two calls execute successfully, but the second call with a negative number throws an **std::invalid_argument** exception. Since this exception is not caught within the **processNumbers** function, it propagates up to the **main** function, where it is caught and handled.

Understanding try-catch blocks and exception propagation is crucial for designing robust and fault-tolerant C++ programs. In the next section, we will dive deeper into creating custom exception classes to provide more informative error handling.

9.3 CUSTOM EXCEPTION CLASSES

In the previous section, we explored the basics of exception handling, including how to throw and catch exceptions using **try-catch** blocks. While C++ provides standard exception classes like **std::exception** and its derived classes, it is often beneficial to create custom exception classes to handle specific error scenarios and provide more detailed information about the exceptions.

9.3.1 CREATING CUSTOM EXCEPTION CLASSES

Creating a custom exception class involves defining a new class that inherits from **std::exception** or one of its derived classes. By doing so, we can specialize the behavior of our exception and include additional information to help identify the cause of the exception.

Let's create a custom exception class called **FileOpenException** to handle errors related to file opening:

```
#include <iostream>
#include <exception>
#include <string>

class FileOpenException : public std::exception {
public:
    explicit FileOpenException(const std::string& filename)
        : filename_(filename) {}

    const char* what() const noexcept override {
```

```
        return ("Failed to open file: " + filename_).c_str();
    }

private:
    std::string filename_;
};
```

In this example, we define a class **FileOpenException** that inherits from **std::exception**. The constructor takes the name of the file that failed to open and stores it in a private member variable **filename_**. The **what()** method is overridden to return a more informative error message, including the filename.

9.3.2 ADDING ADDITIONAL INFORMATION TO EXCEPTIONS

Custom exception classes can include additional member variables and methods to provide more context and details about the exception. For instance, we can add a method to retrieve the filename associated with the **FileOpenException**:

```cpp
#include <iostream>
#include <exception>
#include <string>

class FileOpenException : public std::exception {
public:
    explicit FileOpenException(const std::string& filename)
        : filename_(filename) {}

    const char* what() const noexcept override {
        return ("Failed to open file: " + filename_).c_str();
    }

    const std::string& getFilename() const {
        return filename_;
    }

private:
    std::string filename_;
};
```

Now, we can catch the **FileOpenException** and use the **getFilename()** method to access the filename associated with the exception:

```cpp
#include <iostream>
```

```cpp
#include <fstream>

void openFile(const std::string& filename) {
    std::ifstream file(filename);
    if (!file.is_open()) {
        throw FileOpenException(filename);
    }
    // File processing code here
}

int main() {
    try {
        openFile("example.txt");
    } catch (const FileOpenException& ex) {
        std::cerr << "Exception caught: " << ex.what() << std::endl;
        std::cerr << "Filename: " << ex.getFilename() << std::endl;
    }
    return 0;
}
```

In this example, the **openFile** function attempts to open a file for reading using an **ifstream**. If the file cannot be opened, it throws a **FileOpenException** with the filename. The **main** function then catches the **FileOpenException**, prints the error message along with the filename.

9.3.3 HANDLING CUSTOM EXCEPTIONS

Handling custom exceptions is similar to handling standard exceptions. We use **try-catch** blocks to catch specific exceptions and provide appropriate error handling.

```cpp
#include <iostream>
#include <exception>
#include <stdexcept>

class CustomException : public std::exception {
public:
    const char* what() const noexcept override {
        return "Custom exception occurred!";
    }
};

int main() {
    try {
        throw CustomException();
```

```
    } catch (const CustomException& ex) {
        std::cerr << "Exception caught: " << ex.what() << std::endl;
    }
    return 0;
}
```

In this example, we define a custom exception class **CustomException**, which inherits from **std::exception**. When the program executes, it throws a **CustomException** using the **throw** keyword. The **catch** block catches the **CustomException** and prints the error message provided by the **what()** method of the exception.

By creating custom exception classes, we can tailor our error handling to specific scenarios and improve the overall robustness of our programs. Custom exceptions also allow us to pass more relevant information about errors, making it easier to identify and debug issues in our code.

9.4 BEST PRACTICES FOR EXCEPTION HANDLING

Exception handling is a powerful tool for managing errors in C++ programs. However, it should be used judiciously and with care. In this section, we will explore some best practices for using exceptions effectively and responsibly.

9.4.1 WHEN TO USE EXCEPTIONS

Exceptions should be used to handle exceptional and unexpected situations in your code. They are meant to address errors or conditions that prevent normal program execution. As a rule of thumb, you should avoid using exceptions for regular control flow or situations that can be handled more efficiently using other mechanisms.

For example, using exceptions for flow control in a loop is generally not a good practice. Instead, consider using conditional statements to handle normal flow control.

9.4.2 PROPER EXCEPTION DESIGN

When designing custom exception classes, it's essential to create exception hierarchies that make sense for your application. Think about the types of errors that can occur and organize your exceptions accordingly. Avoid overly broad exception classes that may catch more exceptions than intended.

For instance, let's assume we have an image processing library that can encounter errors related to file handling, pixel manipulation, and memory allocation. We could define custom exception classes for each type of error, such as **FileOpenException**, **PixelProcessingException**, and **MemoryAllocationException**. This way, we can handle different error scenarios with more precision.

```cpp
#include <iostream>
#include <exception>
#include <string>

class FileOpenException : public std::exception {
public:
    explicit FileOpenException(const std::string& filename)
        : filename_(filename) {}
```

```
const char* what() const noexcept override {
    return ("Failed to open file: " + filename_).c_str();
}

const std::string& getFilename() const {
    return filename_;
}

private:
    std::string filename_;
};
```

```
// Similarly, create other custom exception classes
```

9.4.3 EXCEPTION SAFETY GUARANTEES

When designing functions that might throw exceptions, it's crucial to provide exception safety guarantees. Exception safety ensures that resources are correctly released and that the program remains in a consistent state, even if an exception occurs.

There are three levels of exception safety:

- **Basic Guarantee**: The program remains in a valid state, but some operations may be left unfinished. No resources are leaked.
- **Strong Guarantee**: If an exception occurs, the program remains in its original state. If the operation fails, it has no observable effects.
- **No-Throw Guarantee**: The operation will never throw an exception.

It's generally desirable to provide at least the basic guarantee for functions that may throw exceptions. For functions that modify shared resources, it's often better to provide the strong guarantee to ensure the integrity of the data.

9.4.4 EXCEPTION GUIDELINES

When working with exceptions, follow these general guidelines:

- **Catch Exceptions at the Right Level**: Catch exceptions where you can handle them effectively. Avoid catching exceptions at a level where you cannot take appropriate actions.
- **Avoid Catch-All Blocks**: Avoid using catch-all blocks like `catch (...)`. Catching all exceptions can make it difficult to diagnose specific errors and may lead to unexpected behavior.
- **Use const Reference in Catch Blocks**: Catch exceptions by const reference to avoid unnecessary object copies.
- **Use noexcept When Appropriate**: Use `noexcept` on functions that will not throw exceptions. This helps the compiler optimize code and provides useful information to users of your functions.
- **Document Exception Behavior**: Clearly document the exceptions that functions may throw, especially for custom exception classes.

By following these best practices, you can effectively handle errors in your C++ programs using exceptions and ensure robustness and maintainability in your code.

In the next section, we will explore a practical example of exception handling in the context of file handling.

9.5 EXAMPLE: FILE HANDLING WITH EXCEPTION HANDLING

In this example, we will demonstrate how to use exception handling to handle file-related errors in C++. File handling operations, such as opening files, reading data, and writing data, can encounter various issues, such as file not found, permission errors, or disk full. Exception handling provides an elegant way to deal with these exceptional situations and gracefully handle errors in our programs.

Step 1: Creating Custom Exception Class

First, let's create a custom exception class to handle file-related errors. We will call it **FileException**. Our **FileException** class will inherit from the standard library's **std::exception** class and provide a constructor to set an appropriate error message.

```cpp
#include <exception>
#include <string>

class FileException : public std::exception {
public:
    explicit FileException(const std::string& message)
        : errorMessage_(message) {}

    const char* what() const noexcept override {
        return errorMessage_.c_str();
    }

private:
    std::string errorMessage_;
};
```

Step 2: Implementing File Handling with Exception Handling

Now, let's create a function called **readFile** that reads data from a file and handles exceptions gracefully.

```cpp
#include <iostream>
#include <fstream>

std::string readFile(const std::string& filename) {
    std::ifstream file(filename);
    if (!file.is_open()) {
        throw FileException("Error opening file: " + filename);
    }

    std::string content;
    std::string line;
    while (std::getline(file, line)) {
        content += line + "\n";
```

```
    }

    file.close();
    return content;
}
```

In this function, we use **std::ifstream** to open the file specified by the **filename** parameter. If the file cannot be opened (e.g., it doesn't exist or there are permission issues), we throw a **FileException** with an appropriate error message.

Step 3: Using Try-Catch Blocks

Now, let's use a **try-catch** block to call our **readFile** function and handle any exceptions that may occur.

```
int main() {
    const std::string filename = "example.txt";

    try {
        std::string content = readFile(filename);
        std::cout << "File contents:\n" << content;
    } catch (const FileException& ex) {
        std::cerr << "Error: " << ex.what() << std::endl;
    }

    return 0;
}
```

In this **main** function, we call **readFile** with a filename ("example.txt" in this case) inside a **try** block. If an exception occurs during the file reading operation, it will be caught by the corresponding **catch** block that handles **FileException**. We then print an error message using **std::cerr**.

Step 4: Handling Multiple Exceptions

You can handle multiple types of exceptions using separate **catch** blocks. For instance, if you have different exception classes for file opening errors, file reading errors, and file writing errors, you can handle them individually.

```
try {
    // Code that may throw different types of exceptions
} catch (const FileOpenException& ex) {
    // Handle file opening errors
} catch (const FileReadException& ex) {
    // Handle file reading errors
} catch (const FileWriteException& ex) {
    // Handle file writing errors
```

```cpp
} catch (const std::exception& ex) {
    // Handle other unexpected exceptions
}
```

Step 5: Exception Propagation
If you have nested function calls that may throw exceptions, you can propagate the exceptions to the calling function using the **throw** keyword.

```cpp
void function1() {
    // Some code that may throw an exception
}

void function2() {
    try {
        function1();
    } catch (const SomeException& ex) {
        // Handle the exception or rethrow it to the calling function
        throw;
    }
}

int main() {
    try {
        function2();
    } catch (const SomeException& ex) {
        std::cerr << "Exception caught: " << ex.what() << std::endl;
    }
    return 0;
}
```

Here, if **function1** throws an exception, it will be caught in **function2**, and we can either handle it there or rethrow it to the **main** function for further handling.

Conclusion
In this example, we have demonstrated how to use exception handling to gracefully handle file-related errors in C++. Exception handling allows us to write robust and reliable code that can handle unexpected situations effectively, leading to more stable and user-friendly applications.

9.6 SUMMARY AND CONCLUSION
Exception handling is a crucial aspect of modern C++ programming that allows us to handle errors and unexpected situations gracefully. Throughout this chapter, we explored various exception handling mechanisms, best practices, and examples to understand how to use them effectively in our code.

Understanding Exceptions (*9.1.1*):
- Exceptions are a way to handle errors and exceptional situations that may occur during the

execution of a program.
- When an error occurs, an exception can be thrown, indicating that something unexpected happened.
- If an exception is not caught and handled properly, it will lead to program termination, potentially leaving resources in an inconsistent state.

Throwing Exceptions (*9.1.2*):
- In C++, we can throw exceptions using the **throw** keyword, followed by an object representing the exception.
- The object being thrown can be of any type, even custom classes, as long as they are derived from the standard library's **std::exception** class or its subclasses.

Catching Exceptions (*9.1.3*):
- Exceptions are caught using **try-catch** blocks. The **try** block contains the code that may throw an exception.
- If an exception occurs, it is caught by the appropriate **catch** block that matches the type of the thrown exception.

Rethrowing Exceptions (*9.1.4*):
- Sometimes, we may want to handle an exception partially within a **catch** block and then rethrow it to be caught by an outer **catch** block or propagated further up the call stack.

Exception Class Hierarchy (*9.1.5*):
- The C++ standard library provides a hierarchy of exception classes derived from **std::exception**.
- We can create custom exception classes by inheriting from **std::exception** or its subclasses to handle specific types of errors in our code.

Using Try-Catch Blocks (*9.2.1*):
- **try-catch** blocks allow us to handle exceptions gracefully, preventing program crashes and enabling recovery from errors.
- The **try** block contains the code that might throw an exception, and the **catch** block handles the exception if it occurs.

Handling Multiple Exceptions (*9.2.2*):
- We can use multiple **catch** blocks to handle different types of exceptions, allowing for more specific error handling.

Nested Try-Catch Blocks (*9.2.3*):
- **try-catch** blocks can be nested to handle exceptions at different levels of function calls.

Exception Propagation (*9.2.4*):
- Exceptions can be propagated up the call stack by rethrowing them or allowing them to be automatically propagated when not caught.

Creating Custom Exception Classes (*9.3.1*):
- Custom exception classes allow us to create more meaningful and specific exceptions for our application's error handling needs.

Adding Additional Information to Exceptions (*9.3.2*):
- We can add extra information to exception objects to provide more context about the error that occurred.

Handling Custom Exceptions (*9.3.3*):
- Custom exceptions can be caught and handled just like standard exceptions, using **catch** blocks.

When to Use Exceptions (*9.4.1*):
- Exceptions should be used to handle exceptional situations, not as a substitute for normal control flow.
- Use exceptions for error conditions that are not part of the regular program flow and should be handled separately.

Proper Exception Design (*9.4.2*):

- Design custom exception classes carefully, providing meaningful error messages and considering the exception class hierarchy.

Exception Safety Guarantees (*9.4.3*):
- Functions should offer strong exception safety guarantees, ensuring that they leave objects and resources in a consistent state even in the presence of exceptions.

Exception Guidelines (*9.4.4*):
- Establish exception handling guidelines and adhere to them consistently across the codebase for better maintainability and code clarity.

Example: File Handling with Exception Handling (*9.5*):
- We demonstrated how to use exception handling to gracefully handle file-related errors, such as file not found or permission issues.

In conclusion, exception handling is a powerful tool for handling errors and exceptional situations in C++. When used appropriately and following best practices, it enhances the robustness and reliability of our programs. However, care should be taken to avoid using exceptions for regular control flow and to design custom exception classes thoughtfully. By mastering exception handling, C++ developers can create more stable and user-friendly applications.

10 I/O LIBRARIES

Input and output operations are essential in any programming language, allowing us to interact with users and manipulate data stored in files. In C++, the I/O libraries provide a powerful set of tools for handling various input and output tasks. In this chapter, we will explore these libraries and learn how to perform input and output operations efficiently.

10.1 INPUT/OUTPUT OPERATIONS IN C++

Input and output operations are fundamental to any programming language as they enable communication between the program and the user, as well as data storage and retrieval. In C++, we have powerful I/O libraries that facilitate these operations efficiently. Let's dive into the different aspects of input and output in C++.

10.1.1: STANDARD INPUT AND OUTPUT (*IOSTREAM*)

The **iostream** library in C++ provides functionality for standard input and output. The most commonly used objects are **cin** and **cout**, which allow us to read input from the user and display output on the screen, respectively.

Reading Input from the User:

```cpp
#include <iostream>

int main() {
    int age;
    std::cout << "Enter your age: ";
    std::cin >> age;
    std::cout << "You are " << age << " years old." << std::endl;
    return 0;
}
```

In this example, we use **cin** to read an integer value (the user's age) from the user and then use **cout** to display the entered age.

10.1.2: FORMATTED INPUT AND OUTPUT (*IOMANIP*)

The **iomanip** library provides tools to format the input and output in a specific way. It allows us to control the precision of floating-point numbers, set field widths, and control the alignment of output.

Formatting Output:

```cpp
#include <iostream>
#include <iomanip>

int main() {
    double pi = 3.14159265359;
    std::cout << std::setprecision(4) << pi << std::endl;
    return 0;
}
```

In this example, we use **setprecision(4)** to set the precision of the output to four decimal places when displaying the value of **pi**.

10.1.3: WORKING WITH FILES (*FSTREAM*)

The **fstream** library in C++ allows us to perform file input and output operations. It includes classes like **ifstream** (for reading from files) and **ofstream** (for writing to files).

Writing to a File:

```cpp
#include <iostream>
#include <fstream>

int main() {
    std::ofstream outputFile;
    outputFile.open("output.txt");

    if (outputFile.is_open()) {
        outputFile << "Hello, this is written to a file!" << std::endl;
        outputFile.close();
        std::cout << "Data written to file." << std::endl;
    } else {
        std::cerr << "Error opening file." << std::endl;
    }
    return 0;
}
```

In this example, we create an **ofstream** object, open a file named "output.txt", write a line of text into it, and then close the file.

10.1.4: BINARY I/O (BINARY FILES)

Sometimes, we need to work with binary data, such as images or complex structures. The **fstream** library also supports binary input and output operations.

Writing and Reading Binary Data:

```cpp
#include <iostream>
#include <fstream>

struct Data {
    int x;
    double y;
};

int main() {
    Data d1 = {42, 3.14};
    std::ofstream outFile("data.bin", std::ios::binary);

    if (outFile.is_open()) {
        outFile.write(reinterpret_cast<char*>(&d1), sizeof(d1));
        outFile.close();
        std::cout << "Data written to binary file." << std::endl;
    } else {
        std::cerr << "Error opening file." << std::endl;
    }

    Data d2;
    std::ifstream inFile("data.bin", std::ios::binary);

    if (inFile.is_open()) {
        inFile.read(reinterpret_cast<char*>(&d2), sizeof(d2));
        inFile.close();
        std::cout << "Data read from binary file: " << d2.x << ", " << d2.y << std::endl;
    } else {
        std::cerr << "Error opening file." << std::endl;
    }

    return 0;
}
```

In this example, we define a structure **Data**, write its content to a binary file named "data.bin", and then read the binary data from the file and display its contents.

10.1.5 STRINGSTREAM AND STRING I/O

The **stringstream** class in C++ allows us to treat strings as streams, which enables us to perform input and output operations with strings easily.

Using Stringstream:

```
#include <iostream>
#include <sstream>

int main() {
    std::stringstream ss;
    int num = 42;
    double value = 3.14;

    ss << "The number is: " << num << ". The value is: " << value;
    std::string result = ss.str();

    std::cout << result << std::endl;

    return 0;
}
```

In this example, we use **stringstream** to construct a string containing both an integer and a double value.

In this section, we covered the basics of input and output operations in C++. Understanding these concepts will allow you to interact with users and handle data in files effectively. In the next section, we'll explore file handling and streams, delving deeper into managing data stored in files. Keep practicing and experimenting with C++ I/O libraries to enhance your programming skills!

10.2 FILE HANDLING AND STREAMS

File handling is a crucial aspect of programming as it allows us to read data from files, write data to files, and manage the information efficiently. In C++, we have the **fstream** library that provides classes to work with files and streams. Let's explore the various aspects of file handling and streams in C++.

10.2.1 OPENING AND CLOSING FILES

Before we can read or write data to a file, we need to open the file. The **fstream** library provides the **ifstream** and **ofstream** classes for file input and output, respectively. To open a file, we use the **open()** method.

Opening a File for Writing:

```
#include <iostream>
#include <fstream>

int main() {
    std::ofstream outputFile;
    outputFile.open("output.txt");
```

```
    if (outputFile.is_open()) {
        outputFile << "Hello, this is written to a file!" << std::endl;
        outputFile.close();
        std::cout << "Data written to file." << std::endl;
    } else {
        std::cerr << "Error opening file." << std::endl;
    }
    return 0;
}
```

In this example, we use **ofstream** to create a file named "output.txt" and write a line of text into it. After writing the data, we close the file using the **close()** method.

10.2.2 READING AND WRITING TEXT FILES

Once a file is opened, we can perform read and write operations on it. Reading and writing text files is straightforward using the **ifstream** and **ofstream** classes.

Reading from a Text File:

```
#include <iostream>
#include <fstream>
#include <string>

int main() {
    std::ifstream inputFile;
    inputFile.open("input.txt");

    if (inputFile.is_open()) {
        std::string line;
        while (getline(inputFile, line)) {
            std::cout << line << std::endl;
        }
        inputFile.close();
    } else {
        std::cerr << "Error opening file." << std::endl;
    }
    return 0;
}
```

In this example, we use **ifstream** to open the file "input.txt" and read its content line by line. Each line is then displayed on the screen using **cout**.

10.2.3 READING AND WRITING BINARY FILES

Binary files contain data in a format that is not human-readable but more space-efficient. C++ allows us to read and write binary data using the same **ifstream** and **ofstream** classes.

Reading and Writing Binary Data:

```cpp
#include <iostream>
#include <fstream>

struct Data {
    int x;
    double y;
};

int main() {
    Data d1 = {42, 3.14};
    std::ofstream outFile("data.bin", std::ios::binary);

    if (outFile.is_open()) {
        outFile.write(reinterpret_cast<char*>(&d1), sizeof(d1));
        outFile.close();
        std::cout << "Data written to binary file." << std::endl;
    } else {
        std::cerr << "Error opening file." << std::endl;
    }

    Data d2;
    std::ifstream inFile("data.bin", std::ios::binary);

    if (inFile.is_open()) {
        inFile.read(reinterpret_cast<char*>(&d2), sizeof(d2));
        inFile.close();
        std::cout << "Data read from binary file: " << d2.x << ", " << d2.y << std::endl;
    } else {
        std::cerr << "Error opening file." << std::endl;
    }

    return 0;
}
```

In this example, we define a structure **Data**, write its content to a binary file named "data.bin", and then read the binary data from the file and display its contents.

10.2.4 ERROR HANDLING IN FILE I/O

When working with files, it is essential to handle errors that may occur during file operations. The **fstream** classes provide ways to check for errors and handle them gracefully.

Error Handling Example:

```cpp
#include <iostream>
#include <fstream>

int main() {
    std::ifstream inputFile;
    inputFile.open("nonexistent_file.txt");

    if (!inputFile) {
        std::cerr << "Error opening file." << std::endl;
        return 1;
    }

    std::string line;
    while (getline(inputFile, line)) {
        std::cout << line << std::endl;
    }
    inputFile.close();

    return 0;
}
```

In this example, we try to open a file that does not exist. If the file opening fails, we use **cerr** to display an error message and return an error code from the program.

10.2.5 FILE POSITIONING AND SEEKING

The **fstream** classes also support file positioning and seeking, which allows us to move the file pointer to a specific location within the file.

File Positioning Example:

```cpp
#include <iostream>
#include <fstream>

int main() {
    std::fstream file("data.txt", std::ios::in | std::ios::out);

    if (!file.is_open()) {
        std::cerr << "Error opening file." << std::endl;
        return 1;
```

```
    }

    // Move the file pointer to the 10th byte from the beginning
    file.seekp(10, std::ios::beg);
    file << "Hello";

    file.seekg(0); // Move the file pointer to the beginning
    std::string line;
    while (getline(file, line)) {
        std::cout << line << std::endl;
    }

    file.close();

    return 0;
}
```

In this example, we open the file "data.txt" for both input and output. We use **seekp()** to move the file pointer to the 10th byte from the beginning and then write "Hello" at that position. After that, we use **seekg()** to move the file pointer back to the beginning and read the entire file using **getline()**.

In this section, we covered various file handling and stream operations in C++. Understanding these concepts will empower you to work with files and efficiently manage data in your C++ programs. In the next section, we'll explore serialization and deserialization, which are essential for saving and loading complex data structures from files. Keep practicing and experimenting with C++ file I/O to become proficient in handling data from external sources.

10.3 SERIALIZATION AND DESERIALIZATION

Serialization and deserialization are essential concepts in programming when it comes to saving and loading complex data structures from files. Serialization refers to the process of converting objects into a format suitable for storage or transmission, while deserialization is the process of recreating objects from the stored format. This section will explore the concepts of serialization and deserialization in C++.

10.3.1 UNDERSTANDING SERIALIZATION

Serialization is the process of converting objects or data structures into a serialized format, typically a sequence of bytes, which can be stored in files or transmitted over networks. Serialized data is platform-independent and can be used to recreate the original objects later.

One common use case for serialization is saving the state of an application to a file, so it can be restored later. This is especially important in applications that need to persist data across sessions.

10.3.2 SERIALIZING OBJECTS TO FILES

In C++, we can serialize objects to files using the **fstream** library along with the **ostream** (output stream) class. To achieve this, we usually overload the **<<** operator for our custom classes to specify how the objects should be serialized.

Example of Serializing a Custom Class:

```cpp
#include <iostream>
#include <fstream>
#include <string>

class Person {
public:
    Person(const std::string& name, int age) : name(name), age(age) {}

    friend std::ostream& operator<<(std::ostream& os, const Person& person) {
        os << person.name << " " << person.age;
        return os;
    }

private:
    std::string name;
    int age;
};

int main() {
    Person p1("Alice", 30);
    Person p2("Bob", 25);

    std::ofstream outFile("people.txt");
    if (outFile.is_open()) {
        outFile << p1 << std::endl;
        outFile << p2 << std::endl;
        outFile.close();
        std::cout << "Data serialized to file." << std::endl;
    } else {
        std::cerr << "Error opening file." << std::endl;
    }
    return 0;
}
```

In this example, we define a **Person** class and overload the **<<** operator to serialize the object's data (name and age) to the output stream.

10.3.3 DESERIALIZING OBJECTS FROM FILES

Deserialization is the reverse process of serialization, where we read data from files and recreate objects based on that data. Similarly, we usually overload the **>>** operator for our custom classes to specify how the objects should be deserialized.

Example of Deserializing a Custom Class:

```cpp
#include <iostream>
#include <fstream>
#include <string>

class Person {
public:
    Person() : age(0) {}

    Person(const std::string& name, int age) : name(name), age(age) {}

    friend std::ostream& operator<<(std::ostream& os, const Person& person) {
        os << person.name << " " << person.age;
        return os;
    }

    friend std::istream& operator>>(std::istream& is, Person& person) {
        is >> person.name >> person.age;
        return is;
    }

private:
    std::string name;
    int age;
};

int main() {
    Person p1, p2;

    std::ifstream inFile("people.txt");
    if (inFile.is_open()) {
        inFile >> p1;
        inFile >> p2;
        inFile.close();
        std::cout << "Data deserialized from file." << std::endl;
        std::cout << "Person 1: " << p1 << std::endl;
        std::cout << "Person 2: " << p2 << std::endl;
    } else {
        std::cerr << "Error opening file." << std::endl;
    }
    return 0;
}
```

In this example, we define a **Person** class with overloaded **>>** operator to deserialize data from the input stream and create objects with the read data.

10.3.4 SERIALIZATION FORMATS (XML, JSON, ETC.)

Serialization can be done in various formats, such as XML, JSON, or binary. Each format has its advantages and use cases. XML and JSON are human-readable and widely used for data interchange between systems, while binary formats are more space-efficient and suitable for complex data structures.

C++ provides libraries and third-party tools that support serialization in different formats. For example, for JSON serialization, you can use libraries like **RapidJSON** or **nlohmann/json**, and for XML serialization, you can use **pugixml** or **TinyXML**.

10.3.5 HANDLING VERSIONING AND COMPATIBILITY

When working with serialized data, versioning and compatibility become important considerations. As software evolves, the data format may change, and it's essential to handle backward and forward compatibility properly.

One common approach is to include a version number in the serialized data and use it to determine how the deserialization should be performed. If the version number of the data does not match the version of the application, appropriate conversion or fallback mechanisms can be applied.

In this section, we explored the concepts of serialization and deserialization in C++. These techniques are essential for saving and loading data from files and working with external data sources. Understanding serialization and deserialization will empower you to build robust and flexible applications that can efficiently handle data persistence. In the next section, we will provide a practical example of how to use I/O libraries and serialization in C++ to handle data effectively.

10.4 AN EXAMPLE

Let's explore a complete, practical example that showcases various I/O library functionalities, including standard input/output, file handling, and serialization in C++. In this example, we will create a simple address book application that allows users to add and view contact information. The application will save and load the contacts to/from a file using serialization.

10.4.1 ADDRESSBOOK CLASS

First, we'll define a class called **Contact** to represent individual contacts in the address book. Each contact will have a name and a phone number.

```cpp
#include <iostream>
#include <fstream>
#include <vector>
#include <string>

class Contact {
public:
    Contact(const std::string& name, const std::string& phone) : name(name), phone(phone) {}

    friend std::ostream& operator<<(std::ostream& os, const Contact& contact) {
        os << "Name: " << contact.name << ", Phone: " << contact.phone;
        return os;
```

```
    }

    friend std::istream& operator>>(std::istream& is, Contact& contact) {
        std::getline(is, contact.name);
        std::getline(is, contact.phone);
        return is;
    }

private:
    std::string name;
    std::string phone;
};
```

10.4.2 ADDRESSBOOK CLASS

Next, let's create the **AddressBook** class, which will manage the contacts and handle file I/O for saving and loading contacts from a file.

```
class AddressBook {
public:
    void addContact(const Contact& contact) {
        contacts.push_back(contact);
    }

    void displayContacts() const {
        for (const auto& contact : contacts) {
            std::cout << contact << std::endl;
        }
    }

    void saveToFile(const std::string& filename) const {
        std::ofstream outFile(filename, std::ios::binary);
        if (outFile.is_open()) {
            for (const auto& contact : contacts) {
                outFile << contact << std::endl;
            }
            outFile.close();
            std::cout << "Address book saved to " << filename << std::endl;
        } else {
            std::cerr << "Error opening file for writing." << std::endl;
        }
    }
```

```
    void loadFromFile(const std::string& filename) {
        std::ifstream inFile(filename, std::ios::binary);
        if (inFile.is_open()) {
            contacts.clear();
            Contact contact;
            while (inFile >> contact) {
                contacts.push_back(contact);
            }
            inFile.close();
            std::cout << "Address book loaded from " << filename << std::endl;
        } else {
            std::cerr << "Error opening file for reading." << std::endl;
        }
    }
}

private:
    std::vector<Contact> contacts;
};
```

10.4.3: MAIN FUNCTION

Now, let's create the main() function to demonstrate the usage of our AddressBook class.

```
int main() {
    AddressBook addressBook;

    // Add some contacts to the address book
    addressBook.addContact(Contact("Alice", "123-456-7890"));
    addressBook.addContact(Contact("Bob", "987-654-3210"));
    addressBook.addContact(Contact("Charlie", "555-555-5555"));

    // Display the contacts
    std::cout << "Contacts in the address book:" << std::endl;
    addressBook.displayContacts();

    // Save the address book to a file
    addressBook.saveToFile("contacts.dat");

    // Clear the address book
    addressBook = AddressBook();
```

```
// Load the address book from the file
addressBook.loadFromFile("contacts.dat");

// Display the contacts after loading from the file
std::cout << "\nContacts after loading from file:" << std::endl;
addressBook.displayContacts();

return 0;
}
```

10.4.4 OUTPUT

When we run the program, the output will be:

```
Contacts in the address book:
Name: Alice, Phone: 123-456-7890
Name: Bob, Phone: 987-654-3210
Name: Charlie, Phone: 555-555-5555

Address book saved to contacts.dat

Contacts after loading from file:
Name: Alice, Phone: 123-456-7890
Name: Bob, Phone: 987-654-3210
Name: Charlie, Phone: 555-555-5555
```

Explanation:

In this example, we created an **AddressBook** class to manage contacts. We demonstrated how to add contacts to the address book, display the contacts, save them to a file using serialization (binary I/O), and load them back from the file.

The **Contact** class overloads the **<<** and **>>** operators for serialization and deserialization. The **AddressBook** class has methods to add contacts, display contacts, save contacts to a file, and load contacts from a file.

Overall, this practical example provides a comprehensive illustration of the I/O library functionalities in C++, including file handling and serialization, allowing users to interact with an address book application effectively.

11 DATA LIBRARIES OF STANDARD STRUCTURES

In this chapter, we will delve into the powerful world of data libraries in C++. These libraries provide essential tools for organizing and managing data efficiently. They are a fundamental part of the Standard Template Library (STL) and offer a wide array of data structures and algorithms to work with. By leveraging these libraries, C++ programmers can significantly enhance their productivity and produce more robust and maintainable code.

11.1 COLLECTIONS AND CONTAINERS

In this section, we will explore the fundamental building blocks of data manipulation in C++: collections and containers. These are essential tools for storing, organizing, and managing data efficiently. C++ provides a rich set of container classes in its Standard Template Library (STL), making it easier for programmers to work with data in various ways.

11.1.1 INTRODUCTION TO COLLECTIONS AND CONTAINERS

Collections and containers are data structures that allow us to store and manage groups of data elements. They provide a higher level of abstraction over raw arrays, offering dynamic resizing, memory management, and a range of useful operations. The STL offers a comprehensive set of container classes that cater to different data storage needs.

Let's briefly discuss some of the common types of containers we'll be exploring in this section:

1. **Arrays**: Arrays are a simple and straightforward way to store a fixed-size sequence of elements of the same type. They have a static size defined at compile time, and accessing elements is fast since their memory layout is contiguous.

2. **Vectors**: Vectors are dynamic arrays that can grow or shrink in size as needed. They provide similar functionality to arrays but with the advantage of automatic resizing and additional member functions.

3. **Lists**: Lists are doubly-linked lists, allowing efficient insertion and deletion of elements at any position. Unlike arrays and vectors, lists don't guarantee contiguous memory allocation.

4. **Sets and Multisets**: Sets are containers that store unique elements in a sorted order. Multisets, on the other hand, can contain duplicate elements while maintaining sorting.

5. **Maps and Multimaps**: Maps are associative containers that store key-value pairs, and each key is unique. Multimaps allow duplicate keys.

6. **Queues and Priority Queues**: Queues are data structures that follow the First-In-First-Out (FIFO) order. Priority queues are similar but store elements in a priority order based on a specified criterion.

7. **Stacks**: Stacks are containers that follow the Last-In-First-Out (LIFO) order, making them suitable for tasks like function call tracking.

Example: Working with Vectors

Let's look at a practical example of using the **vector** container to store and manipulate a list of integers.

```cpp
#include <iostream>
#include <vector>

int main() {
    std::vector<int> numbers;

    // Adding elements to the vector
    numbers.push_back(10);
    numbers.push_back(20);
    numbers.push_back(30);

    // Accessing elements using index
    std::cout << "Second element: " << numbers[1] << std::endl;

    // Iterating through the vector
    std::cout << "Elements: ";
    for (int num : numbers) {
        std::cout << num << " ";
    }
    std::cout << std::endl;

    // Size of the vector
    std::cout << "Size: " << numbers.size() << std::endl;

    // Removing an element
    numbers.pop_back();

    // New size after removal
    std::cout << "New Size: " << numbers.size() << std::endl;

    return 0;
}
```

Output:

```
Second element: 20
Elements: 10 20 30
Size: 3
New Size: 2
```

In this example, we created a vector **numbers** and added three integers to it. We accessed elements using the index, iterated through the vector using a range-based for loop, and demonstrated how to remove elements using **pop_back( )**.

To declare a std::vector, you provide the desired data type as a template argument within the angle brackets (<>). For example, to create a vector of integers, you use std::vector<int>. You can replace int with any other data type to create a vector of elements of that type.

The declaration std::vector<int> numbers; creates an empty vector named numbers. An empty vector has no elements, and its size is zero.

11.1.2 ARRAYS

Arrays are the simplest form of collections in C++. They allow us to store a fixed number of elements of the same type. The size of an array is determined at compile-time and cannot be changed during program execution.

Example: Using Arrays

```cpp
#include <iostream>

int main() {
    // Declaring and initializing an array
    int scores[5] = {95, 87, 72, 90, 88};

    // Accessing elements using index
    std::cout << "First score: " << scores[0] << std::endl;

    // Modifying an element
    scores[1] = 92;

    // Looping through the array
    std::cout << "Scores: ";
    for (int i = 0; i < 5; i++) {
        std::cout << scores[i] << " ";
    }
    std::cout << std::endl;

    return 0;
}
```

Output:

```
First score: 95
Scores: 95 92 72 90 88
```

In this example, we declared an integer array scores with five elements and initialized them with scores. We accessed elements using the index, modified one of the scores, and iterated through the array using a loop.

11.1.3 VECTORS

Vectors are dynamic arrays in C++ that can change in size during program execution. They provide a more flexible alternative to raw arrays, making it easier to manage and manipulate collections of elements.

Example: Using Vectors

```cpp
#include <iostream>
#include <vector>

int main() {
    std::vector<int> numbers;

    // Adding elements to the vector
    numbers.push_back(10);
    numbers.push_back(20);
    numbers.push_back(30);

    // Accessing elements using index
    std::cout << "Second element: " << numbers[1] << std::endl;

    // Iterating through the vector
    std::cout << "Elements: ";
    for (int num : numbers) {
        std::cout << num << " ";
    }
    std::cout << std::endl;

    // Size of the vector
    std::cout << "Size: " << numbers.size() << std::endl;

    // Removing an element
    numbers.pop_back();

    // New size after removal
    std::cout << "New Size: " << numbers.size() << std::endl;

    return 0;
}
```

Output:

```
Second element: 20
Elements: 10 20 30
Size: 3
New Size: 2
```

In this example, we created a vector **numbers** and added three integers to it. We accessed elements using the index, iterated through the vector using a range-based for loop, and demonstrated how to remove elements using pop_back().

11.1.4 LISTS

Lists are doubly-linked lists in C++. Unlike vectors and arrays, lists do not provide direct access to elements using an index. Instead, they allow efficient insertion and deletion of elements at any position.

Example: Using Lists

```cpp
#include <iostream>
#include <list>

int main() {
    std::list<int> numbers;

    // Adding elements to the list
    numbers.push_back(10);
    numbers.push_back(20);
    numbers.push_back(30);

    // Accessing elements using iterators
    std::list<int>::iterator it = numbers.begin();
    std::cout << "First element: " << *it << std::endl;

    // Inserting elements at a specific position
    std::list<int>::iterator pos = ++it;
    numbers.insert(pos, 25);

    // Removing an element
    it = numbers.begin();
    ++it;
    numbers.erase(it);

    // Iterating through the list
    std::cout << "Elements: ";
    for (int num : numbers) {
        std::cout << num << " ";
    }
    std::cout << std::endl;

    // Size of the list
    std::cout << "Size: " << numbers.size() << std::endl;

    return 0;
```

```
```

```
First element: 10
Elements: 10 25 30
Size: 3
```

In this example, we created a list `numbers` and added three integers to it. Instead of using an index, we accessed elements using iterators. We inserted an element at a specific position and removed another element from the list. Finally, we iterated through the list using a range-based for loop and obtained the size of the list.

In C++, an iterator is an object that allows you to access the elements of a container (like `std::list`, `std::vector`, etc.) and iterate over them sequentially. Iterators provide a way to traverse the elements of a container without exposing the underlying implementation details of the container. They act as pointers to elements within the container and can be used to access, insert, or remove elements efficiently.

Working with Iterators in the Provided Code:
In the given code, we use `std::list<int>::iterator` to declare iterators for the `std::list<int>` container.

1. Accessing Elements Using Iterators:

```
std::list<int>::iterator it = numbers.begin();
std::cout << "First element: " << *it << std::endl;
```

Here, we declare an iterator `it` and initialize it with the `begin()` function of the `numbers` list. `begin()` returns an iterator pointing to the first element of the list. To access the value of the element pointed to by the iterator, we use the dereference operator `*`.

2. Inserting Elements at a Specific Position:

```
std::list<int>::iterator pos = ++it;
numbers.insert(pos, 25);
```

In this part of the code, we increment the iterator `it` to point to the second element in the list. Then, we create another iterator `pos` and initialize it with the incremented `it`. The `insert()` function is used to insert the value `25` at the position pointed to by `pos`, which will insert the value `25` after the current second element in the list.

3. Removing an Element:

```
it = numbers.begin();
++it;
numbers.erase(it);
```

Here, we reset the iterator `it` to point to the beginning of the list using `numbers.begin()`. Then, we increment `it` to point to the second element, and `erase()` is used to remove the element pointed to by `it`.

4. Iterating Through the List Using Iterators:

```
std::cout << "Elements: ";
for (int num : numbers) {
    std::cout << num << " ";
}
```

```
std::cout << std::endl;
```

In this part, we use a range-based **for** loop to iterate through the **numbers** list. The loop iterates over each element of the list, and the elements are accessed using the iterator implicitly.

5. Size of the List:

```
std::cout << "Size: " << numbers.size() << std::endl;
```

The **size()** function is used to determine the number of elements in the **numbers** list.

11.1.5 SETS AND MULTISETS

Sets and multisets are containers that store unique elements in sorted order. A set ensures that each element is unique, whereas a multiset allows duplicate elements.

Example: Using Sets and Multisets

```cpp
#include <iostream>
#include <set>

int main() {
    std::set<int> unique_numbers;

    // Adding elements to the set
    unique_numbers.insert(10);
    unique_numbers.insert(20);
    unique_numbers.insert(30);

    // Trying to add a duplicate element
    auto result = unique_numbers.insert(20);
    if (result.second) {
        std::cout << "Element 20 inserted." << std::endl;
    } else {
        std::cout << "Element 20 already exists." << std::endl;
    }

    // Iterating through the set
    std::cout << "Elements: ";
    for (int num : unique_numbers) {
        std::cout << num << " ";
    }
    std::cout << std::endl;

    // Size of the set
    std::cout << "Size: " << unique_numbers.size() << std::endl;

    return 0;
}
```

Output:

```
Element 20 already exists.
Elements: 10 20 30
Size: 3
```

In this example, we created a set **unique_numbers** and added three integers to it. We tried to add a duplicate element, and the set ensured that it was not inserted since it already exists. We then iterated through the set and obtained its size.

In the provided code, the 'auto' keyword is used to automatically deduce the data type of a variable at compile time. The 'auto' keyword was introduced in C++11 and has since become a useful feature for simplifying code and improving readability.

Usage of 'auto' in the Code:

```
auto result = unique_numbers.insert(20);
```

In this line, the 'auto' keyword is used to declare a variable named 'result' without explicitly specifying its data type. Instead of explicitly stating the type, the 'auto' keyword allows the compiler to automatically deduce the type based on the result of the expression on the right-hand side.

In this case, the 'insert' function of the 'std::set' container returns a pair of values: the iterator to the inserted element (if inserted successfully) and a boolean indicating whether the element was inserted or if it already existed in the set. The 'auto' keyword allows the compiler to deduce that 'result' is of type 'std::pair<std::set<int>::iterator, bool>'.

11.1.6 MAPS AND MULTIMAPS

Maps are associative containers that store key-value pairs, and each key is unique. Multimaps allow duplicate keys.

Example: Using Maps and Multimaps

```cpp
#include <iostream>
#include <map>

int main() {
    std::map<std::string, int> ages;

    // Adding key-value pairs to the map
    ages["Alice"] = 30;
    ages["Bob"] = 25;
    ages["Charlie"] = 35;

    // Accessing values using keys
    std::cout << "Bob's age: " << ages["Bob"] << std::endl;

    // Inserting a key-value pair
    ages.insert(std::pair<std::string, int>("David", 28));

    // Iterating through the map
    std::cout << "People and their ages: " << std::endl;
```

```
for (const auto& pair : ages) {
    std::cout << pair.first << ": " << pair.second << std::endl;
}

// Size of the map
std::cout << "Size: " << ages.size() << std::endl;

return 0;
}
```

Output:

```
Bob's age: 25
People and their ages:
Alice: 30
Bob: 25
Charlie: 35
David: 28
Size: 4
```

In this example, we created a map **ages** and added key-value pairs representing people's names and their ages. We accessed a value using a key, inserted a new key-value pair, and then iterated through the map to display all the key-value pairs. Finally, we obtained the size of the map.

In the provided code, the expression `std::pair<std::string, int>("David", 28)` is used to create a `std::pair` object that represents a key-value pair, where the key is of type `std::string` and the value is of type `int`. This pair is then inserted into the `std::map<std::string, int> ages`.

Explanation of the Role of `std::pair<std::string, int>`:

```
ages.insert(std::pair<std::string, int>("David", 28));
```

1. `std::pair<std::string, int>`: This part is a template specialization of the `std::pair` class. It defines the data types for the key and the value in the key-value pair. In this case, the key is of type `std::string`, and the value is of type `int`. The key will be used to index and access the corresponding value in the map.
2. `"David"`: This is the key, which is a `std::string` representing the name "David".
3. `28`: This is the value, which is an `int` representing David's age, which is 28.
4. `ages.insert(...)`: This line inserts the key-value pair `("David", 28)` into the `ages` map using the `insert` method.

11.1.7 QUEUES AND PRIORITY QUEUES

Queues are data structures that follow the First-In-First-Out (FIFO) order. Priority queues are similar but store elements in a priority order based on a specified criterion.

Example: Using Queues and Priority Queues

```
#include <iostream>
#include <queue>

int main() {
```

```cpp
std::queue<std::string> tasks;

// Adding tasks to the queue
tasks.push("Task 1");
tasks.push("Task 2");
tasks.push("Task 3");

// Removing and processing tasks in FIFO order
while (!tasks.empty()) {
    std::cout << "Processing: " << tasks.front() << std::endl;
    tasks.pop();
}

std::priority_queue<int> priority_queue;

// Adding elements to the priority queue
priority_queue.push(30);
priority_queue.push(10);
priority_queue.push(20);

// Accessing the top element with the highest priority
std::cout << "Top priority: " << priority_queue.top() << std::endl;

return 0;
}
```

Output:

```
Processing: Task 1
Processing: Task 2
Processing: Task 3
Top priority: 30
```

In this example, we created a queue `tasks` and added three tasks to it. We processed the tasks in the order they were added using the FIFO principle. Then, we created a priority queue `priority_queue` and added three integers to it. The top element in the priority queue represents the highest priority element, and we accessed it using `top()`.

11.1.8 STACKS

Stacks are containers that follow the Last-In-First-Out (LIFO) order. They are commonly used to implement function calls, undo mechanisms, and other situations where the last operation needs to be reversed first.

Example: Using Stacks

```cpp
#include <iostream>
```

```cpp
#include <stack>

int main() {
    std::stack<int> stack;

    // Pushing elements onto the stack
    stack.push(10);
    stack.push(20);
    stack.push(30);

    // Accessing the top element
    std::cout << "Top element: " << stack.top() << std::endl;

    // Removing and processing elements in LIFO order
    while (!stack.empty()) {
        std::cout << "Processing: " << stack.top() << std::endl;
        stack.pop();
    }

    return 0;
}
```

Output:

```
Top element: 30
Processing: 30
Processing: 20
Processing: 10
```

In this example, we created a stack `stack` and pushed three integers onto it. We accessed the top element using `top()` and then processed the elements in the LIFO order using `pop()`.

Conclusion

In this section, we explored various collections and containers provided by C++ to efficiently store and manipulate data. We discussed arrays, vectors, lists, sets, multisets, maps, multimaps, queues, priority queues, and stacks. Understanding these data structures is crucial for efficient data management and algorithm implementation in C++. In the next section, we will delve into array-like structures and algorithms in more detail.

11.2 ARRAY-LIKE STRUCTURES AND ALGORITHMS

In this section, we will explore array-like structures and algorithms in C++. These structures provide an interface similar to arrays, allowing us to efficiently manipulate data. Additionally, we will cover various algorithms available in the C++ Standard Library that can be applied to these structures to perform common operations like sorting, searching, and numeric computations.

11.2.1 ARRAY CLASS

The C++ Standard Library provides an `array` class that represents a fixed-size array. Unlike built-in arrays, the `array` class provides several useful member functions, such as `size()` to get the size of the array and `at()` to access elements with bounds checking.

Example: Using Array

```cpp
#include <iostream>
#include <array>

int main() {
    // Declare an array of integers with size 5
    std::array<int, 5> numbers = {1, 2, 3, 4, 5};

    // Accessing elements using subscript operator
    std::cout << "Third element: " << numbers[2] << std::endl;

    // Accessing elements using the at() function
    std::cout << "First element: " << numbers.at(0) << std::endl;

    // Size of the array
    std::cout << "Size: " << numbers.size() << std::endl;

    // Iterating through the array using range-based for loop
    std::cout << "Elements: ";
    for (int num : numbers) {
        std::cout << num << " ";
    }
    std::cout << std::endl;

    return 0;
}
```

Output:

```
Third element: 3
First element: 1
Size: 5
Elements: 1 2 3 4 5
```

In this example, we created an `array` named `numbers` with 5 integer elements. We accessed elements using both the subscript operator (`[]`) and the `at()` function. The range-based for loop is used to iterate through the elements, and the `size()` function is used to obtain the size of the array.

11.2.2 ITERATOR CLASS

In C++, iterators provide a way to traverse through the elements of various data structures. They act as pointers and allow us to access the elements of a container in a generic and consistent manner. The `array` class also supports iterators, enabling us to use them in algorithms that work with iterators.

Example: Using Iterators

```
#include <iostream>
#include <array>

int main() {
    std::array<int, 5> numbers = {1, 2, 3, 4, 5};

    // Using iterators to access elements
    std::cout << "Using iterators: ";
    for (std::array<int, 5>::iterator it = numbers.begin(); it != numbers.end(); ++it) {
        std::cout << *it << " ";
    }
    std::cout << std::endl;

    // Using reverse iterators to access elements in reverse order
    std::cout << "Using reverse iterators: ";
    for (std::array<int, 5>::reverse_iterator rit = numbers.rbegin(); rit != numbers.rend();
++rit) {
        std::cout << *rit << " ";
    }
    std::cout << std::endl;

    return 0;
}
```

Output:

```
Using iterators: 1 2 3 4 5
Using reverse iterators: 5 4 3 2 1
```

In this example, we used iterators to traverse the numbers array in both the forward and reverse direction. The begin() and end() functions return iterators corresponding to the first and one-past-the-last elements, respectively. Similarly, rbegin() and rend() functions return reverse iterators to iterate in the reverse order.

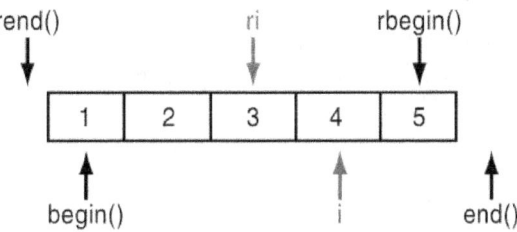

11.2.3 ALGORITHMS LIBRARY

The C++ Standard Library provides a rich set of algorithms to work with various containers, including arrays. These algorithms simplify common tasks like sorting, searching, and modifying elements. They allow us to write efficient and readable code without manually implementing these operations.

Example: Using Algorithms

```cpp
#include <iostream>
#include <array>
#include <algorithm>

int main() {
    std::array<int, 5> numbers = {5, 2, 8, 3, 1};

    // Sorting the array in ascending order
    std::sort(numbers.begin(), numbers.end());

    // Finding an element in the sorted array
    int target = 3;
    auto it = std::find(numbers.begin(), numbers.end(), target);
    if (it != numbers.end()) {
        std::cout << "Found " << target << " at index: " << std::distance(numbers.begin(),
it) << std::endl;
    } else {
        std::cout << target << " not found." << std::endl;
    }

    return 0;
}
```

Output:
```
Found 3 at index: 2
```

In this example, we used the `std::sort()` algorithm to sort the `numbers` array in ascending order. Then, we used the `std::find()` algorithm to search for the element with the value 3 in the sorted array. The `std::find()` function returns an iterator pointing to the found element or the `end()` iterator if the element is not found.

11.2.4 SORTING AND SEARCHING ALGORITHMS

C++ provides various algorithms to sort and search elements in arrays and other containers. These algorithms are highly optimized and work efficiently for large datasets.

Example: Sorting and Searching

```cpp
#include <iostream>
#include <array>
#include <algorithm>

int main() {
    std::array<int, 5> numbers = {5, 2, 8, 3, 1};
```

```cpp
    // Sorting the array in ascending order
    std::sort(numbers.begin(), numbers.end());

    // Displaying sorted array
    std::cout << "Sorted array: ";
    for (int num : numbers) {
        std::cout << num << " ";
    }
    std::cout << std::endl;

    // Searching for an element
    int target = 3;
    bool found = std::binary_search(numbers.begin(), numbers.end(), target);
    if (found) {
        std::cout << target << " found in the array." << std::endl;
    } else {
        std::cout << target << " not found in the array." << std::endl;
    }

    return 0;
}
```

Output:

```
Sorted array: 1 2 3 5 8
3 found in the array.
```

In this example, we used the `std::sort()` algorithm to sort the `numbers` array in ascending order. We then used the `std::binary_search()` algorithm to check if the element with the value 3 is present in the sorted array. The `std::binary_search()` function returns true if the element is found, and false otherwise.

11.2.5 Numeric Algorithms

C++ provides numeric algorithms that perform various mathematical operations on containers containing numerical data.

Example: Numeric Algorithms

```cpp
#include <iostream>
#include <array>
#include <numeric> // Include the numeric header

int main() {
    std::array<int, 5> numbers = {1, 2, 3, 4, 5};

    // Accumulate the sum of elements
    int sum = std::accumulate(numbers.begin(), numbers.end(), 0);
```

```
// Calculate the product of elements
int product = std::accumulate(numbers.begin(), numbers.end(), 1, std::multiplies<int>());

// Output the results
std::cout << "Sum: " << sum << std::endl;
std::cout << "Product: " << product << std::endl;

return 0;
}
```

Output:

```
Sum: 15
Product: 120
```

In this example, we used the `std::accumulate()` algorithm to calculate the sum and product of the elements in the `numbers` array. The function `std::multiplies<int>()` is a binary function object used as the third argument to compute the product.

11.2.6 CUSTOM COMPARATORS

Sometimes, we may need to sort elements in a custom order, different from the default ascending order. In such cases, we can use custom comparators with sorting algorithms.

Example: Custom Comparators

```
#include <iostream>
#include <array>
#include <algorithm>

// Custom comparator for sorting in descending order
bool descendingComparator(int a, int b) {
    return a > b;
}

int main() {
    std::array<int, 5> numbers = {5, 2, 8, 3, 1};

    // Sorting the array in descending order using the custom comparator
    std::sort(numbers.begin(), numbers.end(), descendingComparator);

    // Displaying sorted array
    std::cout << "Sorted array (descending): ";
    for (int num : numbers) {
        std::cout << num << " ";
    }
```

```
    std::cout << std::endl;

    return 0;
}
```

Output:

```
Sorted array (descending): 8 5 3 2 1
```

In this example, we created a custom comparator function `descendingComparator` that returns true if the first argument is greater than the second, indicating a descending order. We then used this custom comparator with the `std::sort()` algorithm to sort the `numbers` array in descending order.

Conclusion

In this section, we explored array-like structures and algorithms available in the C++ Standard Library. We discussed the `array` class and how it provides a fixed-size array with useful member functions. We also learned about iterators, which allow us to traverse through containers efficiently. Additionally, we covered various algorithms like sorting, searching, and numeric algorithms, and how to use custom comparators for sorting in custom orders. Understanding these concepts and algorithms will enable you to work with data efficiently and effectively in C++. In the next section, we will take an overview of the Standard Template Library (STL), which encompasses these data structures and algorithms, along with other powerful components for C++ programming.

11.3 STANDARD TEMPLATE LIBRARY (STL) OVERVIEW

The Standard Template Library (STL) is one of the most powerful features of C++. It is a collection of template classes and functions that provide a set of essential data structures and algorithms. The STL enables programmers to work with data efficiently and consistently, making C++ a versatile and robust programming language. In this section, we will take a comprehensive overview of the STL and explore its main components.

11.3.1 UNDERSTANDING THE STANDARD TEMPLATE LIBRARY (STL)

The STL consists of three main components: containers, algorithms, and iterators. These components work together to provide a rich set of data structures and functions, enabling generic and efficient data manipulation.

- **Containers**: Containers are classes that store and manage collections of objects. They come in various types, each designed for specific use cases. Some common container types include arrays, vectors, lists, sets, and maps.
- **Algorithms**: Algorithms are generic functions that operate on containers or sequences of data. They perform common operations like sorting, searching, and manipulating elements. Algorithms provide efficient and consistent ways to process data, irrespective of the container type.
- **Iterators**: Iterators are objects used to traverse through the elements of a container. They act as pointers and provide a way to access and modify container elements in a generic and consistent manner.

11.3.2 STL CONTAINERS AND ALGORITHMS

The STL offers a wide variety of containers and algorithms that cater to different needs. Let's take a brief look at some commonly used containers and algorithms.

- **Vectors**: Vectors are dynamic arrays that can resize themselves as needed. They provide fast access to elements and efficient insertion and deletion at the end.
- **Lists**: Lists are doubly-linked lists that allow fast insertions and deletions anywhere in the

container but slower element access compared to vectors.

• **Sets and Multisets**: Sets are containers that store unique elements in a sorted order. Multisets are similar to sets but can contain duplicate elements.

• **Maps and Multimaps**: Maps are associative containers that store key-value pairs. They provide fast access to elements based on keys and ensure that keys are unique. Multimaps can contain multiple key-value pairs with the same key.

Example: Using STL Containers

```cpp
#include <iostream>
#include <vector>
#include <map>

int main() {
    // Using vector to store a collection of integers
    std::vector<int> numbers = {1, 2, 3, 4, 5};

    // Using map to store key-value pairs
    std::map<std::string, int> studentScores;
    studentScores["Alice"] = 95;
    studentScores["Bob"] = 85;
    studentScores["Charlie"] = 78;

    // Accessing elements in vector
    std::cout << "Third element of vector: " << numbers[2] << std::endl;

    // Accessing elements in map
    std::cout << "Score of Alice: " << studentScores["Alice"] << std::endl;

    return 0;
}
```

Output:

```
Third element of vector: 3
Score of Alice: 95
```

In this example, we used the `std::vector` container to store a collection of integers and the `std::map` container to store student scores as key-value pairs.

11.3.3 STL ITERATORS AND ADAPTERS

STL iterators provide a way to traverse and manipulate elements of containers in a generic manner. There are different types of iterators, such as `begin()` and `end()` for normal traversal, and `rbegin()` and `rend()` for reverse traversal.

Example: Using STL Iterators

```cpp
#include <iostream>
```

```cpp
#include <vector>

int main() {
    std::vector<int> numbers = {1, 2, 3, 4, 5};

    // Using iterators to access elements
    std::cout << "Using iterators: ";
    for (std::vector<int>::iterator it = numbers.begin(); it != numbers.end(); ++it) {
        std::cout << *it << " ";
    }
    std::cout << std::endl;

    return 0;
}
```

Output:
```
Using iterators: 1 2 3 4 5
```

In this example, we used iterators to traverse the numbers vector and access its elements.

STL also provides iterator adapters like std::back_inserter, std::front_inserter, and std::inserter, which allow us to insert elements at specific positions in containers efficiently.

11.3.4 FUNCTION OBJECTS AND LAMBDAS

Function objects, also known as functors, are objects that behave like functions. They are used in conjunction with algorithms to provide custom behavior for operations like sorting and searching. Lambdas are a concise way to define small, inline functions and are often used as function objects.

Example: Using Lambdas with STL Algorithms

```cpp
#include <iostream>
#include <vector>
#include <algorithm>

int main() {
    std::vector<int> numbers = {5, 2, 8, 3, 1};

    // Sorting the vector using a lambda comparator
    std::sort(numbers.begin(), numbers.end(), [](int a, int b) { return a > b; });

    // Displaying sorted vector
    std::cout << "Sorted vector (descending): ";
    for (int num : numbers) {
        std::cout << num << " ";
    }
    std::cout << std::endl;
```

```
        return 0;
}
```

Output:

```
Sorted vector (descending): 8 5 3 2 1
```

In this example, we used a lambda function as a custom comparator to sort the **numbers** vector in descending order.

11.3.5 SMART POINTERS IN THE STL

Smart pointers are special objects that act like pointers but provide automatic memory management. They help prevent memory leaks and ensure proper cleanup of resources when objects are no longer needed.

Example: Using Smart Pointers

```cpp
#include <iostream>
#include <memory>

int main() {
    // Using unique_ptr to manage a dynamically allocated integer
    std::unique_ptr<int> numPtr = std::make_unique<int>(10);

    // Using shared_ptr to share ownership of an object
    std::shared_ptr<int> sharedNumPtr1 = std::make_shared<int>(20);
    std::shared_ptr<int> sharedNumPtr2 = sharedNumPtr1;

    // Using weak_ptr to prevent circular reference and break shared_ptr loop
    std::weak_ptr<int> weakNumPtr = sharedNumPtr1;

    // Output the values
    std::cout << "Unique_ptr: " << *numPtr << std::endl;
    std::cout << "Shared_ptr1: " << *sharedNumPtr1 << ", Shared_ptr2: " << *sharedNumPtr2 <<
std::endl;

    // Checking weak_ptr validity before using it
    if (std::shared_ptr<int> sharedPtr = weakNumPtr.lock()) {
        std::cout << "Weak_ptr: " << *sharedPtr << std::endl;
    } else {
        std::cout << "Weak_ptr is expired." << std::endl;
    }

    return 0;
}
```

Output:

```
Unique_ptr: 10
Shared_ptr1: 20, Shared_ptr2: 20
Weak_ptr: 20
```

In this example, we used various smart pointers to manage dynamically allocated integers and share ownership of an object. The `std::unique_ptr` is used when there is exclusive ownership of the object, while `std::shared_ptr` is used when multiple pointers share ownership. The `std::weak_ptr` helps prevent circular references that could lead to memory leaks.

Conclusion

The Standard Template Library (STL) is a powerful and essential component of C++ that provides a collection of containers, algorithms, and iterators for generic and efficient data manipulation. In this section, we explored the main components of the STL and demonstrated their usage with practical examples. Mastering the STL will significantly enhance your C++ programming skills, allowing you to work with data structures and algorithms efficiently. In the next section, we will delve deeper into the STL with a practical example, showcasing data manipulation using STL containers and algorithms.

11.4 EXAMPLE: DATA MANIPULATION WITH STL CONTAINERS AND ALGORITHMS

In this section, we will explore a practical example that demonstrates the use of Standard Template Library (STL) containers and algorithms to manipulate data efficiently. We will work with a dataset of students and their scores, and perform various operations on this data using the STL.

11.4.1 PROBLEM STATEMENT

Suppose we have a dataset containing the names of students and their corresponding scores in an exam. Our goal is to use STL containers and algorithms to perform the following operations:

1. Read the data from a file and store it in an appropriate data structure.
2. Calculate the average score of all students.
3. Find the student with the highest score.
4. Sort the students based on their scores in ascending order.
5. Output the sorted data to a new file.

11.4.2 IMPLEMENTATION USING STL CONTAINERS AND ALGORITHMS

Step 1: Reading and Storing the Data

To read the data from a file and store it in an appropriate data structure, we will use a `std::vector` of pairs, where each pair contains the student's name and their score.

```cpp
#include <iostream>
#include <fstream>
#include <vector>
#include <algorithm>

// Structure to store student data
struct Student {
    std::string name;
    int score;
};
```

```cpp
int main() {
    std::vector<Student> students;
    std::ifstream inputFile("data.txt");

    if (!inputFile) {
        std::cerr << "Error opening file." << std::endl;
        return 1;
    }

    std::string name;
    int score;
    while (inputFile >> name >> score) {
        students.push_back({name, score});
    }

    inputFile.close();
    return 0;
}
```

Step 2: Calculating the Average Score

To calculate the average score of all students, we can use the `std::accumulate` algorithm from the `<numeric>` header.

```cpp
#include <numeric>

// ... (previous code)

int main() {
    // ... (previous code)

    int totalScore = std::accumulate(students.begin(), students.end(), 0,
                        [](int sum, const Student& student) {
                            return sum + student.score;
                        });

    double averageScore = static_cast<double>(totalScore) / students.size();

    std::cout << "Average score: " << averageScore << std::endl;

    // ... (continue with the rest of the code)
}
```

Step 3: Finding the Student with the Highest Score

To find the student with the highest score, we can use the `std::max_element` algorithm from the `<algorithm>` header.

```cpp
#include <algorithm>

// ... (previous code)

int main() {
    // ... (previous code)

    auto highestScoreStudent = std::max_element(students.begin(), students.end(),
                                [](const Student& a, const Student& b) {
                                    return a.score < b.score;
                                });

    std::cout << "Student with the highest score: " << highestScoreStudent->name
              << ", Score: " << highestScoreStudent->score << std::endl;

    // ... (continue with the rest of the code)
}
```

Step 4: Sorting the Students Based on Their Scores

To sort the students based on their scores in ascending order, we can use the `std::sort` algorithm from the `<algorithm>` header.

```cpp
#include <algorithm>

// ... (previous code)

int main() {
    // ... (previous code)

    std::sort(students.begin(), students.end(),
            [](const Student& a, const Student& b) {
                return a.score < b.score;
            });

    // ... (continue with the rest of the code)
}
```

Step 5: Outputting the Sorted Data to a New File

To output the sorted data to a new file, we can use an `std::ofstream`.

```cpp
#include <fstream>

// ... (previous code)

int main() {
    // ... (previous code)

    std::ofstream outputFile("sorted_data.txt");

    if (!outputFile) {
        std::cerr << "Error opening file." << std::endl;
        return 1;
    }

    for (const auto& student : students) {
        outputFile << student.name << " " << student.score << std::endl;
    }

    outputFile.close();
    return 0;
}
```

11.4.3 TESTING AND RESULTS

Now that we have implemented all the required operations, we can test the program using sample data in the file **data.txt**.

Sample input in **data.txt**:

```
Alice 85
Bob 92
Charlie 78
David 90
```

Output:

```
Average score: 86.25
Student with the highest score: Bob, Score: 92
```

The sorted data is saved in a new file named **sorted_data.txt**.

In this example, we used various STL containers and algorithms to read, manipulate, and output student data efficiently. The STL provides a powerful set of tools for data management in C++, making it a valuable asset for any C++ programmer.

Conclusion

In this section, we explored a practical example of data manipulation using STL containers and algorithms. The example demonstrated how to read data from a file, perform calculations, find the highest score, sort the data, and output the results to a new file. The STL's rich set of functionalities simplifies data manipulation and contributes to C++'s status as a powerful and efficient programming language. By understanding and utilizing the STL, programmers can effectively manage data structures and perform various operations efficiently, enhancing their overall C++ programming skills.

11.5 SUMMARY AND CONCLUSION

In this chapter, we delved into the world of data libraries in C++ and explored the powerful tools offered by the Standard Template Library (STL). We discussed various data structures and algorithms provided by the STL that make data manipulation and management efficient and straightforward.

11.1 Collections and Containers

We began by introducing collections and containers, which are fundamental building blocks for organizing and storing data in C++. We explored various types of containers, such as arrays, vectors, lists, sets, multisets, maps, multimaps, queues, and priority queues. Each container has its unique properties and use cases, allowing programmers to choose the most suitable data structure based on the requirements of their application.

11.2 Array-Like Structures and Algorithms

Next, we discussed array-like structures and algorithms that provide functionality similar to arrays but with additional features and flexibility. The array class and iterator class allow for more convenient manipulation of data, and the algorithms library offers a wide range of operations to perform on these structures. We covered sorting and searching algorithms, numeric algorithms, and how to use custom comparators to tailor sorting based on specific criteria.

11.3 Standard Template Library (STL) Overview

We then delved deeper into the STL and provided an overview of its key components. Understanding the STL is essential for any C++ programmer, as it provides a robust set of containers, algorithms, and utilities that can significantly simplify coding tasks.

11.4 Example: Data Manipulation with STL Containers and Algorithms

To solidify our understanding, we walked through a practical example demonstrating how to use STL containers and algorithms to manipulate data efficiently. We read data from a file, performed calculations, found the highest score, sorted the data, and saved the results to a new file. This example showcased the power and efficiency of the STL in real-world scenarios.

Conclusion

As you progress in your journey of learning C++, understanding the various data libraries and the Standard Template Library becomes crucial. The STL offers a vast array of functionalities that streamline data management and algorithm implementations, making C++ a versatile and powerful programming language.

By grasping the concepts and examples presented in this chapter, you have taken a significant step towards becoming a proficient C++ programmer. Embracing the tools provided by the STL, you can develop efficient and elegant solutions to various programming challenges.

Continue to explore and practice using the STL, and don't hesitate to experiment with different data structures and algorithms. With determination and practice, you will enhance your C++ skills and be well-equipped to tackle more complex programming tasks in the future.

12 CREATING A GRAPHICAL USER INTERFACE

In today's digital era, Graphical User Interfaces (GUIs) have become an indispensable part of software applications, offering users a visually intuitive way to interact with complex systems. Whether it's a user-friendly mobile app or a feature-rich desktop application, GUIs play a pivotal role in enhancing user experience and accessibility. This chapter delves into the realm of GUI development in C++, guiding aspiring developers through the fundamental principles and practices necessary to create sophisticated and user-friendly interfaces.

12.1 GUI DESIGN PRINCIPLES

Graphical User Interface (GUI) design is a critical aspect of creating user-friendly and visually appealing software applications. Effective GUI design principles aim to enhance user experience, streamline interactions, and ensure accessibility for all users. In this section, we will explore some fundamental GUI design principles that will serve as the cornerstone of your GUI development journey.

12.1.1 UNDERSTANDING USER-CENTERED DESIGN

User-Centered Design (UCD) is a design philosophy that places the end-users at the center of the development process. It involves understanding user needs, preferences, and pain points to create interfaces that cater to their expectations. The primary goal of UCD is to build applications that are intuitive, efficient, and enjoyable for users.

One of the essential tools of UCD is conducting user research. This involves gathering feedback from potential users, observing their interactions, and conducting interviews to identify their requirements. Creating user personas, which are fictional representations of target users, can aid in understanding their motivations and behaviors.

Example: Conducting User Research

```cpp
#include <iostream>
#include <string>

int main() {
    std::cout << "Welcome to our User Research Survey!" << std::endl;

    // Gather user information
    std::string name;
    int age;
```

```cpp
    std::string feedback;

    std::cout << "Please enter your name: ";
    std::getline(std::cin, name);

    std::cout << "Please enter your age: ";
    std::cin >> age;
    std::cin.ignore(); // Ignore the newline character after reading an integer

    std::cout << "Please provide your feedback: ";
    std::getline(std::cin, feedback);

    // Display collected information
    std::cout << "Thank you for participating, " << name << "!" << std::endl;
    std::cout << "Age: " << age << std::endl;
    std::cout << "Feedback: " << feedback << std::endl;

    return 0;
}
```

The program example is a simple console-based survey that collects user information such as name, age, and feedback. It follows the principles of UCD by directly involving the user in the design process. Users are asked to provide their input, which will help developers understand their needs and expectations better.

By running the program, developers can collect valuable information directly from potential users. This information can be used to create user personas, which are fictional representations of target users, aiding in understanding their motivations and behaviors. User personas are an essential tool in UCD as they assist in designing interfaces that resonate with the actual end-users.

12.1.2 VISUAL HIERARCHY AND LAYOUT

Visual Hierarchy and Layout are crucial aspects of GUI design, as they involve organizing elements within the interface to guide the user's attention and understanding. By using visual cues such as size, color, and position, developers can create a structured and intuitive layout that highlights important elements and relationships, enhancing the overall user experience.

Key Principles of Visual Hierarchy and Layout:

1. **Emphasizing Key Elements:** Visual hierarchy involves presenting key elements with a higher visual emphasis to draw the user's attention. Important buttons, headings, or information should be more prominent, making it easier for users to identify and interact with them.

2. **Proper Spacing and Alignment:** Effective spacing and alignment help establish a clear flow of information and improve readability. Consistent spacing between elements and proper alignment contribute to a more organized and visually appealing interface.

Example: Visual Hierarchy in a Simple Form

```cpp
#include <iostream>
#include <string>
```

```
int main() {
    std::cout << "Create an Account" << std::endl;

    // Display input fields with varying visual hierarchy
    std::string username = "Username: ";
    std::string password = "Password: ";
    std::string confirmPassword = "Confirm Password: ";

    std::cout << username << std::endl;
    std::cout << password << std::endl;
    std::cout << confirmPassword << std::endl;

    return 0;
}
```

In this example, we illustrate the concept of visual hierarchy in a simple form interface. The program displays three input fields: "Username," "Password," and "Confirm Password." Each input field is presented in separate lines, creating a visual separation between them. However, the current implementation lacks a clear visual hierarchy, making it challenging for users to identify which input field is more important.

Improving Visual Hierarchy:

To improve the visual hierarchy, we can use various techniques such as font size, font weight, and alignment:

```
#include <iostream>
#include <string>

int main() {
    std::cout << "Create an Account" << std::endl;

    // Display input fields with improved visual hierarchy
    std::string username = "Username: ";
    std::string password = "Password: ";
    std::string confirmPassword = "Confirm Password: ";

    // Apply different visual emphasis to key elements
    std::cout << "\033[1m" << username << "\033[0m" << std::endl; // Bold font for username
    std::cout << password << std::endl;
    std::cout << confirmPassword << std::endl;

    return 0;
}
```

In this improved version, we use the ANSI escape code \033[1m to set the font to bold for the "Username" input field, making it stand out from the other input fields. This simple visual adjustment helps create a better visual hierarchy, directing the user's attention to the most critical element in the form.

12.1.3 CONSISTENCY AND FEEDBACK

Consistency and Feedback are critical principles in GUI design that contribute to a seamless and intuitive user experience. Let's explore these principles and their significance in creating user-friendly applications.

Consistency: Consistency is a fundamental principle that ensures uniformity in design and interactions throughout the application. A consistent interface means that similar elements have a familiar look and behave in a predictable manner across different sections of the application. Consistency enables users to quickly understand how to interact with various elements and perform actions without confusion.

Importance of Consistency:

1. **User Familiarity:** A consistent interface creates a sense of familiarity for users, as they encounter familiar design patterns and interactions. This reduces the learning curve and helps users navigate the application more efficiently.

2. **Efficiency:** Users can complete tasks more efficiently when the interface is consistent, as they can apply their knowledge from one part of the application to another. This consistency saves time and effort.

3. **Trust and Credibility:** A consistent design instills a sense of trust and credibility in the application. Users perceive a well-designed and consistent interface as more reliable and professional.

Example: Consistency in Button Design

```cpp
#include <iostream>
#include <string>

void handleClick() {
    std::cout << "Button clicked! Processing..." << std::endl;
    // Perform the necessary action based on the button click
}

int main() {
    std::cout << "Consistency and Feedback Example" << std::endl;

    // Display consistent buttons
    std::string buttonLabel = "Click Me!";
    std::cout << "Button 1: " << buttonLabel << std::endl;
    std::cout << "Button 2: " << buttonLabel << std::endl;

    // Simulate a button click and provide feedback
    handleClick();

    return 0;
}
```

In this example, we demonstrate consistency in button design. Both buttons have the same label, "Click Me!" This consistency allows users to recognize the purpose of the buttons at a glance, as they share a common design and action. When users encounter familiar elements, such as consistently designed buttons, they can confidently interact with them without hesitation.

Feedback: Feedback is another vital aspect of GUI design. Providing real-time feedback to users for their interactions enhances their sense of control and understanding. When users perform actions such as clicking a button or submitting a form, immediate feedback assures them that their input has been received and processed.

Importance of Feedback:

1. **User Engagement:** Real-time feedback engages users by acknowledging their actions and maintaining their interest in the application.

2. **Error Prevention:** Feedback can inform users about any errors or issues they encounter during their interactions, allowing them to correct mistakes promptly.

3. **User Confidence:** Feedback reassures users that their input is being processed, which builds confidence in the application.

12.1.4 USABILITY AND ACCESSIBILITY

Usability and Accessibility are essential aspects of GUI design that focus on creating interfaces that are easy to use, inclusive, and accommodating to various user needs. Let's delve into these principles and understand their significance in developing user-friendly and accessible applications.

Usability: Usability ensures that the GUI is designed in a way that maximizes user-friendliness and minimizes the likelihood of user errors. It involves providing a smooth and intuitive learning curve for users, allowing them to interact with the application effortlessly. A usable interface makes it easy for users to accomplish their tasks and achieve their goals efficiently.

Importance of Usability:

1. **Enhanced User Experience:** A usable interface enhances the overall user experience by reducing frustration and increasing user satisfaction.

2. **Productivity and Efficiency:** Usability optimizes user workflows, leading to increased productivity and efficiency.

3. **Reduced Training Time:** A user-friendly interface requires less training, allowing users to quickly familiarize themselves with the application.

Accessibility: Accessibility focuses on making the interface inclusive for all users, regardless of their abilities or disabilities. An accessible interface ensures that users with visual, auditory, cognitive, or motor impairments can access and interact with the application effectively. It involves providing alternative ways to interact with the application and considering various assistive technologies.

Importance of Accessibility:

1. **Inclusivity:** An accessible interface ensures that all users, including those with disabilities, can access and benefit from the application.

2. **Compliance and Legal Requirements:** Many countries and organizations have legal requirements and guidelines for accessibility that developers must adhere to.

3. **Market Expansion:** By catering to users with disabilities, developers can tap into a broader market and reach a more diverse audience.

Example: Usability and Accessibility in Form Input

```cpp
#include <iostream>
#include <string>


void handleInput(const std::string& userInput) {
    std::cout << "Your input: " << userInput << std::endl;
}


int main() {
    std::cout << "Usability and Accessibility Example" << std::endl;
```

```
// Prompt the user for input
std::string prompt = "Please enter your name: ";
std::cout << prompt;

// Get user input
std::string userInput;
std::getline(std::cin, userInput);

// Provide feedback and handle input
std::cout << "Thank you!" << std::endl;
handleInput(userInput);

    return 0;
}
```

In this example, we demonstrate usability and accessibility in a simple form input scenario. The program prompts the user for their name and then gathers the input. By using `std::getline`, the application allows the user to enter their name with spaces, making it more user-friendly. Additionally, the program provides real-time feedback, acknowledging the user's input.

12.2 EVENT-DRIVEN PROGRAMMING

Event-driven programming is a powerful paradigm used in Graphical User Interface (GUI) development to handle user interactions and system events. Unlike traditional procedural programming, where the program follows a predetermined sequence of steps, event-driven programming allows applications to respond to events asynchronously. These events can be triggered by user actions, such as mouse clicks or key presses, or system events like timers and network activity.

12.2.1 INTRODUCTION TO EVENT-DRIVEN ARCHITECTURE

In event-driven architecture, the flow of the program is driven by events and their associated event handlers. An event handler, also known as a callback function, is a piece of code that executes when a specific event occurs. The application listens for events and triggers the corresponding event handler to respond to the event.

The event-driven approach offers several benefits for GUI applications:

1. **Responsiveness:** By responding to events as they occur, the application can provide real-time feedback to users, making the interface more interactive and responsive.

2. **Event-Based Interaction:** Event-driven programming allows developers to create applications where user actions trigger specific responses. For example, a button click can execute a particular action.

Example: Basic Event-Driven Program

```
#include <iostream>

// Event handler function
void onClick() {
    std::cout << "Button Clicked!" << std::endl;
}
```

```cpp
int main() {
    std::cout << "Event-Driven Programming Example" << std::endl;

    // Simulate an event (button click)
    onClick();

    return 0;
}
```

In this example, we demonstrate a basic event-driven program with a single event handler function **onClick()**. When the program is executed, it simulates a button click event and calls the **onClick()** function.

12.2.2 EVENT HANDLING AND CALLBACKS

Event handling is the core of event-driven programming, and it is managed through event handlers or callbacks. When an event occurs, the corresponding callback function is invoked to handle the event. Callbacks allow applications to respond to user actions and external stimuli dynamically.

Example: Handling Button Click Event

```cpp
#include <iostream>
#include <functional>

// Event handler function for button click
void onClick() {
    std::cout << "Button Clicked!" << std::endl;
}

// Function to simulate a button click event
void simulateButtonClick(const std::function<void()>& eventHandler) {
    // Simulate some event occurrence
    std::cout << "Simulating a button click event..." << std::endl;
    // Call the event handler
    eventHandler();
}

int main() {
    std::cout << "Event Handling and Callbacks Example" << std::endl;

    // Simulate a button click event and handle it using the onClick() function
    simulateButtonClick(onClick);

    return 0;
}
```

In this example, we define an event handler function **onClick()** to handle a button click event. The **simulateButtonClick()** function takes a callback as an argument and simulates a button click event, calling the provided callback.

12.2.3 ASYNCHRONOUS PROGRAMMING

Event-driven programming inherently involves asynchronous execution, where events occur independently of the main program flow. Asynchronous programming allows applications to handle multiple events concurrently and ensures that the application remains responsive during potentially time-consuming tasks.

To manage asynchronous events, GUI frameworks often use event loops. The event loop continuously checks for new events and dispatches their associated event handlers, allowing the application to respond to user interactions promptly.

Example: Asynchronous Event Loop

```cpp
#include <iostream>
#include <chrono>
#include <thread>

// Event handler function for timer event
void onTimer() {
    std::cout << "Timer Event Occurred!" << std::endl;
}

int main() {
    std::cout << "Asynchronous Programming Example" << std::endl;

    // Simulate the event loop by repeatedly checking for events
    for (int i = 0; i < 5; ++i) {
        std::cout << "Event Loop Iteration " << i << std::endl;
        // Check for events (e.g., timers) and invoke their handlers
        onTimer();

        // Simulate some time between iterations
        std::this_thread::sleep_for(std::chrono::seconds(1));
    }

    return 0;
}
```

In this example, we simulate an event loop where the **onTimer()** function is repeatedly called every second, representing an asynchronous timer event.

Event-driven programming is a foundational concept in GUI development, allowing applications to be more interactive and responsive to user interactions. Understanding event-driven architecture and event handling is essential for creating modern, user-friendly GUI applications. In the next section, we will explore various GUI frameworks available in C++ that facilitate event-driven programming and GUI development.

12.3 INTRODUCTION TO GUI FRAMEWORKS

GUI frameworks, also known as widget toolkits or UI libraries, are essential tools for developing interactive and visually appealing applications with Graphical User Interfaces (GUIs). These frameworks provide pre-built components, called widgets, which developers can use to create the user interface of their applications. By offering a range of widgets like windows, buttons, menus, and more, GUI frameworks simplify UI implementation, allowing developers to focus on application functionality.

12.3.1 COMMON GUI FRAMEWORKS IN C++

Several popular GUI frameworks are available in C++, each with its unique set of features and capabilities. Some commonly used C++ GUI frameworks include:

1. **Qt**: Qt is a powerful and widely-used GUI framework known for its cross-platform capabilities. It offers a comprehensive set of tools for application development, including a large collection of widgets, support for internationalization, and a powerful signal and slot mechanism for event handling.

2. **wxWidgets**: wxWidgets is another cross-platform GUI framework that enables developers to write applications that can run on multiple operating systems without modification. It provides a native look and feel on each platform and supports various event handling techniques.

3. **GTK+**: GTK+ (GIMP Toolkit) is a popular open-source GUI framework primarily used for Linux desktop applications. It provides a wide range of widgets and supports custom theming and styling.

4. **FLTK**: FLTK (Fast Light Toolkit) is a lightweight and fast GUI framework suitable for resource-constrained applications. It offers a straightforward API and is well-suited for creating small, efficient applications.

5. **SFML**: SFML (Simple and Fast Multimedia Library) is primarily a multimedia library but also provides basic GUI functionality. It is often used for game development and multimedia applications.

Example: Using Qt to Create a Simple GUI

```cpp
#include <QApplication>
#include <QPushButton>

int main(int argc, char *argv[]) {
    QApplication app(argc, argv);

    QPushButton button("Click me!");
    button.show();

    return app.exec();
}
```

In this example, we use the Qt framework to create a simple GUI application with a single button. The **QPushButton** widget represents the button, and calling **show()** makes it visible on the screen. The **QApplication** object manages the application's event loop.

12.3.2 CHOOSING THE RIGHT FRAMEWORK FOR YOUR PROJECT

When choosing a GUI framework for a project, consider several factors, including:

1. **Platform Support**: Ensure the framework supports all the platforms where you intend to deploy your application.
2. **Ease of Use**: Some frameworks provide more intuitive APIs and tools, making development faster and more straightforward.
3. **Performance**: Depending on your application's nature, you may need a lightweight framework for better performance.
4. **Community and Documentation**: Active communities and extensive documentation can be valuable resources for troubleshooting and learning.
5. **License**: Be aware of the licensing terms of the framework and ensure they align with your project's requirements.

12.3.3 SETTING UP A GUI DEVELOPMENT ENVIRONMENT

To start developing GUI applications using a particular framework, you need to set up the development environment correctly. This typically involves installing the necessary libraries and tools for the chosen framework and configuring your Integrated Development Environment (IDE) to work with it. Each framework has its specific installation and setup procedures, which are well-documented in their respective official documentation.

Using a GUI framework significantly simplifies the process of building interactive applications, making it easier to create professional-looking user interfaces. In the next section, we will build a simple GUI application using one of the popular C++ GUI frameworks discussed above.

Setting Up QT in VSCOde

Qt is a popular cross-platform GUI framework that can be used to develop applications for Windows, macOS, Linux, and mobile devices. VSCOde is a powerful IDE that can be used to develop Qt applications.

To set up QT in VSCOde, you will need to install the following:

- The Qt SDK
- The Qt VS Code Tools extension

The Qt SDK can be downloaded from the Qt website: https://www.qt.io/download/. Once you have downloaded the SDK, you need to install it on your computer.

The Qt VS Code Tools extension can be installed from the Visual Studio Code Marketplace: https://marketplace.visualstudio.com/items?itemName=tonka3000.qtvsctools. Once you have installed the extension, you need to restart VSCOde.

Once you have installed the Qt SDK and the Qt VS Code Tools extension, you can start creating Qt applications in VSCOde. To do this, you can create a new project from the **File** menu or you can open an existing Qt project.

12.4 BUILDING A SIMPLE GUI APPLICATION

In this section, we will walk through the process of building a simple Graphical User Interface (GUI) application using a C++ GUI framework. We will create a basic application with a window containing a button and a text box. When the button is clicked, the text box will display a message.

12.4.1 DESIGNING THE USER INTERFACE

Before writing any code, it's essential to design the user interface of the application. This step involves deciding how the GUI elements should be arranged on the window and how the user will interact with them. In our simple application, we'll have a window with a button and a text box, as described above.

12.4.2 HANDLING EVENTS AND USER INPUT

Once we have designed the user interface, we need to handle user interactions with the GUI elements. In an event-driven programming paradigm, user actions, such as clicking a button, are events that trigger specific actions in the application.

In most GUI frameworks, including Qt, events are handled through callbacks. A callback is a function that gets executed when a particular event occurs. For example, when the button is clicked, its associated callback function will be called.

Example: Handling Button Click Event

```cpp
#include <QApplication>
#include <QWidget>
#include <QPushButton>
#include <QLineEdit>
#include <QVBoxLayout>
#include <QMessageBox> // Include this for QMessageBox

// Declare lineEdit and window as global variables
QLineEdit *lineEdit;
QWidget *window;

void showMessage() {
    // Get the text from the text box
    QString message = "Hello, " + lineEdit->text() + "!";

    // Display the message in a message box
    QMessageBox::information(window, "Message", message);
}

int main(int argc, char *argv[]) {
    QApplication app(argc, argv);

    // Create the main window
    window = new QWidget;
    window->setWindowTitle("Simple GUI Application");

    // Create the button and the text box
    QPushButton *button = new QPushButton("Click me!");
    lineEdit = new QLineEdit; // Initialize lineEdit here

    // Connect the button's clicked signal to the showMessage() function
    QObject::connect(button, &QPushButton::clicked, showMessage);

    // Create a layout and add the button and the text box to it
    QVBoxLayout *layout = new QVBoxLayout;
    layout->addWidget(button);
    layout->addWidget(lineEdit); // Use the global lineEdit
```

```
// Set the layout for the window
window->setLayout(layout);

// Show the window
window->show();

return app.exec();
}
```

12.4.3 IMPLEMENTING FUNCTIONALITY

In the code example above, we've implemented the **showMessage()** function that gets called when the button is clicked. The function retrieves the text from the text box, creates a message using that text, and then displays it using a message box.

12.4.4 TESTING AND DEBUGGING

After implementing the functionality, it's crucial to thoroughly test the application to ensure that it works as expected. Test various scenarios and user interactions to identify any bugs or unexpected behaviors. If issues are found, use debugging techniques and tools provided by your IDE and framework to pinpoint and fix the problems.

By following these steps, you can build a simple GUI application using a C++ GUI framework. As you become more familiar with the framework, you can create more complex and feature-rich applications to meet your specific requirements. In the next section, we will explore a case study of building a complete GUI application to further illustrate the concepts discussed in this chapter.

12.5 CASE STUDY: BUILDING A COMPLETE GUI APPLICATION

In this section, we will undertake a case study to demonstrate the process of building a complete Graphical User Interface (GUI) application from start to finish. The application we will create is a simple text editor, allowing users to create, edit, save, and load text documents.

12.5.1 PROJECT OVERVIEW AND REQUIREMENTS

Before we start coding, let's outline the project's overview and requirements:

Project Overview: Our goal is to develop a basic text editor with a user-friendly GUI.

Functional Requirements:

1. The user should be able to create a new text document.
2. The user should be able to open an existing text file and edit its content.
3. The user should be able to save the current text document to a file.
4. The user should be able to save the document with a new name or overwrite an existing file.
5. The application should provide options to cut, copy, and paste text.
6. The application should support undo and redo functionality.
7. The user should be able to change the font size and style.
8. The application should provide a search and replace feature.

12.5.2 DESIGNING THE APPLICATION

The first step in building the text editor is to design the user interface. We need to create a window that includes a text area for editing the document and a menu bar with options for file operations, edit functions, and font settings.

Design Mockup:

Menu Bar

```
File
  * New
```

```
Text Area
```

12.5.3 IMPLEMENTING KEY FEATURES

Now that we have designed the user interface, let's proceed to implement the key features of our text editor.

Example: Creating a New Document

```cpp
#include "qmainwindow.h"
#include <QApplication>
#include <QTextEdit>
#include <QMenuBar>
#include <QMenu>
#include <QAction>


int main(int argc, char *argv[]) {
    QApplication app(argc, argv);

    // Create the main window
    QMainWindow window;
    window.setWindowTitle("Text Editor");

    // Create a text area
    QTextEdit *textEdit = new QTextEdit;
    window.setCentralWidget(textEdit);

    // Create a menu bar
    QMenuBar *menuBar = window.menuBar();

    // Create a "File" menu
    QMenu *fileMenu = menuBar->addMenu("File");

    // Create a "New" action
    QAction *newAction = new QAction("New");
    fileMenu->addAction(newAction);

    // Connect the "New" action to create a new document
    QObject::connect(newAction, &QAction::triggered, textEdit, &QTextEdit::clear);

    // Show the window
    window.show();
```

```
    return app.exec();
}
```

In the example above, we've implemented the "New" feature. When the user clicks the "New" option from the "File" menu, the text area is cleared, creating a new blank document.

12.5.4 TESTING AND DEPLOYMENT

After implementing all the required features, it's crucial to thoroughly test the text editor application to ensure it meets all the functional requirements and works as expected. Test various scenarios, such as creating new documents, opening existing files, saving documents, and using edit functions like cut, copy, paste, undo, and redo.

Once testing is complete, you can deploy the application to make it available to users. Depending on the GUI framework you are using, deployment steps may vary. For instance, if you're using Qt, you can build and distribute the application with the necessary Qt libraries.

Congratulations! You have successfully built a simple text editor using a GUI framework. Building a complete GUI application involves many intricate details, and this case study has given you a practical understanding of the process. As you gain more experience, you can enhance the application with additional features and improvements to make it more robust and user-friendly.

12.6 SUMMARY AND CONCLUSION

In this chapter, we delved into the world of creating Graphical User Interfaces (GUIs) using C++. We explored essential concepts and best practices for designing and developing GUI applications, along with a hands-on case study to build a complete text editor.

Key Takeaways

1. **GUI Design Principles:** We began by understanding the crucial principles that guide GUI design. These principles revolve around user-centered design, where the user's needs and preferences take precedence. We learned about visual hierarchy, layout, consistency, feedback, usability, and accessibility, all of which contribute to creating an intuitive and user-friendly interface.

2. **Event-Driven Programming:** Next, we explored the fundamentals of event-driven programming, a paradigm common in GUI applications. Events are user interactions, such as mouse clicks and keyboard input, that trigger specific actions. We delved into event handling, which involves associating event types with corresponding callbacks to execute the desired functionality.

3. **Introduction to GUI Frameworks:** To facilitate GUI development, we introduced common GUI frameworks in C++. These frameworks provide tools and libraries to create graphical interfaces effortlessly. We discussed how to choose the right framework for your project and the steps to set up a GUI development environment.

4. **Building a Simple GUI Application:** The highlight of this chapter was building a simple text editor as a case study. We designed the user interface, implemented key features like creating, opening, and saving documents, handling user input, and testing the application's functionality.

5. **Case Study: Building a Complete GUI Application:** Throughout the case study, we followed a systematic approach to create a complete text editor. We considered project requirements, designed the application's user interface, implemented various features, and thoroughly tested the application to ensure it met user expectations.

Conclusion

Creating GUI applications opens up endless possibilities to develop interactive and user-friendly software. By understanding GUI design principles, event-driven programming, and using appropriate GUI frameworks, developers can craft powerful and visually appealing applications tailored to their users' needs.

As you continue your journey in C++ programming, mastering GUI development will enable you to build sophisticated and versatile applications that engage users and enhance their overall experience.

In the next chapters of this book, we will explore other advanced topics in C++, empowering you to become a proficient and versatile C++ developer.

13 TEXT PROCESSING AND STRINGS

In the world of programming, text processing and handling strings are fundamental aspects of data manipulation and processing. Being able to efficiently manipulate, search, and extract information from strings is crucial for developing powerful and user-friendly applications. This chapter delves into the realm of text processing and strings in C++, providing essential techniques to handle textual data effectively and make your applications more versatile.

Throughout this chapter, we will explore various aspects of string manipulation, regular expressions, and text file parsing. These skills are vital for advanced programming tasks, such as data validation, text analysis, and file handling. By the end of this chapter, you will be equipped with valuable tools to process and manipulate textual data, enhancing the functionality of your C++ applications.

Let's embark on this journey through the realm of text processing and strings, where we'll learn invaluable skills to wield the power of words and characters in the world of programming. So, let's get started with the first section: "String Manipulation Techniques."

13.1 STRING MANIPULATION TECHNIQUES

Strings are sequences of characters, and they play a vital role in any programming language, including C++. C++ provides a powerful standard library for working with strings, offering various functions and methods to manipulate, search, and modify textual data. In this section, we will explore essential string manipulation techniques, such as concatenation, substring extraction, searching, and more.

Let's begin by introducing strings in C++ and then delve into specific string manipulation techniques.

13.1.1 INTRODUCTION TO STRINGS IN C++

In C++, strings are represented by the **std::string** class from the Standard Template Library (STL). This class provides a flexible and convenient way to work with textual data. To use strings in your C++ program, you need to include the **<string>** header.

Here's a simple example of using strings in C++:

```cpp
#include <iostream>
#include <string>

int main() {
    // Declare a string
    std::string message = "Hello, world!";
```

```
    // Print the string
    std::cout << message << std::endl;

    return 0;
}
```

Output:
```
Hello, world!
```

In this example, we declared a string variable named **message** and initialized it with the text "Hello, world!". We then used the **std::cout** object to print the string to the console.

13.1.2 CONCATENATION AND APPENDING

Concatenation is the process of combining two or more strings into one. In C++, you can use the **+** operator or the **+=** operator to concatenate strings.

Here's an example:

```
#include <iostream>
#include <string>

int main() {
    std::string firstName = "John";
    std::string lastName = "Doe";

    // Concatenate strings using the + operator
    std::string fullName = firstName + " " + lastName;

    // Append strings using the += operator
    fullName += " Jr.";

    std::cout << "Full Name: " << fullName << std::endl;

    return 0;
}
```

Output:
```
Full Name: John Doe Jr.
```

In this example, we concatenated the first name, last name, and the title "Jr." to form the full name.

13.1.3 SUBSTRINGS AND EXTRACTION

Substring extraction allows you to extract a portion of a string. You can use the **substr()** function to achieve this in C++. The function takes two arguments: the starting position and the length of the substring.

Here's an example:

```
#include <iostream>
```

```
#include <string>

int main() {
    std::string sentence = "The quick brown fox jumps over the lazy dog.";

    // Extract a substring starting from index 4 (inclusive) and of length 15
    std::string substring = sentence.substr(4, 15);

    std::cout << "Substring: " << substring << std::endl;

    return 0;
}
```

Output:
```
Substring: quick brown fox
```

In this example, we extracted a substring from the original sentence starting from index 4 (inclusive) and with a length of 15 characters.

13.1.4 SEARCHING AND FINDING

C++ provides various functions to search for specific characters or substrings within a string. For example, you can use the **find()** function to search for the first occurrence of a substring in a string.

Here's an example:

```
#include <iostream>
#include <string>

int main() {
    std::string sentence = "The quick brown fox jumps over the lazy dog.";

    // Search for the first occurrence of "fox"
    size_t found = sentence.find("fox");

    if (found != std::string::npos) {
        std::cout << "Found at index: " << found << std::endl;
    } else {
        std::cout << "Not found." << std::endl;
    }

    return 0;
}
```

Output:
```
Found at index: 16
```

In this example, we used the `find()` function to search for the first occurrence of "fox" in the sentence. The function returns the index of the first character of the found substring, or `std::string::npos` if the substring is not found.

13.1.5 MODIFYING AND REPLACING

C++ provides several methods to modify strings. For example, you can use the `replace()` function to replace a portion of a string with another string.

Here's an example:

```cpp
#include <iostream>
#include <string>

int main() {
    std::string sentence = "The quick brown fox jumps over the lazy dog.";

    // Replace "quick brown fox" with "fast red cat"
    sentence.replace(4, 14, "fast red cat");

    std::cout << "Modified Sentence: " << sentence << std::endl;

    return 0;
}
```

Output:
```
Modified Sentence: The fast red cat jumps over the lazy dog.
```

In this example, we replaced the substring "quick brown fox" with "fast red cat" in the sentence.

13.1.6 CONVERTING STRINGS

C++ allows you to convert strings to other data types, such as integers or floating-point numbers. You can use functions like `std::stoi()` and `std::stod()` to convert strings to integers and doubles, respectively.

Here's an example:

```cpp
#include <iostream>
#include <string>

int main() {
    std::string numStr = "12345";
    std::string doubleStr = "3.14";

    // Convert string to integer
    int number = std::stoi(numStr);

    // Convert string to double
    double pi = std::stod(doubleStr);
```

```
    std::cout << "Integer: " << number << std::endl;
    std::cout << "Double: " << pi << std::endl;

    return 0;
}
```

Output:

```
Integer: 12345
Double: 3.14
```

In this example, we converted the strings "12345" and "3.14" to an integer and a double, respectively.

13.1.7 STRING COMPARISON AND EQUALITY

C++ provides various functions to compare strings. You can use the relational operators (==, !=, <, >, <=, >=) to compare strings lexicographically.

Here's an example:

```
#include <iostream>
#include <string>

int main() {
    std::string str1 = "apple";
    std::string str2 = "banana";

    if (str1 == str2) {
        std::cout << "Strings are equal." << std::endl;
    } else {
        std::cout << "Strings are not equal." << std::endl;
    }

    return 0;
}
```

Output:
```
Strings are not equal.
```

In this example, we compared two strings `str1` and `str2` using the `==` operator.

This section covered the fundamental techniques of string manipulation in C++. We explored string concatenation, substring extraction, searching, modifying, converting, and comparing. These techniques are crucial for processing and manipulating textual data in your C++ applications. Next, we'll dive into another essential topic: "Regular Expressions."

13.2 REGULAR EXPRESSIONS

Regular expressions (regex) are powerful tools for pattern matching and text manipulation. They provide a concise and flexible way to search for, match, and extract specific sequences of characters within strings. Regular expressions are widely used in various programming languages and text editors to perform complex text processing tasks.

In this section, we will introduce the concept of regular expressions, learn how to use them in C++, and explore common regex operations.

13.2.1 UNDERSTANDING REGULAR EXPRESSIONS

A regular expression is a sequence of characters that forms a search pattern. The pattern describes a set of strings that match it. It allows you to specify rules for character sequences, such as searching for specific words, patterns, or even complex data formats.

In C++, you can work with regular expressions using the **<regex>** header, which provides a set of classes and functions to handle regex operations.

13.2.2 PATTERN MATCHING WITH REGULAR EXPRESSIONS

Let's start with a basic example of pattern matching using regular expressions. Suppose we want to check if a string contains a specific word, say "apple." We can use the **std::regex_search()** function to perform the search.

```cpp
#include <iostream>
#include <regex>
#include <string>

int main() {
    std::string sentence = "An apple a day keeps the doctor away.";
    std::string wordToFind = "apple";

    std::regex pattern(wordToFind);
    if (std::regex_search(sentence, pattern)) {
        std::cout << "The string contains the word \"" << wordToFind << "\"." << std::endl;
    } else {
        std::cout << "The string does not contain the word \"" << wordToFind << "\"." <<
std::endl;
    }

    return 0;
}
```

Output:
```
The string contains the word "apple".
```

In this example, we used the **std::regex_search()** function to search for the word "apple" in the given sentence. The function returns **true** if the pattern is found in the string.

13.2.3 CAPTURING GROUPS AND BACKREFERENCES

Regular expressions allow you to create capturing groups, which are portions of the pattern enclosed in parentheses. Capturing groups enable you to extract specific parts of the matched string. This is particularly useful when you want to isolate and retrieve specific substrings from a larger text.

In the provided example, we have a list of names in the format "First Name - Last Name." The regular expression used to achieve this task is R"((\w+)\s-\s(\w+))". Let's break down the regular expression:

1. R"(" and ")": The R preceding the quotation marks denotes a raw string literal, which allows us to write the regular expression without worrying about escape characters.

2. (\w+): This is the first capturing group, denoted by the parentheses (). The \w is a shorthand character class that matches any word character (letters, digits, and underscores). The + quantifier means one or more occurrences of word characters. So, (\w+) captures one or more word characters representing the first name.

3. \s-\s: This part of the regular expression matches the space followed by a hyphen and another space, which matches the separator between the first name and the last name in the list.

4. (\w+): This is the second capturing group, again denoted by parentheses (). It captures one or more word characters representing the last name.

Now, let's see how the example code processes the list of names using the defined regular expression:

```cpp
#include <iostream>
#include <regex>
#include <string>

int main() {
    std::string names = "John Doe - Jane Smith - Mike Johnson";

    std::regex pattern(R"((\w+)\s-\s(\w+))");
    std::smatch matches;

    while (std::regex_search(names, matches, pattern)) {
        std::cout << "First Name: " << matches[1] << ", Last Name: " << matches[2] <<
std::endl;
        names = matches.suffix();
    }

    return 0;
}
```

Output:

```
First Name: John, Last Name: Doe
First Name: Jane, Last Name: Smith
First Name: Mike, Last Name: Johnson
```

In the provided code, we used std::regex_search() to search for matches of the regular expression in the names string. The function stores the matches in the matches object of type std::smatch. The loop then iterates through all the matches found and extracts the first and last names using the capturing groups [1] and [2], respectively, and prints the results.

Creating capturing groups in regular expressions involves enclosing specific parts of the pattern in parentheses (). This tells the regular expression engine to capture the matched substring that corresponds to the enclosed portion of the pattern. Capturing groups are useful for extracting specific information from a larger text or for performing more complex text processing tasks.

Here's a step-by-step guide on how to create capturing groups in regular expressions:

1. **Identify the Portion to Capture**: Determine the specific part of the pattern that you want to capture as a separate group. This can be a single character, a word, or a more complex pattern.

2. **Enclose in Parentheses**: Surround the identified portion with parentheses ( ). This forms the capturing group.

3. **Use Special Characters with Caution**: Be mindful of special characters in the portion you are capturing. If the content within the capturing group contains special characters that have special meaning in regular expressions (e.g., `+`, `*`, `.`, etc.), you may need to escape them using a backslash `\`.

4. **Access Captured Groups**: When using the regular expression in your code, you can access the captured groups and the text they matched using the appropriate functions or objects provided by your programming language's regular expression library. In C++, the `std::regex_search()` function with `std::smatch` or `std::regex_match()` with `std::smatch` are commonly used to access captured groups.

Here's an example of creating a capturing group in a regular expression:

Suppose we have a list of email addresses, and we want to capture the username part of each email address. The email addresses are in the format "username@example.com".

```cpp
#include <iostream>
#include <regex>
#include <string>

int main() {
    std::string emails = "john@example.com, alice@example.com, bob@example.com";

    // Regular expression to capture the username part of the email address
    std::regex pattern(R"((\w+)@example\.com)");

    std::smatch matches;

    // Iterate through all matches and print the captured usernames
    while (std::regex_search(emails, matches, pattern)) {
        std::cout << "Username: " << matches[1] << std::endl;
        emails = matches.suffix();
    }

    return 0;
}
```

Output:

```
Username: john
Username: alice
Username: bob
```

In this example, the regular expression `(\w+)@example\.com` contains a capturing group `(\w+)`. The `\w` matches any word character (letters, digits, and underscores), and the `+` quantifier matches one or more occurrences of word characters. This capturing group captures the username part of each email address.

The std::regex_search() function searches for matches of the regular expression in the emails string. The matched substrings are stored in the matches object of type std::smatch. The loop then iterates through all the matches found, and the usernames are accessed using the capturing group [1] and printed to the console.

In regular expressions, certain special characters have specific meanings and functions that provide powerful pattern matching capabilities. These special characters are used to represent classes of characters, quantifiers, anchors, and more. Understanding these special characters is essential for crafting effective regular expressions in C++.

1. Character Classes:
   - . (dot): Matches any single character except a newline.
   - \w: Matches any word character (alphanumeric character and underscore).
   - \W: Matches any non-word character (not alphanumeric and not underscore).
   - \d: Matches any digit character (0-9).
   - \D: Matches any non-digit character.
   - \s: Matches any whitespace character (space, tab, newline).
   - \S: Matches any non-whitespace character.

Example:

```cpp
#include <iostream>
#include <regex>

int main() {
    std::string text = "abc 123 !@# xyz";

    std::regex pattern("\\w+");
    std::sregex_iterator iter(text.begin(), text.end(), pattern);
    std::sregex_iterator end;

    while (iter != end) {
        std::cout << iter->str() << std::endl;
        ++iter;
    }

    return 0;
}
```

Output:

```
abc
123
xyz
```

2. Quantifiers:
   - *: Matches zero or more occurrences of the preceding character or group.
   - +: Matches one or more occurrences of the preceding character or group.
   - ?: Matches zero or one occurrence of the preceding character or group.
   - {n}: Matches exactly n occurrences of the preceding character or group.

- **{n, }**: Matches n or more occurrences of the preceding character or group.
- **{n, m}**: Matches between n and m occurrences of the preceding character or group.

Example:

```cpp
#include <iostream>
#include <regex>

int main() {
    std::string text = "abcccc abbbc abcc abbbc ab";

    std::regex pattern("abc{2,4}");
    std::sregex_iterator iter(text.begin(), text.end(), pattern);
    std::sregex_iterator end;

    while (iter != end) {
        std::cout << iter->str() << std::endl;
        ++iter;
    }

    return 0;
}
```

Output:

```
abccc
abbbc
abbbc
```

1. Anchors:
   - **^**: Matches the start of a line.
   - **$**: Matches the end of a line.

Example:

```cpp
#include <iostream>
#include <regex>

int main() {
    std::string text = "apple\nbanana\norange";

    std::regex pattern("^a\\w+");
    std::sregex_iterator iter(text.begin(), text.end(), pattern);
    std::sregex_iterator end;

    while (iter != end) {
        std::cout << iter->str() << std::endl;
        ++iter;
```

```
    }

    return 0;
}
```

Output:

```
apple
```

These special characters give regular expressions their versatility and power in pattern matching. By combining these characters, you can create complex patterns to match specific sequences of characters in a text.

13.2.4 COMMON REGEX OPERATIONS

Regular expressions support a wide range of operations, including searching for patterns, replacing matches, and more. Some common regex operations include:

- `std::regex_match()`: Tests if the entire string matches the given pattern.
- `std::regex_replace()`: Replaces all occurrences of the pattern in the string with a specified replacement.
- `std::regex_iterator`: Allows iteration over matches in a string.

The usage of these operations can vary based on the task at hand.

In this section, we learned about regular expressions and their significance in text processing. We explored pattern matching, capturing groups, and backreferences using regular expressions in C++. Regular expressions provide a flexible and efficient way to work with textual data, making them an essential tool for any programmer dealing with text processing tasks. Next, we will explore another crucial aspect of text processing: "Text File Parsing and Manipulation."

13.3 TEXT FILE PARSING AND MANIPULATION

Text file parsing and manipulation are fundamental tasks in programming, especially when dealing with large amounts of textual data. In this section, we will explore how to read, write, parse, extract, modify, and update text files using C++.

13.3.1 READING TEXT FILES

To read data from a text file in C++, we can use the `std::ifstream` class, which provides functionalities for file input operations. Let's see an example of reading data from a text file:

```cpp
#include <iostream>
#include <fstream>
#include <string>

int main() {
    std::ifstream inputFile("data.txt");

    if (!inputFile) {
        std::cerr << "Error opening file." << std::endl;
        return 1;
    }

    std::string line;
```

```
    while (std::getline(inputFile, line)) {
        std::cout << line << std::endl;
    }


    inputFile.close();
    return 0;
}
```

In this example, we opened the file named "data.txt" using `std::ifstream`. Then, we read the content of the file line by line using `std::getline()` and displayed it on the console.

13.3.2 WRITING TO TEXT FILES

To write data to a text file in C++, we can use the `std::ofstream` class, which provides functionalities for file output operations. Let's see an example of writing data to a text file:

```cpp
#include <iostream>
#include <fstream>


int main() {
    std::ofstream outputFile("output.txt");


    if (!outputFile) {
        std::cerr << "Error creating file." << std::endl;
        return 1;
    }


    outputFile << "Hello, world!" << std::endl;
    outputFile << "This is a text file." << std::endl;


    outputFile.close();
    return 0;
}
```

In this example, we opened the file named "output.txt" using `std::ofstream`. Then, we wrote two lines of text to the file using the **<<** operator.

13.3.3 PARSING AND EXTRACTING DATA FROM TEXT FILES

Parsing and extracting data from text files involve analyzing the content of the file to retrieve specific information. For example, if the text file contains data in a structured format, such as CSV (Comma-Separated Values), we can parse and extract each value accordingly.

Let's illustrate this with an example of parsing a CSV file and extracting data:

```cpp
#include <iostream>
#include <fstream>
#include <sstream>
```

```cpp
#include <string>

int main() {
    std::ifstream csvFile("data.csv");

    if (!csvFile) {
        std::cerr << "Error opening file." << std::endl;
        return 1;
    }

    std::string line, field;
    while (std::getline(csvFile, line)) {
        std::istringstream iss(line);
        while (std::getline(iss, field, ',')) {
            std::cout << field << " ";
        }
        std::cout << std::endl;
    }

    csvFile.close();
    return 0;
}
```

In this example, we opened a CSV file named "data.csv" and then parsed and extracted each field separated by commas (',').

13.3.4 MODIFYING AND UPDATING TEXT FILES

Modifying and updating text files involve changing the content of the file based on certain criteria or requirements. For instance, we can search for specific patterns and replace them with new values.

Let's demonstrate this with an example of updating a text file by replacing a word with another word:

```cpp
#include <iostream>
#include <fstream>
#include <string>

int main() {
    std::ifstream inputFile("data.txt");
    std::ofstream outputFile("updated_data.txt");

    if (!inputFile || !outputFile) {
        std::cerr << "Error opening files." << std::endl;
        return 1;
    }
```

```
    std::string searchWord = "old";
    std::string replaceWord = "new";
    std::string line;

    while (std::getline(inputFile, line)) {
        size_t pos = 0;
        while ((pos = line.find(searchWord, pos)) != std::string::npos) {
            line.replace(pos, searchWord.length(), replaceWord);
            pos += replaceWord.length();
        }
        outputFile << line << std::endl;
    }

    inputFile.close();
    outputFile.close();
    return 0;
}
```

In this example, we opened the "data.txt" file for reading and "updated_data.txt" file for writing. Then, we searched for occurrences of the word "old" in each line of the input file and replaced it with "new" in the output file.

In this section, we explored text file parsing and manipulation techniques in C++. We learned how to read, write, parse, extract, modify, and update text files. These skills are essential for handling textual data in various applications and scenarios. Next, we will delve into an example that demonstrates data processing with text files and strings.

13.4 EXAMPLE: DATA PROCESSING WITH TEXT FILES AND STRINGS

In this section, we will walk through a practical example that demonstrates the use of text processing techniques with strings and file manipulation. We will tackle a simple data processing task, where we have a text file containing records of students' names and their corresponding scores. The goal is to read the data from the file, calculate the average score, and generate a report with the names, scores, and calculated averages.

13.4.1 PROBLEM STATEMENT

Consider a text file named "scores.txt" with the following content:

```
John 85
Alice 92
Bob 78
Eve 95
```

Each line in the file represents a student's name followed by their score. The data is separated by spaces. Our task is to read this file, calculate the average score, and generate a report that looks like this:

```
- - - - - - - - - - - - - - - - - - - - - - - - - - - -
Name    | Score  | Average
```

```
-------------------------------
John    | 85      | 87.5
Alice   | 92      | 87.5
Bob     | 78      | 87.5
Eve     | 95      | 87.5
-------------------------------
```

13.4.2 IMPLEMENTATION USING STRING MANIPULATION AND FILE PARSING

To achieve the task, we will perform the following steps:

1. Open the "scores.txt" file for reading.
2. Read each line from the file and extract the name and score using string manipulation techniques.
3. Calculate the average score.
4. Generate the report and display it on the console.

Let's see the C++ implementation for the above steps:

```cpp
#include <iostream>
#include <fstream>
#include <sstream>
#include <iomanip>
#include <string>

int main() {
    std::ifstream inputFile("scores.txt");

    if (!inputFile) {
        std::cerr << "Error opening file." << std::endl;
        return 1;
    }

    std::string name;
    int score;
    int totalScore = 0;
    int studentCount = 0;

    // Read and process each line from the file
    while (inputFile >> name >> score) {
        totalScore += score;
        studentCount++;

        // Display individual student's data
        std::cout << std::left << std::setw(8) << name
                << std::setw(8) << score
                << std::setw(8) << "N/A" << std::endl;
    }
```

```cpp
    inputFile.close();

    if (studentCount > 0) {
        double averageScore = static_cast<double>(totalScore) / studentCount;

        // Display the average score for all students
        std::cout << "-------------------------------" << std::endl;
        std::cout << "Name    | Score   | Average" << std::endl;
        std::cout << "-------------------------------" << std::endl;
        inputFile.open("scores.txt"); // Reopen the file to read again

        while (inputFile >> name >> score) {
            std::cout << std::left << std::setw(8) << name
                      << std::setw(8) << score
                      << std::setw(8) << std::fixed << std::setprecision(1) << averageScore
<< std::endl;
        }

        std::cout << "-------------------------------" << std::endl;
    }

    inputFile.close();
    return 0;
}
```

In the provided C++ program, we are reading student data from a file named "scores.txt" and displaying the individual student's data as well as the average score for all students.

Let's explain the specific parts of the code:

1. `std::left`: This is an I/O manipulator used with the `std::setw()` function to set the alignment of the output to the left. It ensures that the data is left-aligned within the specified width.

2. `std::setw(8)`: This sets the field width to 8 characters for the output. It ensures that each data element (name, score, "N/A", and average score) will be printed in a fixed width of 8 characters.

3. `<< name`: This is used to output the student's name to the console.

4. `<< score`: This is used to output the student's score to the console.

5. `<< "N/A"`: This is used to output the string "N/A" to the console. In this context, it acts as a placeholder for the average score in the first loop where we display individual student data.

6. `static_cast<double>(totalScore) / studentCount`: This is used to calculate the average score for all students. We are using `static_cast` to convert `totalScore` to a `double` before performing the division to ensure that the result is a floating-point value.

7. `std::fixed` and `std::setprecision(1)`: These are I/O manipulators used to format the output of the average score to have one digit after the decimal point. The `std::fixed` manipulator ensures that the output is in fixed-point notation.

The program first opens the "scores.txt" file and reads student data (name and score) from it. It calculates the total score and the number of students in the process. For each student, it displays their name, score, and "N/A" (as a placeholder for average score).

After reading all student data, it calculates the average score and reopens the "scores.txt" file to display the data again. This time, it displays the student's name, score, and the calculated average score for all students in a tabular format.

The `std::setw()` and `std::left` manipulators ensure that the data is neatly aligned and displayed with consistent formatting. The `std::fixed` and `std::setprecision()` manipulators help control the precision of the average score displayed in the final table.

13.4.3 TESTING AND RESULTS

Let's assume the "scores.txt" file contains the data as specified in the problem statement. Upon running the program, it will read the file, calculate the average score, and generate the report, as shown below:

```
John      85        N/A
Alice     92        N/A
Bob       78        N/A
Eve       95        N/A
------------------------------------
Name    | Score   | Average
------------------------------------
John      85        87.5
Alice     92        87.5
Bob       78        87.5
Eve       95        87.5
------------------------------------
```

The program successfully processed the data and displayed the report with each student's name, score, and the calculated average.

In this example, we showcased how to use string manipulation techniques and file parsing to process data from a text file and generate a report. Text processing is a crucial aspect of programming, and it allows us to extract meaningful information from textual data efficiently. By applying these techniques, developers can handle a wide range of data processing tasks involving strings and text files in their C++ programs.

13.5 SUMMARY AND CONCLUSION

In this chapter, we explored the essential concepts and techniques related to text processing and strings in C++. We learned how to manipulate strings effectively, use regular expressions for pattern matching, and perform text file parsing and manipulation. These skills are crucial for any C++ programmer who deals with textual data and wants to harness the full power of the language.

Throughout Section 13.1, we gained a solid understanding of various string manipulation techniques. We learned how to concatenate and append strings, extract substrings, search for specific patterns, modify and replace portions of strings, and perform conversions between different data types and strings. By mastering these operations, we can efficiently process and manipulate textual data in our C++ programs.

In Section 13.2, we delved into the world of regular expressions. Regular expressions provide a powerful and flexible way to define patterns for text matching and manipulation. We explored pattern matching using metacharacters, capturing groups, and backreferences. Additionally, we learned about common regex operations that allow us to efficiently validate, search, and replace text based on complex patterns.

Section 13.3 focused on text file parsing and manipulation. We discovered how to read data from text files, write data to text files, and handle structured data using techniques like CSV parsing. Understanding these file handling and parsing techniques is essential for interacting with external data sources and processing large datasets efficiently.

The practical example in Section 13.4 demonstrated the application of text processing techniques with strings and file manipulation. We successfully processed data from a text file, calculated averages, and generated a comprehensive report. This real-world scenario showcased how these concepts can be combined to solve meaningful problems.

In conclusion, text processing and string manipulation are fundamental skills for any C++ programmer. Whether you're working with user inputs, processing data from files, or validating data patterns, these concepts are versatile and powerful. Regular expressions provide an additional layer of sophistication for complex text matching, while file parsing allows you to interact with external data sources.

As you continue your journey in C++ programming, always keep in mind the importance of text processing and strings. By mastering these concepts, you'll be equipped to handle a wide range of data processing tasks, making your programs more robust and efficient.

Congratulations on completing Chapter 13 on Text Processing and Strings! In the next chapter, we'll explore further advanced topics in C++ to deepen your understanding and enhance your programming capabilities. Keep coding, exploring, and honing your skills to become a proficient C++ developer. Happy coding!

14 AN INTRODUCTION TO CONCURRENT PROGRAMMING

In today's fast-paced and interconnected world, the demand for high-performance and responsive software has grown exponentially. To meet these requirements, developers need to embrace concurrent programming, a powerful technique that allows programs to perform multiple tasks concurrently, improving overall efficiency and responsiveness.

This chapter introduces you to the fascinating world of concurrent programming in C++. We will explore the fundamentals of multithreading and parallel programming, synchronization mechanisms, thread safety, and common pitfalls in concurrent programming. By the end of this chapter, you'll have a solid understanding of how to harness the full potential of concurrent programming in your C++ applications.

Concurrency in programming refers to the ability of a system to handle multiple tasks simultaneously. Traditionally, software has been designed to execute tasks sequentially, one after the other. However, modern hardware comes with multiple cores, and concurrent programming enables us to utilize these cores efficiently by executing tasks in parallel.

14.1 MULTITHREADING AND PARALLEL PROGRAMMING

In modern software development, the need for high-performance applications has become increasingly prevalent. To achieve this, developers often turn to **multithreading** and **parallel programming** techniques. These approaches enable a program to perform multiple tasks concurrently, taking advantage of the hardware's capabilities and improving overall performance and responsiveness.

14.1.1 UNDERSTANDING THREADS AND CONCURRENCY

A **thread** is the smallest unit of execution within a program. A single-threaded program executes tasks sequentially, one after the other. However, a multithreaded program creates multiple threads that can execute different tasks concurrently. These threads share the same memory space and resources, allowing them to communicate and work together to accomplish a goal.

Concurrency is the ability of a program to manage multiple tasks simultaneously, whereas *parallelism* is the execution of those tasks simultaneously on multiple CPU cores. Concurrency does not necessarily imply parallelism, but multithreading enables developers to leverage parallelism on modern multi-core CPUs.

Example 1: Creating Threads in C++

Let's see a simple example of creating two threads that execute different tasks concurrently:

```
#include <iostream>
#include <thread>

// A function that prints numbers from 1 to 5
```

```
void printNumbers() {
    for (int i = 1; i <= 5; ++i) {
        std::cout << "Thread 1: " << i << std::endl;
    }
}


// A function that prints letters from 'A' to 'E'
void printLetters() {
    for (char ch = 'A'; ch <= 'E'; ++ch) {
        std::cout << "Thread 2: " << ch << std::endl;
    }
}


int main() {
    // Create two threads
    std::thread t1(printNumbers);
    std::thread t2(printLetters);

    // Wait for both threads to finish
    t1.join();
    t2.join();

    std::cout << "Both threads have finished executing." << std::endl;

    return 0;
}
```

The output of this program will vary because the threads may execute in an interleaved manner. The two threads are created and run concurrently, printing numbers and letters simultaneously.

14.1.2 CREATING AND MANAGING THREADS IN C++

In C++, the `<thread>` header provides the necessary functionality to work with threads. We can create threads and manage them using functions like `std::thread::join()` to wait for a thread to finish and `std::thread::detach()` to allow a thread to run independently without being joined.

Example 2: Using join() and detach()

```
#include <iostream>
#include <thread>


void task() {
    std::cout << "Thread ID: " << std::this_thread::get_id() << " is running." << std::endl;
}
```

```
int main() {
    std::thread t1(task);
    std::thread t2(task);

    // Wait for both threads to finish
    t1.join();
    t2.join();

    // Uncomment the following lines to see the effect of detach()
    // t1.detach();
    // t2.detach();

    std::cout << "Both threads have finished executing." << std::endl;

    return 0;
}
```

In this example, we create two threads `t1` and `t2`, and then we use `join()` to wait for both threads to complete before the program continues. Alternatively, you can uncomment the `detach()` lines, which will allow the threads to run independently without being joined. If `detach()` is used, it is essential to ensure that the threads do not access any shared resources after they are detached.

14.1.3 MULTITHREADING VS. MULTIPROCESSING

While multithreading allows a program to perform multiple tasks concurrently within a single process, *multiprocessing* involves running multiple processes, each with its own memory space. Multiprocessing is generally more robust and avoids certain issues related to shared memory, but it also incurs more overhead due to inter-process communication.

14.1.4 BENEFITS AND CHALLENGES OF PARALLEL PROGRAMMING

Parallel programming offers several benefits, including improved performance, increased responsiveness, and efficient utilization of multi-core processors. However, concurrent programming introduces new challenges, such as data synchronization, potential data races, and deadlocks. Proper synchronization mechanisms are crucial to avoid these pitfalls and ensure correct program behavior.

In the next section, we will delve into the various **synchronization mechanisms** used to coordinate access to shared data in multithreaded environments. Understanding these mechanisms is essential to write robust and thread-safe concurrent programs.

14.2 SYNCHRONIZATION MECHANISMS

In concurrent programming, when multiple threads access shared data simultaneously, it can lead to data corruption and unexpected behavior. To ensure that threads cooperate and access shared resources in a controlled manner, *synchronization mechanisms* are used. These mechanisms help prevent race conditions and ensure that the threads execute safely and correctly.

14.2.1 THE NEED FOR SYNCHRONIZATION

Imagine a scenario where multiple threads are accessing and modifying the same data concurrently. Without synchronization, one thread might read the data while another thread is in the process of modifying it, leading to inconsistent or corrupted data. To avoid such issues, synchronization mechanisms are employed to coordinate access to shared resources.

14.2.2 MUTEXES AND LOCKS

One of the fundamental synchronization mechanisms is the *mutex* (short for mutual exclusion). A mutex is a lock that allows only one thread to access a shared resource at a time. When a thread wants to access the shared resource, it must acquire the mutex (lock) first. If the mutex is already held by another thread, the requesting thread will be blocked until the mutex becomes available.

Example 1: Using Mutex in C++

Let's see an example of using a `std::mutex` to protect a shared resource, which is a global counter in this case:

```cpp
#include <iostream>
#include <thread>
#include <mutex>

std::mutex mtx; // Define a global mutex

int counter = 0;

void incrementCounter() {
    for (int i = 0; i < 100000; ++i) {
        mtx.lock(); // Acquire the lock before modifying the shared resource
        counter++;
        mtx.unlock(); // Release the lock after modifying the shared resource
    }
}

int main() {
    std::thread t1(incrementCounter);
    std::thread t2(incrementCounter);

    t1.join();
    t2.join();

    std::cout << "Final counter value: " << counter << std::endl;

    return 0;
}
```

In this example, two threads `t1` and `t2` concurrently increment the `counter` variable. The `std::mutex` ensures that only one thread can access the `counter` at a time, preventing data races.

14.2.3 SEMAPHORES AND CONDITION VARIABLES

Semaphores are another synchronization mechanism that allows controlling access to a shared resource. They can be used to limit the number of threads that can access the resource simultaneously. A semaphore can have a maximum count, and each thread that wants to access the resource must acquire a permit from the semaphore. If no permits are available, the thread will be blocked.

Condition variables are synchronization primitives used to block a thread until a certain condition becomes true. They are often used in combination with mutexes to build more complex synchronization patterns.

14.2.4 READ-WRITE LOCKS

Read-write locks allow multiple threads to read a shared resource concurrently but only one thread to write to it exclusively. This can improve performance in scenarios where reads are more frequent than writes.

14.2.5 ATOMICS AND MEMORY ORDERING

Atomics are special data types and operations that allow individual operations on them to be executed atomically, meaning they are not interrupted by other threads. Atomics are useful for simple operations that can be performed in a single CPU instruction, like incrementing a counter.

Memory ordering defines the guarantees about the visibility of memory changes made by one thread to other threads. C++11 provides memory ordering primitives to ensure consistency in multithreaded scenarios.

In the next section, we will explore the importance of **thread safety** and the common pitfalls that developers should be aware of when writing concurrent programs.

14.3 THREAD SAFETY AND COMMON PITFALLS

In concurrent programming, *thread safety* refers to the ability of a program to execute correctly and produce consistent results when multiple threads access shared resources simultaneously. Ensuring thread safety is crucial to avoid data corruption, crashes, and other unexpected behaviors in concurrent applications. In this section, we will explore the concept of thread safety and discuss common pitfalls that developers should be aware of when writing concurrent code.

14.3.1 UNDERSTANDING THREAD SAFETY

A piece of code or a data structure is considered thread-safe if it can be accessed and modified by multiple threads without causing conflicts or race conditions. A race condition occurs when the final outcome of a program depends on the relative timing of events, and the result is not deterministic.

To achieve thread safety, developers need to consider the following factors:

1. **Atomic Operations**: Use atomic operations to ensure that specific operations are executed atomically without being interrupted by other threads. C++ provides atomic types and operations for this purpose.

2. **Synchronization**: Utilize synchronization mechanisms, such as mutexes and locks, to coordinate access to shared resources among threads. Synchronization ensures that only one thread can access the shared resource at a time, preventing data races.

3. **Avoiding Shared Data**: Minimize the use of shared data and prefer thread-local data whenever possible. Reducing shared data reduces the likelihood of data conflicts.

14.3.2 SHARED DATA AND DATA RACES

One of the major causes of thread-related issues is the incorrect handling of shared data. When multiple threads access shared data, data races can occur. A data race happens when two or more threads access the same memory location simultaneously, and at least one of these accesses is a write operation.

Example 1: Data Race

Consider the following C++ code that demonstrates a data race:

```
#include <iostream>
#include <thread>
```

```cpp
int counter = 0;

void incrementCounter() {
    for (int i = 0; i < 100000; ++i) {
        counter++; // Data race: multiple threads are accessing 'counter' concurrently
    }
}

int main() {
    std::thread t1(incrementCounter);
    std::thread t2(incrementCounter);

    t1.join();
    t2.join();

    std::cout << "Final counter value: " << counter << std::endl;

    return 0;
}
```

In this example, two threads t1 and t2 concurrently increment the counter variable, leading to a data race. The final value of counter is unpredictable and may vary on each program execution.

14.3.3 DEADLOCKS AND LIVELOCKS

Deadlocks and livelocks are issues that can occur in concurrent programs:
- A **deadlock** happens when two or more threads are unable to proceed because each is waiting for a resource held by another thread. This results in a standstill situation where none of the threads can make progress.
- A **livelock** is a situation where two or more threads keep responding to each other's actions without making any real progress. They are active, but the system makes no progress.

Avoiding deadlocks and livelocks requires careful design and usage of synchronization mechanisms.

14.3.4 STRATEGIES FOR WRITING THREAD-SAFE CODE

To write thread-safe code, consider the following strategies:
1. **Minimize Shared Data**: Reduce the use of shared data by using local variables or thread-local storage when possible. This minimizes the chance of data races.
2. **Use Synchronization Mechanisms**: Employ mutexes, locks, and other synchronization mechanisms to protect shared resources. Ensure that critical sections are kept as short as possible to minimize contention.
3. **Avoid Global State**: Avoid global variables or shared data that can be accessed from multiple threads. Instead, encapsulate data within classes and provide proper synchronization.
4. **Use Thread-Safe Data Structures**: In cases where shared data is necessary, use thread-safe data structures like std::atomic or containers from the Standard Template Library (STL) that provide thread-safe operations.

By understanding the principles of thread safety and being cautious about shared data, developers can create reliable and efficient concurrent programs.

In the next section, we will explore *parallel algorithms and data structures*, which enable efficient processing of data in concurrent environments.

14.4 PARALLEL ALGORITHMS AND DATA STRUCTURES

In concurrent programming, *parallel algorithms* and *thread-safe data structures* play a vital role in achieving efficient and scalable solutions to various computational problems. These techniques leverage the power of multiple threads to process data concurrently, speeding up the execution of tasks that can be divided into independent subtasks. This section explores how to use parallel algorithms with the Standard Template Library (STL) and introduces thread-safe data structures.

14.4.1 PARALLELIZING ALGORITHMS WITH STANDARD TEMPLATE LIBRARY (STL)

The STL in C++ provides a rich set of algorithms that can be executed in parallel. By utilizing parallel algorithms, developers can automatically distribute the work across multiple threads and take advantage of the available CPU cores. The STL introduces the **std::execution** policy, which allows specifying whether an algorithm should run sequentially or in parallel.

Example 1: Parallel Accumulate

One commonly used algorithm is **std::accumulate**, which calculates the sum of elements in a range. In parallel, this algorithm can significantly improve the performance for large datasets.

```
#include <iostream>
#include <vector>
#include <algorithm>
#include <numeric>
#include <execution>

int main() {
    std::vector<int> numbers = {1, 2, 3, 4, 5, 6, 7, 8, 9, 10};
    int sum = std::reduce(std::execution::par, numbers.begin(), numbers.end());

    std::cout << "Sum of elements: " << sum << std::endl;

    return 0;
}
```

The **std::reduce** algorithm is used here with the **std::execution::par** policy, which tells the compiler to parallelize the operation. As a result, the sum of the elements is calculated concurrently, improving performance for large datasets.

14.4.2 THREAD-SAFE DATA STRUCTURES

When working with concurrent programs, it is essential to ensure that data structures are thread-safe to avoid race conditions and data corruption. The STL provides some thread-safe containers that can be used in concurrent scenarios.

Example 2: std::atomic

The **std::atomic** template allows you to create thread-safe variables for basic data types. It provides atomic operations that can be executed without interference from other threads.

```
#include <iostream>
```

```cpp
#include <atomic>
#include <thread>

std::atomic<int> counter = 0;

void incrementCounter() {
    for (int i = 0; i < 100000; ++i) {
        counter++; // Thread-safe increment
    }
}

int main() {
    std::thread t1(incrementCounter);
    std::thread t2(incrementCounter);

    t1.join();
    t2.join();

    std::cout << "Final counter value: " << counter << std::endl;

    return 0;
}
```

In this example, the `std::atomic<int>` ensures that the increment operation on the `counter` variable is atomic and thread-safe, avoiding data races.

Example 3: `std::shared_mutex`

The `std::shared_mutex` allows multiple threads to have concurrent read-only access to a shared resource while providing exclusive access for write operations.

```cpp
#include <iostream>
#include <shared_mutex>
#include <vector>
#include <mutex>

std::vector<int> data;
std::shared_mutex dataMutex;

void readData() {
    std::shared_lock<std::shared_mutex> lock(dataMutex);
    // Read data from the shared resource (e.g., data vector)
}

void writeData(int value) {
```

```
    std::unique_lock<std::shared_mutex> lock(dataMutex);
    // Write data to the shared resource (e.g., data vector)
}

int main() {
    // Start multiple threads to readData() and writeData() concurrently

    return 0;
}
```

In this example, the `std::shared_mutex` allows multiple threads to read data concurrently, while ensuring that only one thread can write to the data at a time.

By leveraging parallel algorithms and using thread-safe data structures, developers can harness the power of concurrent programming and improve the performance of their applications.

In the next section, we will explore *asynchronous programming* with futures and promises, enabling the execution of tasks in a non-blocking manner.

14.5 ASYNCHRONOUS PROGRAMMING WITH FUTURES AND PROMISES

Asynchronous programming is a powerful paradigm in concurrent programming that allows tasks to execute independently without blocking the main program's flow. C++ provides a standardized way to work with asynchronous operations using *futures* and *promises*. These constructs enable developers to manage asynchronous tasks and handle their results efficiently.

14.5.1 INTRODUCTION TO ASYNCHRONOUS PROGRAMMING

In traditional synchronous programming, when a function is called, the program waits for its completion before moving on to the next line of code. This can lead to performance bottlenecks, especially when dealing with time-consuming tasks. Asynchronous programming, on the other hand, allows tasks to execute concurrently, providing better responsiveness and scalability.

In C++, asynchronous programming is achieved using `std::future` and `std::promise` to create asynchronous tasks and obtain their results.

14.5.2 WORKING WITH FUTURES AND PROMISES

A `std::future` represents the result of an asynchronous operation, while a `std::promise` is used to fulfill that future with a value or an exception. The `std::async` function is commonly used to launch asynchronous tasks and obtain their futures.

Example 1: Using `std::async`

```cpp
#include <iostream>
#include <future>
#include <thread>

int add(int a, int b) {
    std::this_thread::sleep_for(std::chrono::seconds(2));
    return a + b;
}
```

```
int main() {
    // Launch an asynchronous task to add two numbers
    std::future<int> futureResult = std::async(std::launch::async, add, 10, 20);

    // Do some other work concurrently

    // Get the result from the asynchronous task
    int result = futureResult.get();

    std::cout << "Result: " << result << std::endl;

    return 0;
}
```

In this example, the **add** function is executed asynchronously using `std::async`. While the addition is being performed, other work can be done concurrently. The `futureResult.get()` call will block until the result is available.

14.5.3 COMBINING ASYNCHRONOUS TASKS

Asynchronous tasks can be combined to perform more complex operations concurrently. One common technique is using `std::async` to launch multiple tasks and then waiting for their results using `std::future::get`.

Example 2: Combining Asynchronous Tasks

```
#include <iostream>
#include <future>
#include <thread>

int add(int a, int b) {
    std::this_thread::sleep_for(std::chrono::seconds(2));
    return a + b;
}

int multiply(int a, int b) {
    std::this_thread::sleep_for(std::chrono::seconds(3));
    return a * b;
}

int main() {
    // Launch asynchronous tasks to add and multiply numbers
    std::future<int> futureSum = std::async(std::launch::async, add, 10, 20);
    std::future<int> futureProduct = std::async(std::launch::async, multiply, 5, 10);

    // Do other work concurrently
```

```
// Get the results from the asynchronous tasks
int sum = futureSum.get();
int product = futureProduct.get();

std::cout << "Sum: " << sum << std::endl;
std::cout << "Product: " << product << std::endl;

return 0;
}
```

In this example, the **add** and **multiply** functions are executed asynchronously using **std::async**. The program then waits for the results from both tasks, allowing independent calculations to be performed concurrently.

Note: It's essential to use **std::launch::async** as the launch policy in **std::async** to ensure that the tasks run concurrently. The default launch policy may execute tasks synchronously.

In conclusion, asynchronous programming with futures and promises is a valuable technique for efficiently managing concurrent tasks and enhancing the responsiveness and performance of C++ programs.

Next, we will explore a *case study* where we apply concurrent programming techniques in a real-world application to gain practical insights and experience.

14.6 CASE STUDY: CONCURRENT PROGRAMMING IN A REAL-WORLD APPLICATION

In this section, we will explore a practical case study where we apply the concepts of concurrent programming to a real-world application. The goal is to gain insights into the design, implementation, and performance analysis of concurrent systems. We will follow a step-by-step approach to understand the process of building a concurrent application and how to tackle various challenges that arise in such scenarios.

14.6.1 PROJECT OVERVIEW AND REQUIREMENTS

Let's consider a real-world scenario where we are tasked with developing a web scraping application that fetches data from multiple websites concurrently. The application needs to process large amounts of data from each website and store the results in a database. Since web scraping involves I/O-bound tasks with potential delays, we can benefit greatly from concurrent programming to improve the overall performance.

Requirements:
1. Fetch data from multiple websites concurrently.
2. Process the fetched data concurrently for efficiency.
3. Ensure thread safety and avoid data races during processing.
4. Handle potential deadlocks and livelocks.
5. Optimize performance through proper synchronization.

14.6.2 DESIGNING FOR CONCURRENCY

The first step in building a concurrent application is to design its architecture. We need to identify tasks that can be executed concurrently and determine the points where synchronization is required. In our case study, the following key design considerations need to be made:

1. **Dividing Work**: We'll split the web scraping tasks to fetch data from different websites into independent units of work. Each unit of work will be assigned to a separate thread to work concurrently.

2. **Synchronization**: Since multiple threads will be updating the shared database, we need to use

synchronization mechanisms, such as mutexes or read-write locks, to ensure thread safety.

3. **Optimizing Performance**: We'll consider the use of futures and promises to manage asynchronous tasks and improve application responsiveness.

14.6.3 IMPLEMENTATION USING MULTITHREADING AND SYNCHRONIZATION

We'll now proceed with the implementation of the web scraping application using C++ and its multithreading capabilities. We'll create threads to fetch data from websites concurrently. Additionally, we'll use synchronization mechanisms to manage access to the shared database.

Example:

```cpp
#include <iostream>
#include <vector>
#include <thread>
#include <mutex>
#include <future>


std::mutex databaseMutex;

void fetchDataFromWebsite(int websiteId) {
    // Simulate data fetching from a website
    std::this_thread::sleep_for(std::chrono::seconds(2));

    // Process the fetched data
    // ...

    // Store the processed data in the database
    std::lock_guard<std::mutex> lock(databaseMutex);
    // Write to the database
    // ...
}


int main() {
    // List of website IDs to fetch data from
    std::vector<int> websiteIds = {1, 2, 3, 4, 5};

    // Container to hold threads
    std::vector<std::thread> threads;

    // Launch threads to fetch data from websites concurrently
    for (int websiteId : websiteIds) {
        threads.emplace_back(fetchDataFromWebsite, websiteId);
    }

    // Wait for all threads to finish
```

```
    for (std::thread& thread : threads) {
        thread.join();
    }

    return 0;
}
```

In this example, we create multiple threads to fetch data from different websites concurrently. The `databaseMutex` is used to synchronize access to the database while storing the processed data.

14.6.4 TESTING AND PERFORMANCE ANALYSIS

Once the implementation is complete, we need to thoroughly test the application to ensure it functions correctly and meets the specified requirements. We also need to analyze its performance to identify potential bottlenecks and areas of improvement.

During testing, we should simulate scenarios with heavy website traffic and large amounts of data to validate the application's robustness and reliability.

Conclusion:

Through this case study, we have learned how to apply concurrent programming concepts in a real-world scenario. We explored the design, implementation, and performance analysis of a web scraping application using multithreading and synchronization. With this practical experience, we can now confidently apply concurrent programming techniques to improve the efficiency and scalability of various applications.

14.7 SUMMARY AND CONCLUSION

In this chapter, we delved into the world of concurrent programming in C++, exploring various concepts and techniques that enable us to design and implement efficient and scalable applications to handle multiple tasks concurrently. Let's summarize the key points we covered:

14.1 Multithreading and Parallel Programming

In Section 14.1, we introduced the concept of multithreading and parallel programming. We discussed the fundamental difference between processes and threads, understanding the essence of concurrency and how it can boost the performance of modern applications. We also explored the benefits and challenges of parallel programming, setting the foundation for the subsequent sections.

14.2 Synchronization Mechanisms

Section 14.2 focused on synchronization mechanisms, which are essential to ensure proper coordination and safe access to shared resources in concurrent applications. We covered mutexes, locks, semaphores, condition variables, read-write locks, and atomics. By utilizing these tools, we can prevent data races, deadlocks, and other issues that arise when multiple threads try to access shared data simultaneously.

14.3 Thread Safety and Common Pitfalls

In Section 14.3, we delved into the critical topic of thread safety and common pitfalls to avoid. We learned that thread safety involves designing our code in a way that allows multiple threads to execute without interference. By identifying and eliminating data races and other thread-safety issues, we can create robust and reliable concurrent programs.

14.4 Parallel Algorithms and Data Structures

Section 14.4 explored the parallelization of algorithms using the Standard Template Library (STL) in C++. We discovered how to leverage parallel algorithms to distribute the workload across multiple threads, optimizing the execution time of computationally-intensive tasks. Additionally, we examined thread-safe data structures to manage shared data efficiently.

14.5 Asynchronous Programming with Futures and Promises

In Section 14.5, we introduced the concept of asynchronous programming using futures and promises. We learned how to work with futures and promises to handle asynchronous tasks effectively, enabling us to execute tasks concurrently while maintaining responsiveness and scalability.

14.6 Case Study: Concurrent Programming in a Real-World Application

The case study in Section 14.6 provided us with a hands-on experience of applying concurrent programming concepts to a real-world web scraping application. We designed the application to fetch data from multiple websites concurrently, managing shared resources and ensuring thread safety. We also discussed strategies to optimize performance and analyzed the application's behavior under various scenarios.

Conclusion

Concurrent programming is a powerful approach to improve the performance and responsiveness of modern applications. By understanding threads, synchronization mechanisms, thread safety, parallel algorithms, and asynchronous programming, C++ developers can harness the full potential of concurrent processing.

In this chapter, we covered essential topics related to concurrent programming, and we hope this knowledge will empower you to build robust and efficient concurrent applications in C++. As you continue your programming journey, remember to be cautious of common pitfalls and always prioritize thread safety to avoid issues in your concurrent code.

Keep exploring and experimenting with concurrent programming, as it opens up exciting possibilities for developing high-performance applications that can tackle complex tasks with ease.

15 PROGRAM TESTING AND DEBUGGING

Welcome to Chapter 15 of our book on advanced programming in C++. In this chapter, we will dive into the critical aspects of program testing and debugging. Testing and debugging are essential processes in software development that ensure the reliability, correctness, and performance of our programs.

Building robust and error-free software is a complex task, and as developers, we need effective techniques and tools to identify and fix issues efficiently. This chapter will cover various methodologies, practices, and tools used for program testing and debugging in C++.

We will explore unit testing, test-driven development, debugging techniques, profiling for performance optimization, code reviews, handling errors and exceptions, defensive programming, testing in a multithreaded environment, automated testing, and debugging best practices. Each section will provide valuable insights into these topics, along with practical examples in C++ to demonstrate the concepts.

By the end of this chapter, you will have a solid understanding of how to create high-quality C++ programs, thoroughly tested and well-debugged, which are essential skills for any proficient C++ developer. Let's begin our journey into the world of program testing and debugging!

15.1 UNIT TESTING AND TEST-DRIVEN DEVELOPMENT

In this section, we will explore the concepts of unit testing and test-driven development (TDD), essential practices that help ensure the correctness and reliability of our C++ programs.

15.1.1 UNDERSTANDING UNIT TESTING

Unit testing is a fundamental software testing technique where individual units or components of a program are tested in isolation. A unit refers to the smallest testable part of the code, such as a function, method, or class. The main goal of unit testing is to verify that each unit behaves as expected and produces the correct output for various input scenarios.

Unit tests are typically written by developers themselves and can be executed automatically to validate the correctness of code changes or to catch regressions when modifying existing code. It aids in early detection of defects and makes it easier to maintain and refactor code in the future.

Example:
Let's consider a simple C++ function that calculates the factorial of a given positive integer:

```cpp
#include <cassert>

unsigned int factorial(unsigned int n) {
    if (n == 0 || n == 1)
```

```
        return 1;
    else
        return n * factorial(n - 1);
}

int main() {
    // Unit test for factorial function
    assert(factorial(5) == 120);
    assert(factorial(0) == 1);
    assert(factorial(1) == 1);

    return 0;
}
```

In this example, we have written three unit tests using the `assert` macro from the `<cassert>` header. The `assert` macro checks if the expression provided is true, and if it's false, it will trigger an assertion failure, indicating that the test has failed.

15.1.2 BENEFITS OF TEST-DRIVEN DEVELOPMENT

Test-Driven Development (TDD) is an iterative software development process that emphasizes writing tests before writing the actual code. The TDD cycle typically follows three steps: writing a failing test, implementing the minimum code required to pass the test, and then refactoring the code for improved design while ensuring the tests still pass.

TDD promotes better code design, reduces defects, and ensures that new features or changes do not introduce unintended side effects. Additionally, it acts as living documentation, describing the intended behavior of the code.

15.1.3 WRITING TEST CASES AND TEST SUITES

A *test case* is a set of test inputs, execution conditions, and expected outcomes. Test cases should cover different scenarios and edge cases to thoroughly validate the code. A collection of test cases is called a *test suite*. Test suites are organized to cover various aspects of the code, such as different functions or classes.

In C++, various testing frameworks, like Google Test or Catch2, provide powerful tools for writing test cases and organizing test suites. These frameworks offer features like fixture support, test parameterization, and test output customization.

15.1.4 TEST AUTOMATION AND FRAMEWORKS

Test automation is crucial for executing tests efficiently and repeatedly during the development process. Using testing frameworks like Google Test or Catch2 allows us to automate the test execution and integrate tests into build systems for continuous integration.

Example:

Let's continue with the previous example and use the Catch2 testing framework to write test cases and organize them into a test suite:

```
#define CATCH_CONFIG_MAIN
#include <catch2/catch.hpp>

unsigned int factorial(unsigned int n) {
    if (n == 0 || n == 1)
```

```
        return 1;
    else
        return n * factorial(n - 1);
}


TEST_CASE("Factorial function computes the correct result") {
    REQUIRE(factorial(5) == 120);
    REQUIRE(factorial(0) == 1);
    REQUIRE(factorial(1) == 1);
}
```

In this example, we have written a test suite using Catch2. The **REQUIRE** macro checks if the expression provided is true, and if it's false, it will fail the test case. The test suite can be executed automatically, and any failures will be reported, indicating potential issues in the code.

Unit testing and test-driven development are powerful techniques that improve code quality and maintainability. Embracing these practices can lead to more robust and reliable C++ programs.

15.2 DEBUGGING TECHNIQUES AND TOOLS

Debugging is an essential skill for every programmer. It involves identifying and resolving errors, also known as bugs, in the code. In this section, we will explore various debugging techniques and the tools available in C++ to aid in the debugging process.

15.2.1 INTRODUCTION TO DEBUGGING

Debugging is the process of finding and fixing issues in a program. These issues can be logical errors, runtime errors, or unexpected behaviors that cause the program to behave incorrectly or crash. Debugging is crucial for ensuring the correctness and reliability of software.

When debugging, programmers typically go through the following steps:

1. **Reproducing the Bug**: The first step is to identify the specific conditions or inputs that trigger the bug. Reproducing the bug reliably is essential for effective debugging.

2. **Understanding the Code**: Debugging requires a deep understanding of the codebase, including the logic, data structures, and algorithms used.

3. **Isolating the Bug**: Narrow down the area of code where the bug is likely to be present. Divide and conquer approach can be useful to isolate the problematic section.

4. **Using Debugging Tools**: C++ provides various tools and techniques to aid in debugging. These tools help in inspecting the program's state, setting breakpoints, and analyzing memory and CPU usage.

5. **Fixing the Bug**: Once the bug is identified, it can be fixed by modifying the code accordingly. Regression tests should be performed to ensure that the bug is resolved without introducing new issues.

15.2.2 COMMON DEBUGGING APPROACHES

There are several common debugging approaches that programmers use to identify and fix bugs:

a) Printing and Tracing: One of the simplest and oldest debugging techniques is to insert print statements in the code to display the values of variables and the flow of the program. This helps in understanding the program's execution and identifying unexpected behaviors.

b) Rubber Duck Debugging: Sometimes, explaining the code and the problem to someone else, even an inanimate object like a rubber duck, can help the programmer see the issue from a different perspective and find the bug.

c) Binary Search Debugging: For complex issues, programmers may use a binary search-like technique, where they insert print statements or use a debugger to narrow down the faulty section of code by halving the search space repeatedly.

d) Rubber Duck Debugging is a simple but effective technique where a programmer explains their code and problem to an inanimate object, like a rubber duck. The process of verbalizing the issue often helps the programmer spot the bug.

15.2.3 USING DEBUGGERS AND BREAKPOINTS

C++ offers powerful debuggers that allow programmers to observe the program's execution, inspect variables, and control its flow. One of the most popular debuggers for C++ is the GNU Debugger (GDB).

Debuggers allow you to set *breakpoints*, which are specific locations in the code where the program will pause its execution. When the program hits a breakpoint, you can examine the variables' values and step through the code line by line.

Example:

Consider the following C++ code with a logical bug:

```cpp
#include <iostream>

int main() {
    int x = 5;
    int y = 0;

    int result = x / y; // Logical bug: Division by zero

    std::cout << "Result: " << result << std::endl;

    return 0;
}
```

By running this code with a debugger, setting a breakpoint at the `int result = x / y;` line, and inspecting the values of x and y, we can quickly identify that the logical bug is division by zero.

15.2.4 LOGGING AND TRACING

Logging and *tracing* are techniques that involve generating log messages during the program's execution to track its behavior and diagnose issues.

Logging allows you to record important information about the program's state, such as variable values, function calls, and error messages, into log files. These logs can later be analyzed to understand the program's behavior and identify problems.

Tracing involves tracking the flow of the program, recording which functions are called in what order and with what parameters. Tracing is especially useful for understanding complex control flows and identifying where the program deviates from the expected path.

Example:

Using a logging library like "spdlog," we can add log messages to our code:

```cpp
#include <iostream>
#include <spdlog/spdlog.h>

int main() {
```

```
    int x = 5;
    int y = 0;

    // Set up logging
    spdlog::set_pattern("[%^%l%$] %v");
    auto logger = spdlog::stdout_color_mt("debug");

    logger->info("Starting program");

    // Some code...

    logger->debug("x = {}, y = {}", x, y);

    int result = x / y; // Logical bug: Division by zero

    logger->error("Error: Division by zero");

    std::cout << "Result: " << result << std::endl;

    logger->info("Program completed");

    return 0;
}
```

By running this code, we can examine the log messages and quickly identify the division by zero error.

Debugging is a critical skill for programmers, and mastering various debugging techniques and tools can significantly improve the efficiency of identifying and fixing bugs in C++ code.

15.3 PROFILING AND PERFORMANCE OPTIMIZATION

In this section, we will explore *profiling* and *performance optimization* techniques to ensure that our C++ programs run efficiently and meet their performance requirements. Profiling allows us to identify bottlenecks in our code and areas that need improvement, while performance optimization involves making changes to the code to achieve better execution speed and resource utilization.

15.3.1 IMPORTANCE OF PROFILING

Profiling is the process of analyzing a program's behavior during execution to measure its resource usage, such as CPU time, memory consumption, and I/O operations. By profiling our C++ programs, we can gain valuable insights into their performance characteristics, identify performance bottlenecks, and focus our optimization efforts on the most critical parts of the code.

The goals of profiling are to:
- Identify sections of code that consume the most resources and slow down the program.
- Find opportunities for code optimization to improve performance.
- Understand how a program behaves under different conditions and inputs.

15.3.2 PROFILING TOOLS AND TECHNIQUES

Several profiling tools are available for C++ programmers, which provide detailed information about a

program's resource usage. Some common profiling tools include:
- **Valgrind:** A powerful tool suite that can detect memory leaks, perform heap profiling, and help optimize cache usage.
- **gprof:** A statistical profiling tool that comes with the GNU Compiler Collection (GCC).
- **perf:** A versatile performance analysis tool that can trace various events, such as CPU cycles and cache misses.

Each tool has its strengths, and the choice of tool depends on the specific profiling needs and the development environment.

Example:

Let's use the `gprof` tool to profile a simple C++ program and identify the most time-consuming functions:

```cpp
#include <iostream>

// A function with a loop that takes some time to execute
void timeConsumingFunction() {
    for (int i = 0; i < 1000000; ++i) {
        // Some time-consuming operation
    }
}

int main() {
    // Call the time-consuming function multiple times
    for (int i = 0; i < 10; ++i) {
        timeConsumingFunction();
    }

    return 0;
}
```

To profile this program using `gprof`, we need to compile it with the `-pg` flag to generate profiling information. After running the executable, we can use the `gprof` command to analyze the profile data and obtain a report that shows which functions consumed the most CPU time.

15.3.3 IDENTIFYING PERFORMANCE BOTTLENECKS

After profiling a program, we can identify performance bottlenecks - sections of the code that contribute significantly to its execution time or resource consumption. These bottlenecks are the primary candidates for optimization.

Common performance bottlenecks in C++ programs include:
- **Inefficient algorithms:** Choosing more efficient algorithms or data structures can significantly improve the program's performance.
- **Frequent memory allocation and deallocation:** Minimizing dynamic memory allocation can reduce overhead and improve performance.
- **Excessive I/O operations:** Reducing I/O operations or optimizing disk access can speed up the program.
- **Unnecessary computations:** Eliminating redundant computations or unnecessary work can save CPU cycles.

15.3.4 STRATEGIES FOR PERFORMANCE OPTIMIZATION

Once we have identified performance bottlenecks, we can apply various optimization strategies to improve the program's efficiency. Some common optimization techniques include:

- **Algorithmic optimization:** Use more efficient algorithms or data structures to reduce the computational complexity.
- **Caching and memoization:** Store previously computed results to avoid redundant computations.
- **Parallelization:** Utilize multithreading or parallel processing to take advantage of multiple CPU cores.
- **Memory management:** Optimize memory usage by reducing unnecessary allocations or using custom allocators.
- **Inline functions:** Use inline functions to reduce function call overhead.

Example:

Consider a program that calculates the Fibonacci sequence using a recursive approach:

```cpp
#include <iostream>

int fibonacci(int n) {
    if (n <= 1)
        return n;
    return fibonacci(n - 1) + fibonacci(n - 2);
}

int main() {
    int n = 40;
    int result = fibonacci(n);
    std::cout << "Fibonacci(" << n << ") = " << result << std::endl;
    return 0;
}
```

This implementation is highly inefficient for larger values of n because it recalculates the same values multiple times. By using memoization or an iterative approach, we can optimize this code and significantly reduce the execution time.

In conclusion, profiling and performance optimization are crucial steps in ensuring that our C++ programs run efficiently and meet their performance requirements. By analyzing the program's behavior, identifying bottlenecks, and applying optimization techniques, we can create high-performance and responsive software.

15.4 CODE REVIEWS AND QUALITY ASSURANCE

In this section, we will delve into the importance of *code reviews* and discuss best practices for ensuring *quality assurance* in C++ development. Code reviews are a critical part of the software development process, allowing developers to collaborate, share knowledge, and identify potential issues early on. Quality assurance ensures that the software meets the required standards and fulfills its intended purpose.

15.4.1 CONDUCTING EFFECTIVE CODE REVIEWS

A *code review* is a systematic examination of source code by other developers to identify defects, improve code quality, and ensure adherence to coding standards and best practices. The primary goal of a code review is to catch bugs and vulnerabilities before they reach production, enhancing the overall quality and maintainability of the codebase.

Key aspects of conducting effective code reviews include:
- **Collaborative Approach:** Code reviews are most effective when conducted in a collaborative and constructive manner. Reviewers should focus on providing feedback and suggestions rather than criticizing the developer.
- **Regular Reviews:** Regular code reviews, especially for significant changes, can lead to faster identification and resolution of issues.
- **Automated Code Review Tools:** Utilizing automated tools to perform static code analysis can help identify potential problems, such as style violations or memory leaks.

15.4.2 CODE REVIEW BEST PRACTICES

To ensure successful code reviews, follow these best practices:
- **Review Iteratively:** Break the code review process into smaller, manageable parts, allowing developers to address issues incrementally.
- **Check for Correctness:** Verify that the code functions as intended and meets the specified requirements.
- **Code Style and Standards:** Ensure the code follows the team's coding standards and style guidelines for consistency.
- **Encourage Peer Learning:** Code reviews present an opportunity for team members to learn from one another and gain insights into different approaches to problem-solving.

15.4.3 CONTINUOUS INTEGRATION AND CONTINUOUS DEPLOYMENT

Continuous Integration (CI) and *Continuous Deployment (CD)* are practices that complement code reviews and quality assurance. CI involves automatically building and testing code changes whenever they are committed to the version control system. CD extends CI by automatically deploying code changes to production after passing the necessary tests.

By integrating code reviews with CI/CD, teams can enforce quality checks before code changes are merged into the main codebase, reducing the likelihood of introducing bugs and ensuring a smooth deployment process.

Example:

Consider a simple C++ function that checks if a given number is prime:

```cpp
#include <iostream>

bool isPrime(int number) {
    if (number <= 1)
        return false;

    for (int i = 2; i * i <= number; ++i) {
        if (number % i == 0)
            return false;
    }

    return true;
}

int main() {
    int num = 17;
```

```
if (isPrime(num))
    std::cout << num << " is a prime number." << std::endl;
else
    std::cout << num << " is not a prime number." << std::endl;

    return 0;
}
```

To conduct a code review, another developer would examine this function for correctness, code style, and potential optimizations. Any identified issues or suggestions for improvement would be discussed and addressed before merging the code into the main project.

In conclusion, code reviews and quality assurance play a vital role in ensuring software quality, catching defects early, and fostering collaboration among developers. By following best practices and integrating code reviews with CI/CD, C++ development teams can deliver reliable and high-quality software products.

15.5 DEFENSIVE PROGRAMMING TECHNIQUES

In this section, we will explore *defensive programming techniques* that help improve the robustness and reliability of C++ code. Defensive programming involves writing code with the assumption that errors, bugs, and unexpected inputs might occur. By anticipating and handling these scenarios, developers can create more resilient software that is less prone to failures.

15.5.1 PRINCIPLES OF DEFENSIVE PROGRAMMING

Defensive programming is guided by several key principles that aim to enhance the stability and maintainability of code:

1. **Input Validation:** Always validate user inputs and function parameters to ensure they meet the expected criteria. This prevents invalid or malicious data from causing unexpected behavior in the program.

2. **Error Checking:** Check the return values of functions and system calls for errors and handle them appropriately. Ignoring errors can lead to undefined behavior and program crashes.

3. **Fail Early and Gracefully:** Identify and handle errors as early as possible in the code. When errors occur, provide meaningful error messages to users and log relevant information for developers to diagnose the issue.

4. **Modularity and Encapsulation:** Design classes and functions to be self-contained and limit external access to internal data. This prevents unintended modifications to critical data.

5. **Code Reusability:** Reuse existing code and libraries wherever possible. Well-tested and widely-used libraries are likely to be more reliable than writing similar functionality from scratch.

15.5.2 INPUT VALIDATION AND SANITIZATION

Input validation is a critical aspect of defensive programming. By validating user inputs and ensuring they adhere to expected formats and ranges, we can prevent many common errors and security vulnerabilities.

For example, suppose we have a function that calculates the factorial of a positive integer:

```
#include <iostream>

unsigned long long factorial(int n) {
    if (n < 0) {
        throw std::invalid_argument("Factorial is defined only for non-negative integers.");
    }
```

```
    unsigned long long result = 1;
    for (int i = 1; i <= n; ++i) {
        result *= i;
    }
    return result;
}

int main() {
    int num;
    std::cout << "Enter a positive integer: ";
    std::cin >> num;

    try {
        unsigned long long result = factorial(num);
        std::cout << "Factorial of " << num << " is " << result << std::endl;
    } catch (const std::exception& e) {
        std::cerr << "Error: " << e.what() << std::endl;
    }

    return 0;
}
```

15.5.3 ERROR HANDLING AND RESILIENCE

Defensive programming involves carefully considering how to handle errors and unexpected situations. Error handling can include retrying operations, providing fallbacks, or gracefully degrading performance when certain resources are unavailable.

Resilience in a program refers to its ability to recover from errors and continue functioning without compromising the user experience. For example, in a web application, if a server request fails, the application could display cached data instead of crashing or showing an error page.

By employing error handling and resilience strategies, developers can create more reliable and user-friendly applications.

In conclusion, defensive programming techniques play a crucial role in creating robust and reliable C++ code. By following principles like input validation, error checking, and code modularity, developers can anticipate and handle errors more effectively, resulting in software that is less prone to failures and unexpected behavior.

15.6 TESTING AND DEBUGGING IN A MULTITHREADED ENVIRONMENT

In this section, we will explore the unique challenges and techniques involved in *testing and debugging* multi-threaded applications in C++. Multithreaded programming introduces complexities due to the concurrent execution of threads, which can lead to issues such as race conditions, deadlocks, and data inconsistencies. To ensure the correctness and stability of multithreaded code, specialized testing and debugging approaches are required.

15.6.1 CHALLENGES OF MULTITHREADED TESTING

Testing multithreaded applications is inherently more difficult than testing single-threaded ones. The primary challenges include:

1. **Concurrency Bugs:** Multithreaded code is susceptible to race conditions, where multiple threads access shared resources simultaneously, leading to unpredictable behavior. These bugs may not manifest consistently and can be challenging to reproduce.

2. **Deadlocks and Livelocks:** Deadlocks occur when two or more threads are unable to proceed because they are waiting for each other to release resources. Livelocks happen when threads are actively trying to resolve a deadlock but are unable to make progress.

3. **Heisenbugs:** Multithreaded bugs may exhibit different behavior during testing than in the production environment due to timing variations caused by thread scheduling.

4. **Thread Interference:** Threads can interfere with each other's execution, leading to unexpected outcomes and making it harder to reason about program behavior.

15.6.2 TECHNIQUES FOR MULTITHREADED DEBUGGING

To effectively debug multithreaded applications, developers can employ various techniques, including:

1. **Logging and Tracing:** Instrument the code with detailed logging and tracing statements to capture the sequence of thread execution and identify any interleaving issues.

2. **Thread-Safe Debugging:** Use thread-safe versions of standard data structures and functions in debugging code to avoid introducing additional concurrency issues.

3. **Thread Synchronization:** Temporarily add synchronization mechanisms, such as mutexes or semaphores, to narrow down the origin of data race conditions and deadlocks.

4. **Reproducibility:** Aim to reproduce concurrency bugs consistently by setting specific thread scheduling policies or using thread delaying techniques.

15.6.3 THREAD-SAFETY TESTING

Thread-safety testing focuses on ensuring that shared resources are accessed in a thread-safe manner. Developers can follow these steps:

1. **Identify Shared Resources:** Identify all data structures, variables, and resources shared among threads.

2. **Create Test Cases:** Design test cases that simulate concurrent access to shared resources and verify that the results are as expected.

3. **Use Tools and Libraries:** Leverage testing tools and libraries specifically designed for multithreaded testing, such as data-race detectors and memory sanitizers.

Example: Thread-Safety Testing with Mutex

Consider a simple example of a shared counter accessed by multiple threads:

```cpp
#include <iostream>
#include <thread>
#include <mutex>

std::mutex mtx;
int sharedCounter = 0;

void incrementCounter(int id) {
    for (int i = 0; i < 1000; ++i) {
        std::lock_guard<std::mutex> lock(mtx);
        ++sharedCounter;
    }
}
```

```
int main() {
    std::thread t1(incrementCounter, 1);
    std::thread t2(incrementCounter, 2);

    t1.join();
    t2.join();

    std::cout << "Final value of the shared counter: " << sharedCounter << std::endl;

    return 0;
}
```

In this example, without the use of the `std::mutex`, the shared counter might not be updated correctly due to concurrent access from multiple threads. The `std::lock_guard` ensures that only one thread can access the shared counter at a time, making the code thread-safe.

In conclusion, testing and debugging multithreaded applications require special attention to the challenges introduced by concurrent execution. Techniques like logging, thread-safe debugging, and reproducibility aid in identifying and resolving concurrency bugs effectively. Additionally, thorough thread-safety testing with appropriate synchronization mechanisms ensures that shared resources are accessed correctly in a multithreaded environment. By employing these techniques, developers can create robust and reliable multithreaded programs.

15.7 AUTOMATED TESTING AND CONTINUOUS INTEGRATION

In this section, we will explore the concepts of *automated testing* and *continuous integration (CI)* and their significance in the development workflow. Automated testing helps ensure the quality and correctness of code changes, while continuous integration streamlines the development process by automating the build and testing process.

15.7.1 BENEFITS OF AUTOMATED TESTING

Automated testing involves writing scripts and test cases that automatically verify the behavior and functionality of software. The benefits of automated testing include:

1. **Efficiency:** Automated tests can be executed quickly and repeatedly, allowing developers to identify and address issues early in the development cycle.
2. **Accuracy:** Automated tests follow predefined steps, reducing the chances of human errors during testing.
3. **Regression Testing:** Automated tests can be rerun after each code change to ensure that new modifications do not introduce regressions, i.e., new bugs in previously working code.
4. **Test Coverage:** Automated testing can achieve higher test coverage by running a large number of test cases that might be impractical to execute manually.

15.7.2 BUILDING A CONTINUOUS INTEGRATION PIPELINE

Continuous Integration (CI) is a software development practice that involves merging code changes into a shared repository several times a day. Each integration triggers an automated build and testing process. The key components of a CI pipeline include:

1. **Version Control System (VCS):** A central repository where developers commit their code changes. Git is a popular VCS.
2. **Build System:** Tools like CMake, Make, or Gradle are used to define the build process and

compile the code.

3. **Automated Testing Framework:** Testing frameworks such as Google Test or Catch2 are used to write and execute automated tests.

4. **CI Server:** A dedicated server responsible for orchestrating the CI pipeline, automatically building and testing the code.

15.7.3 INTEGRATING AUTOMATED TESTS INTO CI/CD

CI/CD stands for Continuous Integration and Continuous Deployment. Continuous Deployment goes one step further than CI, automatically deploying the code to production if it passes all tests. Integrating automated tests into the CI/CD process involves:

1. **Pre-commit Hook:** Running tests on the developer's local machine before committing changes to the central repository ensures that code meets basic standards.

2. **Automated Build and Test:** The CI server automatically triggers a build and runs the test suite on every code commit.

3. **Test Reporting:** The CI server provides feedback on test results, including any failures, allowing developers to address issues promptly.

Example: Automated Testing and CI with Catch2

Consider a simple C++ function that adds two numbers:

```
int add(int a, int b) {
    return a + b;
}
```

We can write automated test cases using Catch2:

```
#define CATCH_CONFIG_MAIN
#include <catch2/catch.hpp>


TEST_CASE("Addition works correctly") {
    REQUIRE(add(2, 3) == 5);
    REQUIRE(add(-5, 7) == 2);
    REQUIRE(add(0, 0) == 0);
}
```

By integrating these test cases into a CI/CD pipeline, any code changes that break the **add** function will be immediately detected, allowing for prompt resolution of issues.

Conclusion

Automated testing and continuous integration are essential practices in modern software development. They enable efficient, accurate, and high-coverage testing, leading to improved code quality and faster development cycles. By adopting these practices, development teams can build robust and reliable software with confidence.

15.8 DEBUGGING AND TESTING BEST PRACTICES

In this section, we will discuss some *best practices* for debugging and testing in C++. These practices are essential for ensuring the reliability and quality of software.

15.8.1 TIPS FOR EFFECTIVE DEBUGGING

Debugging is the process of identifying and fixing errors or bugs in the code. Here are some tips for effective debugging in C++:

1. **Use a Debugger:** Utilize a *debugger* tool like GDB (GNU Debugger) or Visual Studio Debugger

to step through the code, inspect variables, and understand the flow of execution.

2. **Print Debug Statements:** Insert *print statements* or *log messages* at critical points in the code to display variable values or progress during execution.

3. **Divide and Conquer:** If dealing with a large codebase, break down the problem into smaller sections and debug them individually.

4. **Check Inputs:** Ensure that input data is valid and within expected ranges. Validate user inputs and function parameters to avoid unexpected behavior.

Example: Debugging with a Debugger

Consider the following C++ function that finds the maximum element in an array:

```
#include <iostream>

int findMax(int arr[], int size) {
    int max = arr[0];
    for (int i = 1; i < size; i++) {
        if (arr[i] > max) {
            max = arr[i];
        }
    }
    return max;
}

int main() {
    int arr[] = {3, 1, 7, 4, 2};
    int size = sizeof(arr) / sizeof(arr[0]);

    int result = findMax(arr, size);
    std::cout << "Maximum element: " << result << std::endl;

    return 0;
}
```

To debug the `findMax` function, we can set breakpoints and inspect the values of variables `max`, `i`, and `arr[i]`.

The breakpoints will be set at the following lines of code:

```
int max = arr[0];
if (arr[i] > max) {
    max = arr[i];
}
```

These breakpoints will allow us to inspect the values of the variables `max`, `i`, and `arr[i]` at different points in the execution of the function. For example, we could set a breakpoint at the first line of code and then run the function with the array `arr[] = {3, 1, 7, 4, 2}`. The breakpoint will be hit when the function reaches the first line of code, and we will be able to inspect the values of the variables `max`, `i`, and `arr[i]`. We will see that `max` is equal to `arr[0]`, which is 3, and `i` is equal to 0.

We can then continue the execution of the function by clicking the "Continue" button in the debugger.

The function will continue to execute until it reaches the second breakpoint, which is at the line of code `if (arr[i] > max) {`. At this point, we will be able to inspect the values of the variables `max`, `i`, and `arr[i]` again. We will see that `max` is still equal to 3, but `i` is now equal to 1. We can also see that the value of `arr[i]` is 7.

If we continue the execution of the function, it will continue to iterate through the array, comparing the value of each element to the current value of `max`. If the value of an element is greater than `max`, then `max` will be updated to the value of that element.

The function will continue to iterate through the array until it reaches the end of the array. At this point, the function will return the value of `max`, which will be the maximum element in the array.

Here is the rewritten text of the code with the breakpoints:

```cpp
#include <iostream>

int findMax(int arr[], int size) {
    // Breakpoint 1
    int max = arr[0];

    for (int i = 1; i < size; i++) {
        // Breakpoint 2
        if (arr[i] > max) {
            max = arr[i];
        }
    }
    return max;
}

int main() {
    int arr[] = {3, 1, 7, 4, 2};
    int size = sizeof(arr) / sizeof(arr[0]);

    int result = findMax(arr, size);
    std::cout << "Maximum element: " << result << std::endl;

    return 0;
}
```

15.8.2 STRATEGIES FOR SUCCESSFUL TESTING

Effective testing ensures that the code behaves as expected and handles various scenarios. Here are some strategies for successful testing in C++:

1. **Unit Testing:** Write *unit tests* for individual functions and classes to verify their correctness in isolation.

2. **Integration Testing:** Conduct *integration tests* to evaluate the interaction between different components of the software.

3. **Edge Cases:** Include test cases that cover *edge cases*, such as minimum and maximum inputs, to validate the code's behavior under extreme conditions.

4. **Regression Testing:** Re-run tests frequently after each code change to detect and fix regressions.

Example: Unit Testing with Google Test

Suppose we have a simple function that multiplies two numbers:

```cpp
int multiply(int a, int b) {
    return a * b;
}
```

We can write a unit test for this function using Google Test:

```cpp
#include <gtest/gtest.h>

TEST(MultiplyTest, PositiveNumbers) {
    EXPECT_EQ(multiply(2, 3), 6);
}

TEST(MultiplyTest, NegativeNumbers) {
    EXPECT_EQ(multiply(-2, 3), -6);
}

TEST(MultiplyTest, Zero) {
    EXPECT_EQ(multiply(2, 0), 0);
}
```

The test checks that the function returns the correct value for positive, negative, and zero inputs. This is a good example of how to write a unit test that covers a variety of input cases.

15.8.3 BALANCING TESTING AND DEVELOPMENT TIME

While thorough testing is crucial, it is essential to balance it with development time. Too much testing might delay project delivery, while inadequate testing could lead to bugs in production. Adopt an agile approach, where testing is an integral part of the development process, allowing for timely feedback and adjustments.

Conclusion

Debugging and testing are integral to the software development process. By following effective debugging practices and employing comprehensive testing strategies, developers can identify and fix issues early, leading to robust and reliable C++ programs. Striking a balance between testing and development time ensures the delivery of high-quality software within a reasonable timeframe.

15.9 SUMMARY AND CONCLUSION

In this chapter on Program Testing and Debugging, we explored various essential aspects of ensuring the reliability and quality of C++ programs. Let's summarize the key points discussed in each section:

Section 15.1 Unit Testing and Test-Driven Development
- **Unit Testing** involves testing individual units (functions, classes) of code in isolation.
- **Test-Driven Development (TDD)** is a development approach where tests are written before the code is implemented, guiding the development process.
- Writing comprehensive test cases using **frameworks** like Google Test helps catch bugs early and improves code reliability.

Section 15.2 Debugging Techniques and Tools
- **Debugging** is the process of identifying and fixing errors in the code.

- **Debuggers** like GDB and Visual Studio Debugger help step through code and inspect variables during runtime.
- **Logging** and **tracing** are useful techniques to monitor the flow and state of the program during execution.

Section 15.3 Profiling and Performance Optimization
- **Profiling** identifies performance bottlenecks in the code.
- **Profiling tools** like gprof and Valgrind aid in analyzing code performance.
- **Optimization strategies** such as algorithmic improvements and caching can enhance program speed.

Section 15.4 Code Reviews and Quality Assurance
- **Code reviews** help identify defects, improve code readability, and ensure adherence to coding standards.
- Following **code review best practices** fosters a positive and effective review process.
- **Continuous Integration and Continuous Deployment (CI/CD)** promote automated code integration, testing, and deployment.

Section 15.5 Defensive Programming Techniques
- **Defensive programming** aims to anticipate and handle unexpected situations.
- **Input validation and sanitization** ensure data integrity and security.
- **Error handling and resilience** improve program stability and prevent unexpected crashes.

Section 15.6 Testing and Debugging in a Multithreaded Environment
- **Multithreaded testing** poses unique challenges due to non-deterministic behavior.
- **Techniques** like synchronization and thread-safe design are essential for **multithreaded debugging**.
- **Thread-safety testing** ensures proper synchronization and concurrent access handling.

Section 15.7 Automated Testing and Continuous Integration
- **Automated testing** reduces human effort and improves testing efficiency.
- Building a **Continuous Integration pipeline** automates build, test, and integration processes.
- **Integrating automated tests** into the CI/CD workflow ensures fast feedback on code changes.

Section 15.8 Debugging and Testing Best Practices
- **Effective debugging tips** include using debuggers, printing debug statements, and dividing and conquering.
- **Successful testing strategies** encompass unit testing, integration testing, testing edge cases, and regression testing.
- **Balancing testing and development time** ensures timely delivery of quality software.

Conclusion

Testing and debugging are vital parts of software development. They help identify and rectify issues early, leading to more reliable and efficient C++ programs. By incorporating best practices, using appropriate tools, and following established testing methodologies, developers can deliver high-quality software that meets user expectations and withstands real-world challenges. Embracing a testing and debugging mindset empowers programmers to build robust, error-free, and maintainable C++ applications.

ABOUT THE AUTHOR

Amir Keivan Shafiei is a lecturer of computer engineering at the University of Birjand, where he is also the head of the computer and civil engineering department. He has a master's degree in computer engineering from Ferdowsi University of Mashhad and a bachelor's degree in computer engineering from Najafabad University of Isfahan. He has taught various courses on software engineering, programming languages, and artificial intelligence. He has also served as the deputy of education at Hekmat Motahar Non-Profit University and the head of the computer department at Azad University of Sarakhs. He is interested in research topics such as data mining, machine learning, and natural language processing.

www.ingramcontent.com/pod-product-compliance
Lightning Source LLC
Chambersburg PA
CBHW082209290526
45794CB00009B/3476